D1379899

THE STATIONERS' COMPANY

A HISTORY OF THE LATER YEARS 1800-2000

The Stationers' Company

A History of the Later Years 1800-2000

EDITED BY ROBIN MYERS
Honorary Archivist & Liveryman of the Company

THE WORSHIPFUL COMPANY OF STATIONERS
& NEWSPAPER MAKERS · 2001

Published for The Worshipful Company of Stationers & Newspaper Makers
by PHILLIMORE & CO LTD
Shopwyke Manor Barn, Chichester, West Sussex PO20 6BG

ISBN 1 86077 140 8

Typeset in ITC Galliard, 11½ on 15pt
Printed in Great Britain at Unwin Brothers, the Gresham Press, Woking
on 'Natural' 120gm² acid-free paper from Robert Horne Paper Company Ltd
and bound by The Bath Press

FRONTISPIECE: The Hall *en fête*; The Court celebrates the award of the
Company's Silver Medal to Sir Derek Greenaway, June 1984.

Contents

CONTENTS

List of Illustrations

Acknowledgements

I have accumulated many debts of gratitude.

My first, which is also a debt of the Company, is to the late George Mandl, who wanted the Company to have a history of its later years. He encouraged and supported me personally, and gave the project financial backing (which his widow, Mrs Giselle Mandl, has generously continued since his death). The late Past Master Allen Thompson was another friend who encouraged and advised me while he was chairman of the library and archive trust and up to the last weeks of his life. Since their untimely deaths, their mantle has fallen on Bob Russell, the present Upper Warden and their successor as chairman of the trust; he aided and abetted my efforts and, when I flagged, gave me cheer and hospitality.

Many have taken time from other work to help and advise. Among them, Iain Bain laid the foundations of the design of the book and Noel Osborne provided the services of a publisher. J.D. Lee, in indexing the book, has saved us from a number of inconsistencies.

The book would not have been possible without those who gave help in kind—Sir Clive Martin, Lord Mayor, 1999-2000, and Past Master of the Company, printed the book. The Bath Press kindly donated the binding, and Toby Marchant of Robert Horne generously provided the paper.

I am grateful to Past Master Christopher Rivington, who wrote the Foreword, as well as offering editorial comment throughout and supplying a great deal of information on the Company's recent past, from his personal and collective Rivington store of knowledge of the last two centuries of our history. Christopher Rivington, Keith Hutton and Roy Coxhead spent many hours in proof-reading the entire book.

Last, but far from least, I thank the contributors, Michael Berlin, Richard Bowden, Michael Harris, Penny Hunting, Ann Saunders and David Whitaker. Their hard work and long-suffering and good-natured patience in the face of more than normal editorial interference was wonderful—huge slashings of their deathless prose, rearranging of their material, even moving whole sections from one chapter to another in order to avoid overlap and turn a collection of essays by various hands into a coherent whole. In doing this I was assisted by Giles Mandelbrote of the British Library, who, out of the kindness of his heart, gave me many, many hours of time he could ill spare, to help me with the final editing, sorting and rearranging chapters, and then reading the final result.

Of the contributors, one in particular, Penny Hunting, must be singled out. She did far more research than appears in her two chapters as published, and her material helped to underpin others, particularly Michael Berlin and Robin Myers's chapter on the membership of the Company, and Michael Harris's on the relations of the Company with the Corporation of London.

Without all these, and others who I thank without naming, this book would not have seen the light of day. I hope they will think themselves thanked and rewarded if our combined efforts have produced a book which is read and used inside the Company and outside in the world of book history.

ROBIN MYERS
Stationers' Hall

Foreword

But for his untimely death, Past Master George Mandl would have written this book's Foreword. This history of the later years of the Stationers' Company is indeed his brainchild, and it owes much to his initial encouragement and to his generous financial support. Like many others in the Company, I feel sad that George has not been able to enjoy this book's fruition and give it his blessing in a characteristic Mandlian foreword. I feel honoured to have been asked to take his place.

After George's death, the Company's Archivist, Robin Myers, agreed to continue with the project; happily they had worked on the outlines of the book together. It is indeed fitting that Robin Myers should be the Editor. She has thoroughly researched the Company's archives, and written widely and authoritatively on them in the last twenty years; she almost certainly now knows more about the history of our Company than any one else. For the writing of the book Robin Myers assembled six other scholars, each a specialist in an area relevant to the Company's history, to contribute individual chapters, and she has written several of the chapters herself. The way the book was conceived and the way it has turned out make this history of the Company's last 200 years a complement to Blagden's classic history of the first 550 years; and it is a partial sequel to it, for Blagden deliberately treated the 19th and 20th centuries somewhat cursorily. Moreover many members of the Company have found Blagden's book, despite its authority and much fascinating content, difficult to read. For this new work the Editor has asked her contributors to make their chapters readable as well as authoritative, with an appeal to members of the Company, to the interested general reader and to academics.

The book is not a chronicle but a history of every aspect of our guild's life, covered aspect by aspect, rather than sequentially. I think you will agree that Robin Myers has succeeded in taking ten very individual chapters by seven separate contributors and blending them skilfully into a whole. She has let each author speak in his or her own voice and yet has managed to produce a unity, which the inclusion of various appendices and a chronology of Company and trade events, helps to strengthen. The result is a book of variety (and all the more readable for it), which members of the Company and the general reader, whether academically minded or not, will enjoy reading, while learning much about, for example, the history of the English Stock, the Company's handling of legal deposit, its membership, its historic archives, its relations with the City, and its property.

None of the authors of the main text of the book, other than the Editor, is a Stationer (although each has thoroughly researched the relevant aspect of the Company). Because the authors have felt no editorial constraints, they have not feared to be critical of the Company from time to time, balancing its successes with its failures. Each contributor has held independent views but has been fair in what he or she has written. The book is thus very different from most guild histories, and I believe more readable and more penetrating. It will surely become an acknowledged reference work for historians of the book trade, of copyright, of the City of London, and of other subjects. Its full index allows it to be used as such. Personally, I have found it revealing how much new information on some of these subjects the contributors' research has brought to light.

The new history is, I consider, a fine addition to the publications on our guild. Its publication is most timely and significant, as we approach the sexcentenary of our foundation in 1403. I wish this book the success it merits, and I commend it to you, the readers.

CHRISTOPHER RIVINGTON, PAST MASTER

Notes on Contributors

Michael Berlin: historian, lecturer and author; is currently working on a history of the Farmers' Company.

Richard Bowden is currently archivist to the Howard de Walden estate. He previously worked for Westminster City Archives, 1972-95, during which time he published books and articles on aspects of London's history.

Michael Harris PHD, FSA, Birkbeck College; author of *London Newspapers in the Age of Walpole*; co-editor, with Robin Myers, of the Publishing Pathways series on the history of the British book trade, 20 vols. 1981- ; is currently working on a history of news in the 18th century.

Penelope Hunting PHD, architectural historian and the author of the histories of the Drapers' Company, the Leathersellers' Company and the Society of Apothecaries; she is currently working on a history of the Royal Society of Medicine.

Robin Myers, MA, FSA, has been the Company's Honorary Archivist since 1978; she was President of the Bibliographical Society (1996-98) and is an honorary member of the Antiquarian Booksellers' Association; she has published widely on the Stationers' Company and the history of the book trade.

Ann Saunders PHD, FSA: historian, writer, editor and lecturer; honorary editor to the London Topographical Society; author of *The Art and Architecture of London* and several other books on the capital.

David Whitaker OBE, is the great-grandson of Joseph Whitaker, founding editor of both *Whitaker's Almanack* and *The Bookseller*. Four of his great uncles, and his father, were Stationers, as is his sister Sally. David Whitaker has been chairman of J. Whitaker & Sons, editor of *The Bookseller*, and chairman of many book trade committees ranging from Standard Book Numbering to Public Lending Right.

Abbreviations

Printed Books

Arber Arber, Edward, *A Transcript of the Registers of the Company of Stationers of London, 1554-1640 A.D.* 5 vols., 1875-94.

Blagden Blagden, Cyprian, *The Stationers' Company, a History, 1403-1959*, 1960.

McKenzie McKenzie, D.F., *Stationers' Company Apprentices, 1605-1800*, 3 vols. 1961-78.

Maxted Maxted, Ian, *The London Book Trades, 1775-1800*, 1977.

Myers Myers, Robin, *The Stationers' Company Archive, an Account of the Records, 1554-1984*, 1990.

Plomer Plomer, H.R. *et al.*, *A Dictionary of Printers and Booksellers who were at work in England, Scotland and Ireland, 1557-1775*, 4 vols. 1907-32, reprinted in 1 vol. 1977.

Unwin Unwin, Philip, *The Stationers' Company 1918-1977, a Livery Company in the Modern World*, 1978.

Archival Material (see Select List of Records)

Series I Miscellaneous documents in 40 boxes, listed, 1984.

Series II 664 legal and miscellaneous documents, calendared, 1950.

List of Subscribers

Cdr. Anthony Evan Adlard, RN
William Adlard
Hugh Amory
John Andrew-James
Society of Antiquaries of London
Patricia Aske
Raymond G. Astbury
Michael Barnard
Roger S. Bates
P.J. Batley
A.D. Baynes-Cope
Stuart Behn
Bill Bell
Derek Bell-Jones
Elizabeth Benn
Sir Jonathan Benn, Bt
Charles Benson
Paul N. Benwell
James L. Binnie
B.C. Bloomfield
Herbert Bohlhalter
J.H. Bowman
Clive Bradley
Richard S.W. Braithwaite
Jacqueline Branschi
Douglas Bristow
Andrew S. Brode
Alan Brooker
Robert Brooker
K. Allan Brunton-Reed
Eric Buckley
Arthur C.E. Buckwell
Gillis A. Burgess
A.T. Cameron
Ursula Carlyle
Melissa Cater
Arthur E. Chapman
H. Frank Chappell
Chetham's Library, Manchester
C. Paul Christianson
Elisa Civale
Geoffrey W.H.C. Claydon
Roger Cline
George B. Clouter

Lesley Cole
Robert H. Cole
Michael Collie
Vincent H. Conran
T.S. Corrigan
Richard John Cossens
Geoffrey Croughton
Neville Cusworth
Nicholas Cusworth
Leonard E. Davidge
John Evan Davies
N.E.M. Davies
Donald Davis
Jonathan Dean
James T. Donald
Douglas East
Colin R. Edwards
Sir Jeremy Elwes
Alison Emblow
Terence Eustance
J.A. Faiers
John Feather
Christine Ferdinand
Colin H. Fergusson
Ian D.F. Fidler
Elizabeth Ann Field
Barbara L. Fitzpatrick
Keith R. Fletcher
C.R.S. Fowler
Jane Francis
Norman Franklin
Gernot Gabel
Norman J. Garrod
Major R.J.A. Gazzard
Peter Gell
Jeff Green
Rémy J.B. Green
The Grolier Club Library
Geoffrey Groom
D.J. Hall
Ramsay Hampton
Christopher Harrison
Richard Harrison
T.W. Harrison

Michael J. Hart
Eric Haylock
Nicholas Heffer
Wilfrid B. Hodgson
Tom Hoffman
Brian J. Homersham
Peter Homewood
Jonathan Horne
Arnold Hunt
W.G. Hunt
Jeremy Hutton
Keith Hutton
Institute of Historical Research,
    University of London
Peter Isaac
Jessica Mary Jacob
Jennifer F. Jones
Philip Henry Jones
Anna and Gloria Kasket
Raymond Kilgarriff
Wallace Kirsop
Sarah Knowles
Leslie T. Lack
Lambeth Palace Library
John Lancaster
Chris Latham
Robert Laurie
Edwin Charles Lawrence
E.A. Quarmby Lawrence
Colin Lee
Elisabeth Leedham-Green
R. John Leighton
John M. Lettin
Richard A. Linenthal
Rosemary Lines
The London Library
Peter and Angela Lucas
Magdalen College Library, Oxford
Alexander Malcolm
The Marshall Library of Economics,
    University of Cambridge
Keith and Marjorie Maslen
Colin D. McDermid
Warren and Joanne McDougall

James Noel McGarry

Christopher McKane

Derek Melluish

The Warden and Fellows of Merton
College, Oxford

Serge and Michelle Meyer

Roy Millington

John and Susan Mitchell

Richard Model

Dennis Monckton

E.G.H. Moody

Brigadier R.S. Mountford

Rodney Mountford

The Heirs of Dr Robert Murray

Sheila J. Needham

Capt. A.G. Newing, RM

Doris R. Nicholson

Mark Ockelton

S.A.J. Oram

Dennis G. Osborne

Noel Osborne

Alan John Ousey

John R. Paine

Robert M. Palmer

Parker Library, Corpus Christi
College, Cambridge

R. Grant Paton

David Pearson

Michael A.E. Pegge

M.A. Pelham

Roger Pertwee

Jonathan Pewtress

Sir Edward Pickering

Guthrie Pickering

Harry Pollak

Julian Pooley

Esther Potter

Bernard Quaritch Ltd

John Quinney

Roger Reeve

P.T. Rippon

Christopher Rivington

Denis Hammond Roberts

Margaret Rodgers

D.A. Ross

The Royal Library, Windsor Castle

R.J. Russell

J.D. Ryman

St John's College, Oxford

Peter Sargent

William K. Sessions

Alasdair Shand

Terrence Shapland

Ivy Sharp

Clive J. Sharples

Elizabeth Mary Shelbourne

Alison Shell

Anthony A. Shipton

Michael Silverman

Roy Simpson

Sir John Sparrow

Russell C.R. Spencer

Michael G.R. Stamford

Colin Stanley

Alan J. Steel

John Stidolph

Peter Stockham

H. Martin Stuchfield

V.F. Sullivan

G. Thomas Tanselle

Ashley A. Teape

James Thompson

Josephine Thompson

Robert Threlfall

Sir Ray Tindle

George K. Todorovitch

Mark F. Tollit

J.R. Topham

Melville Topper

Michael Townsend

Donald Trelford

Jean Tsushima

Michael L. Turner

Dominique Varry

Charles Villiers

Laurence Viney

Mair Waldo-Thomas

John Walwyn-Jones

D.A.W. Ward

Dudley Ward

Nigel S. Wass

Sarah and Philip Watkins

L.J. Weaver

Eva M. Weininger

J. Elizabeth Wheatley

Peter L. Whiting

Owen H. Whittaker

Colin Whurr

D.E. Wickham

Peter M. Williams

Janice Conway Wood

Denis Woodfield

Martin Woodhead

Mary Woodroffe

The Worshipful Company of
Butchers

The Worshipful Company of Cutlers

The Worshipful Company of Dyers

The Worshipful Company of
Founders

The Worshipful Company of
Framework Knitters

The Worshipful Company of
Glovers of London

David Wyndham-Smith

Bill Young

To the memory of George T. Mandl,
Master of this Company, 1992 to 1993,
who, to our great regret, did not live to see
the publication of this history which he originated.

Introduction

The view of St Paul's, seen through the central window in the east wall of the Hall, provides the frontispiece to Blagden's history of the Company's first 550 years. In the 36 years since his death, that view has been blotted out by two concrete developments—the Colonial Mutual building, now converted to an hotel, in the foreground and Paternoster Square beyond. Blagden would no longer recognise the area surrounding the Hall.

The *History of the Later Years* examines every aspect of the Company's last two centuries, from its relations with the trades of its guild to those with the Corporation of the City; the main body of the book describes and evaluates the later years of the Company's composition and organisation, property and records. Not all the chapters span the entire period: the registry for copyright and legal deposit ended in the early years of the 20th century; the English Stock was wound up in 1961; the Company's library was not founded until 1974. The original intention was to end at 1990 but as the end of the century approached, it seemed better to continue to the year 2000, neatly rounding off with two events—the celebration of our 27th Lord Mayor, who happens also to be the book's printer, and, rather less jubilant but more final, the closure of the voluntary copyright registry which followed the termination of the Company's official registry, itself a sort of legacy of the censorship measures begun in 1556. Whereas the contributors have attempted to analyse and evaluate the events and personalities of the 19th and early 20th centuries, the nearer we got to the present, the more we merely chronicled events, avoiding opinions which might be invidious.

The present work is, in part, a revision and an expansion of Blagden's final chapters on the years 1800 to 1959, which have not stood the test of time as well as those on the Company's first 250 years. Nineteenth-century studies were not considered worth much serious research 40 years ago and Blagden himself, born in 1906, was too close to the period to see its worth. In common with leading bibliographers and book trade historians from Arber to McKenzie, he held the view that the Company lost its *raison d'être* with the ending of its statutory control of printing and bookselling, and that during the 19th century it gradually dwindled into little more than a club whose history could only be of domestic interest. It is a view which the present volume reassesses.

Blagden's opinion was that it 'was during the 19th century that the Company "retired" from the book trade'. It might be truer to say it was the other way round, for the Company continued to bind apprentices in large numbers throughout the 19th century, proof that it was still closely involved with its trades. More accurately, the trade retreated from the Company owing to a number of circumstances, some of them beyond the control of either the trade or the Company. In the course of the two centuries covered by the present work, London expanded, taking workers farther and farther afield, firms moved out, first to the periphery and then into the regions; printing, bookselling and publishing, split into separate subdivisions and founded specialised associations and unions, were overtaken by increasing industrialisation and, in recent years, by the technological revolution. The Hall, for so long the epicentre of printing and publishing, was, even in Blagden's day, more and more isolated from the industry it was linked to. The dispersal which began with the bombing of Paternoster Row and St Paul's Churchyard (now rebuilt, not as a street but as a carpark) in the 1940s, resulted in a mass exodus of publishing after the War. Blagden, in 1959, hoped that the traditional ties with the book trades would be maintained and 'the recent association with Fleet Street' fostered, making the Company more useful and prosperous. He could not have foreseen the final departure of 1985 when the press abruptly deserted Fleet Street, for so long the street of the press. Today almost none of the Livery lives or works in the vicinity.

Whatever it had done, the Stationers' Company could not have changed the course of events, but it has kept its links with the book and allied trades, and everyone, except the minority who enter by patrimony, must work in one or other of the trades of the guild. Among them, the old names are still to be found, although those who bear them no longer head the firms bearing their name. Two world wars have sparked off a social revolution—sons and daughters no longer follow fathers in family firms. The decline and final abolition of apprenticeship as a system of training, the technological revolution of the last two decades, the amalgamation of firms culminating in the globalisation of printing and publishing has produced a world which Blagden, historian and publisher, only 40 years ago, would have found it hard to envisage.

There is next to nothing, among the wealth of archival and published documentation on the Company's history, describing daily life at Stationers' Hall between 1800 and 2000. There is no doubt that the Hall, situated at the heart of the trade, must have been a hive of activity in the early 19th century—with apprentices coming to be bound, books being brought to be registered and copies being deposited for forward transmission to the legal deposit libraries, regular Courts, Stockboard meetings, dividend, quarterage and pension courts, convivial dinners and informal gatherings as well as trade committees. The Beadle's Book records that one liveryman died in his chair while talking to the Clerk, Henry Rivington, in his office.

The rare, anonymous pamphlet *Entered at Stationers' Hall*, cited in Chapter Four, contains a graphic, if satirical, description of searching for entered books in the registering office—it is unlikely, though nowhere stated, that the Warehouse Keeper dealt with the day-to-day running of registry. His duties as Treasurer of the English Stock, involving the wine committee and other more convivial matters, no doubt kept him too busy; the vivid descriptions by Charles Knight and T.F. Dibdin, which are quoted in Chapter Four, bring to life the November Almanack Days when the hall was thronged with porters making wholesale collections; elsewhere there are also references to Almanack

Day in the unpublished letters and diaries of members of the Nichols family. Until 1888, when the house attached to the Hall was refurbished and turned into offices, the Beadle (or Warehouse Keeper) lived on the premises; Joseph Greenhill, later Warehouse Keeper, was born there in 1803, and before that, a predecessor, George Hawkins, died there in 1760. The Beadle continued to live on the premises until William Poulten was granted leave to live elsewhere in 1905, as described in Chapter Six.

The Hall would have been daily visited by those living and working and storing their stock in the warehouses in Stationers' Hall Court. The Rivington Clerks came in and out from their solicitor's office in Fenchurch Buildings. Such are the haphazard glimpses of daily life at Stationers' Hall in the years before the First World War, but none gives the extended picture of it which would provide the connecting thread.

In the second half of the 20th century, life at the Hall was increasingly different. During the Second World War, in the wake of the Blitz, it must sometimes have been almost deserted. Then between the end of the war and the 1970s, the Hall was used almost exclusively for Company or trade functions. There followed a period of little outside use except for occasional researchers in the muniment room; but from the mid-1980s, a more commercially-minded Clerk and Court saw the Hall's potential for income. Lucrative Hall lettings make the Company once again prosperous, and concerts, marriage ceremonies, wedding feasts and barmitzvahs now make it hum with activity, even at weekends.

It is the impact on the organisation and membership of the Company and its synthesis with ancient tradition which is the subject of the present history. The pace will continue to quicken as we enter the new century and who knows how much of the old Company will be left intact by the year 2100? It is to be hoped that some will.

ROBIN MYERS
Stationers' Hall

CHAPTER ONE

The Company and the Trades of the Guild

D A V I D   W H I T A K E R

The 19th century saw a gradual erosion of the importance of the Company to the business lives of its members. In 1835 it became possible to buy the Freedom of the City of London—a prerequisite for trading within its boundaries—outside the structure of the old Companies. The requirement was abolished altogether in 1856. There was a steady growth of organised labour in the manufacturing industries after the repeal of the Combination Acts in 1824, and, more rapidly, after the passing of the Trades Union Act of 1871. Employers' organisations, on a national basis, were perceived as a necessary response. In the bookselling trade a defensive organisation which Lord Campbell had held to be an 'illegal conspiracy' in 1852 was reconstituted in 1895, when the tides of belief in *laissez-faire* economics were on the ebb. So far as their business affairs were concerned, members of the Company took themselves off.

The structures of the traditional trades also altered, as did the location of many of their factories and workshops. The use of water and steam-driven machinery in book production in the 19th century, and the Education Act of 1870, combined to provide a huge capacity to supply, with a market which steadily increased its ability to consume. Overseas markets also grew. As Victorian publishers did well by doing good, the papermakers, printers and binders who supplied them prospered too. But, increasingly, they did so out of London.

The growth of the market at home and expanding markets in the USA and the colonies meant that, 'After about 1875 the corporate interest in the protection of copyright had almost ceased to exist and many publishers were not members of the Society; but a vested interest in formal registration had taken its place'.[1] This vested interest was to receive its death blow from the 1911 Copyright Act which put an end to the power of the mantra 'Entered at Stationers' Hall' by abolishing formal registration. With that went the registration fees the Company had been collecting in recent years.[2] Another plank had been removed from the Company's reasons for being.

For Blagden other events which marked 'the otherwise imperceptible slither into old age' were the disposal of the Company's fire engine in 1844, the sale of its barge in 1850 and, in 1883, the treasurership of the English stock ceasing to be a full-time or salaried office.[3] In his chapter on the English stock Richard Bowden shows how important were

1. The composing room at the St Bride Institute in 1898, as illustrated in the prospectus for the 1900-1 session of letterpress and lithographic printing classes. The Company's connection with the Institute was to become a strong one in the 1920s, when students came to the Hall for lectures and examinations as well as to receive awards.

---

1 Blagden, p.274.
2 Before 1883 the fees went to the Registering Officer, after that date they went to the Company. See p.72.
3 Blagden, p.265.

diaries and almanacs, *Old Moore* prominent among them, to the financial state of the Company in the late 19th and early 20th centuries. He suggests that, without the English stock and, in particular, the sale of its property on Ludgate Hill in 1959, the Company might not have been given the time to conduct its long search for a new role.

Blagden described the property sale as

> the most exciting—and potentially the most significant—event of the last, somewhat featureless, 50 years in the history of the Stationers' Company. If the great sum received from the sale is invested with imagination and the income used with discretion, if the traditional ties with the book trade are maintained and the recent association with Fleet Street fostered, the Company may be, in the years to come, not only prosperous, but once again of service.[4]

This search for a role in which to be 'of service' had been going on for much of the previous half century, but without any great success; certainly not enough success to counter Blagden's view of the period as 'somewhat featureless'. And the search was to continue right through the 20th century.

The Departure of the Trades

Today's Papermakers Association was established in the 1850s. Among its predecessors were the Papermakers of Great Britain which met in 1765 at the George and Vulture inn, in Cornhill. It set up a committee to petition on excise matters which, according to D.C. Coleman, by 1790 described itself as a Committee of Master Papermakers.[5] In 1803, still at the George and Vulture, it was calling itself the United Society of Master Papermakers of Great Britain. In 1830, again with excise duty foremost in mind, manufacturers of paper and pasteboard met to draw up plans for excise repeal. This time the venue was the London Coffee House. While many papermakers were members of the Company, their business was done outside it.

By the end of the 18th century bookbinders also had an organisation which was outside of the Company. Pressured by their employees—who went on strike in 1786 to reduce their working week to 83 hours only, and again in 1806 for 30 minutes off for tea— and pressured too by their customers the bookseller-publishers who wanted lower prices, bookbinders did not look to the Hall for what little strength they could muster. The price book of 1813, issued in an effort to stabilise prices, came from the Associated Bookbinders of London and Westminster.[6]

The London Master Printers Association, dormant since the middle years of the century, was revived in 1890 with the object of embracing the whole City. In 1897 after its committee meeting of 29 April the Secretary asked the Stationers' Company if it would be willing to allow the printers to use the Hall for their annual meeting, which

---

4 Blagden, p.283.
5 D.C. Coleman, *The British Paper Industry 1495-1860: a study in industrial growth* (Oxford, 1958).
6 Mary Sessions, *The Federation of Master Printers—How it Began* (1950).

they hoped would be followed by a dinner. (This took place on 26 November, morning dress was worn, and Alderman George Wyatt Truscott was in the chair.)

It was the Glasgow printers who proposed, in 1897, that there be a National Federation.[7] This was fully realised on 28 May 1901 when the first official meeting of the British Federation of Master Printers took place in the Holborn Restaurant in London. Printers supplied 22 Masters between 1800 and 1899, compared with 43 who were stationers. In the 20th century the printers came to dominate the Company. But their business was done elsewhere.

The youngest recruit was in the same mould. The Newspaper Makers Company was formed in 1931 when Britain was in the economic doldrums which had followed the First World War. Still not quite sure of themselves despite their great wealth and growing influence, the Newspaper Makers were glad in 1933 to combine with the Stationers. They added vigour and colour at a time when the Company, for very different reasons, was not sure of its own role in the world. However, their business decisions—insofar as they were made jointly anywhere at all—were made at the Newspaper Society or at the Newspaper Publishers Association.[8]

Booksellers and Publishers

Blagden wrote, sadly, that

> ... no organisation in the trade, whether of master printers, or of bookbinders, or of publishers, developed out of or had any direct association with the Stationers' Company. The disputes about published prices in the 1850s and the 1890s caused no stir in the Court Room ... and the closest relationship was that of landlord and tenant ... it was during the 19th century that the Stationers' Company 'retired' from the book trade.[9]

While Blagden has a point in this, two trade associations were actually formed in the Hall itself. The story of booksellers and publishers is worth telling at greater length because it demonstrates how deeply rooted, even visceral, was their attachment to the Company which, as Blagden says, 'retired' from them. It also demonstrates the changes that took place in Victorian days to two of the traditional trades of the Guild.

The 19th century was not kind to booksellers. For much of the time the conviction was dominant that unregulated *laissez-faire* was the proper way to conduct the economy of the country. The combining together of tradesmen to provide mutual support and a regulation of the market place was out of fashion. In 1852 Charles Dickens chaired a meeting of authors to support the principle of free trade in books. (This is part of the 1850s dispute to which Blagden refers.) Following this meeting, and in the same year, members of the Booksellers Association asked Lord Campbell, Dean Milman and

---

7 Sessions, *op. cit.*
8 Librarians—who organised themselves in the Library Association in 1877, have only been eligible to join the Company since 1989. Authors were briefly admitted to the Company in the early 1930s, with journalists; they had founded their own professional association, the Society of Authors, in 1884.
9 Blagden, p.275.

George Grote to arbitrate on the matter. Lord Campbell declared that the Association—whose leading members were almost all members of the Stationers' Company—was an illegal conspiracy. The consequent disbanding of the Booksellers Association, and the end to the price stability it had sought, was followed by widespread discounting, a decline in stockholding, and a thinning of the ranks of the specialist tradesman.

The second half of the century also saw an acceleration of the separation of the roles of the bookseller and publisher. The booksellers remained tradesmen, and struggling tradesmen at that, while the publishers moved up a notch or two in the social hierarchy. Perhaps the writing might have been seen to be on the wall from that moment in 1812, with the publication of *Childe Harold*, of which it was written that 'Byron woke up to find himself famous and his publisher John Murray woke up a gentleman'.

By the 1880s *laissez-faire* was no longer seen as akin to God's Commandments, and it was accepted that quality bookselling was in dire straits. As the new decade opened London booksellers sought to form a new association and where more suitable to do it than at Stationers' Hall? On 29 May 1890 Messrs. Stott, Calder, Turner, Stoneham, Waters, Burleigh and J.V. Whitaker—editor of *The Bookseller*, which recorded the event—decided to ask the Company to lend its Hall for a meeting to propose that 'It is desirable to form a London Booksellers Society'. The meeting was held on 9 June, and the motion was passed.[10]

Five years later, on 11 January 1895, a special general meeting was called, to be held on 23 January, again at Stationers' Hall. The object was to 'report on negotiations with publishers', and to record the change of name of the London Booksellers Society to the Associated Booksellers of Great Britain and Ireland. The 'negotiations with publishers' were to do two things: to persuade them to lend their weight to stop the discounting which had brought the retail trade to its knees, and to persuade publishers themselves to form an association which could negotiate on behalf of its members with the Associated Booksellers.

The negotiations with publishers took a long time and their history illustrates the changing relationship between the two bodies of members of the Company. For instance, the minute book of the Associated Booksellers (from 23 January 1894 to 14 September 1899) records that its meeting of 10 October 1895 was held at the Anderton Hotel because the Stationers 'declined to lend their Hall for the purpose of holding a conference'.

The minutes of the meeting at the Anderton Hotel—'To discuss certain propositions put forward by the Associated Booksellers of Great Britain and Ireland'—show that Colonel Routledge proposed and W.F.Warne seconded 'That a meeting of publishers be summoned to consider the desirability of appointing a committee to meet the committee of the Associated Booksellers.' The proposal was adopted. Both proposer and seconder were publishers. Stationers' Hall was booked for 21 November. This time the booking was accepted.

---

10 The rare book trade formed their own association, the Antiquarian Booksellers' Association, in 1906.

Almost all of those who attended the 21 November meeting were publishers and members of the Company. C.J. Longman was in the chair. John Murray proposed that a committee be appointed to draw up rules for the formation of the Publishers Association to be submitted to publishers on 23 January 1896. The rules were adopted, and the minute book of the new Association shows that on 15 April 1896 its Council learned that the Stationers had agreed to 'allow us to hold our meetings and to have our office at Stationers' Hall and would allow their Clerk Mr Poulten to act as our paid Secretary'. The publishers were *persona grata*.

It should be noted that Mr Poulten was 'their Clerk' not *the* Clerk, an altogether more exalted person who at that time was C.R. Rivington of the family which ran the Stationers' Company for so many years. Mr Poulten's official title was Beadle, a post which he held from 1890 to 1940. Philip Unwin, Master 1971-72, recalled him as wearing a high 'stick-up' collar and being the very image, to a young man, of a Victorian beadle. 'As Liveryman number 351,' Unwin wrote, 'I recall sitting next to him at a civic dinner and, nourished as I had been in a teetotal household, was greatly intrigued to see the relish with which he carefully warmed his brandy then tipped it into his coffee.' Mr Poulten also, until old age, bathed every morning, and all year round, in the Highgate Pond.[11]

Mr Poulten got £175 a year and a house for being Beadle at the Stationers' Company; the Publishers Association minutes for 5 April 1896 record that the publishers were to negotiate a fee of 'not more than £75 a year' for his new and additional role. At its meeting on 21 April the Publishers Association Council was told that Mr Poulten was now its Secretary, at £1 a week, paid weekly. This was generous in today's 'real terms'. (In February of 1897 Mr Poulten got a rise to £1 10s. a week, 'the duties of the office having considerably increased'; and, perhaps, because he had read the minutes of 5 April Mr Poulten served the Publishers Association until 1934.) At that same 21 April meeting C.J. Longman, first President of the Publishers Association, noted that it was receiving legal assistance from C.R. Rivington, the Clerk.

On 17 December 1896 a sub-committee of the Publishers Association met at Stationers' Hall to prepare comments on a new draft bill on copyright. This was another defining moment. For from then on the minutes of the monthly meetings of the Council of the Publishers Association show it taking into its hands those matters which it saw as essential to the maintenance of the health of its business, but which had once been the concern of the Stationers' Company itself.

In Mr Longman's inaugural address he gave the concerns of the new Association as (1) copyright, (2) relations between publishers and authors and (3) 'excessive discounts' given to retailers. Having been instrumental in persuading the publishers to form an association at all, the booksellers' interest, stopping underselling, was put last on the list of concerns of the publishers. This was not the only slight that they were to receive.

11 Unwin, p.25.

Meetings of the Associated Booksellers were held at Stationers' Hall from 1896 to 1907. Permission was renewed in April 1901 'upon the express condition that Stationers' Hall is not to be deemed the offices of the Association and that communications relating to the business of the Association are not to be addressed from Stationers' Hall by the Association or any officer thereof'.[12] Perhaps they forgot, for on 16 January 1907 Mr Poulten wrote to the President of the Associated Booksellers that there would be in future 'a charge of 21 shillings per meeting for the use of this Hall, and as the Court and Card Room will not be available it will be necessary that any meeting you may hereafter desire to hold should take place either in the Hall itself or in the lobby adjoining the Court Room'. Mr Poulten added, unconvincingly, 'I trust that these new arrangements will not cause you any inconvenience'.

The Associated Booksellers' minutes for February record that 'Much regret was felt at the thought of severing association with the Hall in which meetings had been held for so long', and an appeal was made higher up the hierarchy, but to no avail. The April minutes end the story: 'The President reported that he had been in communication with the Clerk to the Court of Assistants of the Stationers' Company, and as it was quite evident no change in the conditions for the Council's accommodation would be made, he could not advise the holding of further meetings in the rooms offered.' The Associated Booksellers moved its meetings to Essex Hall, in Essex Street, 'at a very considerably reduced charge'.

The booksellers who had become publishers and gentlemen had, cuckoo like, ousted the booksellers who had remained as retailers and tradesmen.

The Draw of a Good Dinner

While none of these associations, not even the Associated Booksellers or the Publishers Association, had truly 'developed out of or had any direct association with the Stationers' Company ... other than as landlord and tenant', to use Blagden's phrases, their sentimental attachment to it remained strong. And even if the Company was on a 'slither into old age', people important in its traditional trades continued to join. The attraction of the Hall, and its famous dinners, was enhanced by its proximity to the offices and warehouses of so many of the leading publishers who were clustered in and around Warwick Lane, Amen Court, Ave Maria Lane and in Carter Lane on the other side of Ludgate Hill. Newspaper makers too, in Printing House Square or clustered in and around Fleet Street, were within walking distance. Many of the warehouses of paper merchants and the London works or offices of leading printers and binders were also only a short walk away. This continued to be true until the great German firebomb raids in 1941 destroyed the trade's traditional heartland.

The Company's dinners were famous not just for years, but for centuries. On 14 April 1795 *The Times* wrote, sharply, that

12 Court Book E, 1 April 1901.

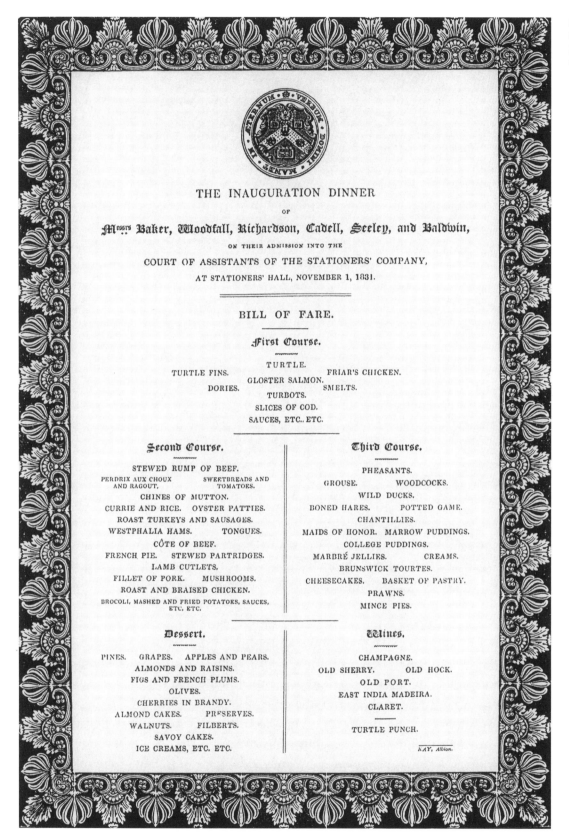

2. Menu for the Inauguration Dinner, 1 November 1831.

THE INAUGURATION DINNER

OF

Messrs Baker, Woodfall, Richardson, Cadell, Seeley, and Baldwin,

ON THEIR ADMISSION INTO THE

COURT OF ASSISTANTS OF THE STATIONERS' COMPANY,

AT STATIONERS' HALL, NOVEMBER 1, 1831.

BILL OF FARE.

First Course.

TURTLE.

TURTLE FINS.   FRIAR'S CHICKEN.

GLOSTER SALMON.

DORIES.   SMELTS.

TURBOTS.

SLICES OF COD.

SAUCES, ETC., ETC.

Second Course.

STEWED RUMP OF BEEF.

PERDRIX AUX CHOUX   SWEETBREADS AND
AND RAGOUT,   TOMATOES.

CHINES OF MUTTON.

CURRIE AND RICE.   OYSTER PATTIES.

ROAST TURKEYS AND SAUSAGES.

WESTPHALIA HAMS.   TONGUES.

CÔTE OF BEEF.

FRENCH PIE.   STEWED PARTRIDGES.

LAMB CUTLETS.

FILLET OF PORK.   MUSHROOMS.

ROAST AND BRAISED CHICKEN.

BROCOLI, MASHED AND FRIED POTATOES, SAUCES,
ETC. ETC.

Third Course.

PHEASANTS.

GROUSE.   WOODCOCKS.

WILD DUCKS.

BONED HARES.   POTTED GAME.

CHANTILLIES.

MAIDS OF HONOR.   MARROW PUDDINGS.

COLLEGE PUDDINGS.

MARBRÉ JELLIES.   CREAMS.

BRUNSWICK TOURTES.

CHEESECAKES.   BASKET OF PASTRY.

PRAWNS.

MINCE PIES.

Dessert.

PINES.   GRAPES.   APPLES AND PEARS.

ALMONDS AND RAISINS.

FIGS AND FRENCH PLUMS.

OLIVES.

CHERRIES IN BRANDY.

ALMOND CAKES.   PRESERVES.

WALNUTS.   FILBERTS.

SAVOY CAKES.

ICE CREAMS, ETC. ETC.

Wines.

CHAMPAGNE.

OLD SHERRY.   OLD HOCK.

OLD PORT.

EAST INDIA MADEIRA.

CLARET.

TURTLE PUNCH.

KAY, Albion.

Yesterday the Stationers' Company had their annual dinner at Stationers' Hall. Having determined, in consequence of the great scarcity of flour, to abolish the use of pies, they contented themselves with several haunches of venison, and a number of *venison pasties*, which consumed flour sufficient for 50 fruit pies. And in order to adopt the above resolution of no pies, the Court of Assistants had privately a snug dinner, consisting of all the delicacies of the season. Of public dinners, those of the Stationers' Company rival every other. We have not yet heard of the Company's having contributed anything to the relief of the poor.

On 1 November 1831, at an inauguration dinner for Messrs Baker, Woodfall, Richardson, Cadell, Seeley and Baldwin, on their admission to the Court of Assistants, the first course was turtle fins, turtle, friar's chicken, Gloster (*sic*) salmon, dories, smelts, turbots, slices of cod, and sauces; the second course was stewed rump of beef, chines of mutton, currie and rice, oyster patties, roast turkeys and sausages, Westphalia hams, tongues, côte of beef, French pie, stewed partridges, lamb cutlets, fillet of pork, mushrooms, roast and braised chicken, with broccoli, mashed and fried potatoes and sauces.

For those who could cope with it, there was a third course: pheasants, grouse, woodcocks, wild ducks, boned hares, potted game, chantillies, maids of honor (*sic*), marrow puddings, college puddings, Marbré jellies, creams, Brunswick tortes, cheesecakes, a basket of pastry, prawns and mince pies. For dessert there were pines, grapes, apples and pears, almonds and raisins, figs and French plums, olives, cherries in brandy, almond cakes, preserves, walnuts, filberts, Savoy cakes, ice creams, and more. The wines were described simply as Champagne, Old Sherry, Old Hock, Old Port, East India Madeira and Claret.

Twenty-nine years later, on Thursday, 8 November 1860, not a lot had changed. The Company sat down to mock turtle, mulligatawny or oxtail soups; turbot, codfish or stewed eels; turkey, ham, pigeon pie, boiled chicken, stewed beef, or tongues; roast chicken, chines of mutton, sirloin of beef, or *caneton aux navets*; pheasants, grouse, widgeon or partridges; plum pudding, blancmangers (*sic*), mince pies, pastry, wine jelly, cheesecakes, apple tarts, cabinet pudding, marrow pudding or *Charlottes à la Bohémienne*.

Forty years on the menu for the Presentation Dinner held on Wednesday, 24 October 1900 for Alderman Frank Green (Lord Mayor Elect) shows that the heavy eating of the height of Victoria's era had stopped. But even this menu seems hearty when looked back on from the age of Weight Watchers. The Company enjoyed as much as it could manage of *anchois aux oeufs*, sardines *à la Bordelaise*, clear turtle soup, thick turtle soup, John Dory *à la Pelissier*, soles *à la Normande*, oyster cutlets *à la crème*, grouse puddings *à l'essence*, saddles of mutton, *pommes de terre sautés*, York ham, French salad, roast pheasants and grilled mushrooms. For puddings there were *gelées d'abricots à la crème*, maids of honor, *gelées au marasquin, compôtes de fruits, bombe glacé au citron* ending, for those who were still capable, with bloater roe on toast. There was Turtle Punch, Amontillado, Hock, Rudesheimer, Pommery & Greno champagne, Bollinger champagne (both of vintage 1893), Cockburn's port, and Château Palmer Margaux (1890) followed by liqueurs and brandy.

Famed not just for the Food

And if the food did not draw them, the sense of occasion might. Dinners of the Company were reported in the press. *The Times*—less sharp by Victorian days—had its offices and works three minutes' walk away in Printing House Square. On 13 June 1889 the paper recorded that

> At a dinner given by the Master, Mr John Miles, the Wardens, and Court of Assistants of the Stationers' Company this week there were among those present Lord Houghton, Mr W.H. Smith, M.P., Sir F. Bramwell, Archdeacon Farrar, Canon Gregory, Sir John Gilbert, R.A., Sir T. Spencer Wells, the Rev. Dr Wace (Principal of King's College), the Astronomer Royal, Mr H.T. Cole, Q.C. (Treasurer of the Middle Temple), the Rev. Dr Haig Brown, Mr John Evans, F.R.S., Mr Warren De La Rue, F.R.S., Mr Ewan Christian (President of the Royal Institute of British Architects), Major-General Clarke, Dr Owen Rees, F.R.S., Professor Jebb, Mr Briton Rivière, R.A., Professor Henry Morley, Mr Philip Magnus, Mr H. Austen Dobson, Mr H. Trueman Wood, Mr T.C. Hansard, Dr Symes Thompson, Mr G. Bentley, Mr Owen Roberts, and Mr C.R. Rivington.
>
> Lord Houghton in replying for the House of Lords, said that in all Constitutions that had been elaborated in our time or in the time before us, the framers of Constitutions had never omitted a second Chamber. We none of us trusted our first thoughts, and we assimilated the mind politic to the mind individual. Mr W.H. Smith, M.P., returned thanks for the toast of the House of Commons. That House, it might be said, expressed the first thoughts of the multitude, and in doing so he ventured to hope they would long hold the position of representatives rather than of delegates. The toasts of Science, Literature, and Art, severally proposed by Sir F. Bramwell, Professor Jebb, and the Rev. Prebendary Wace, were responded to by the Astronomer Royal, Archdeacon Farrar, and Sir John Gilbert, R.A., and Mr Briton Rivière, R.A.

Ten years later, on 16 May 1898, the company was even more distinguished. The next day *The Times* reported that 'The Master, Wardens, and Court of Assistants of the Stationers' Company gave a dinner last night in their hall 'to meet his Grace the Archbishop of Canterbury, patron of the company'. The Master, C.J. Clay, presided and among the guests there were three Bishops, the Vice Chancellors of Oxford and Cambridge Universities, the Masters, Presidents or Rectors of 16 Oxford or Cambridge Colleges, and numerous other luminaries.

The Master proposed the health of the Archbishop of Canterbury, and the Archbishop's reply indicated that his briefing may have been less accurate than it was enthusiastic. According to *The Times* report he said

> The Stationers' Company was distinguished from all the other Livery Companies of London—it stood alone, because all the other companies, as far as he could see, had become somewhat lazy, and had turned away from their proper business. For instance, they heard a good deal about the Fishmongers' Company. How many fish did they catch? Then there was the Drapers' Company. He did not believe that that company could supply him with enough cloth to make him a pair of breeches (laughter). It seemed to him that they had

really given up their proper place in the economy of this great City. The Stationers' Company, however, still acted up to the excellent old English proverb of 'mind your own business.' They looked after books—the most important part of stationery—and in all ways they were true to their original calling. They had still to register all the books that were brought to them to be registered, and he believed that an Act of Parliament was going to be passed shortly which would give them still more authority in connection with this subject.

When the Bishop of Bristol proposed a toast to 'Education' his sentiments might well be echoed by his successor today. He hoped that 'the Vice-Chancellors would forever keep raising the standard of those to whom they assigned their honours, and that they would jealously keep open the avenues to the Universities, so that they should be freely accessible to talent and genius for every rank in society, down to the very lowest.'

There were also luncheons, arranged from 1920 on by the Livery Committee (see below). Among speakers were Hugh Walpole in 1922, Sir Sefton Brancker on Commercial Aviation in 1926, Gilbert Frankau, Charles Ffoulkes (Curator of the Tower of London) and Edgar Wallace as part of a strong programme in 1928, Gordon Selfridge on Romance in Business in 1933, Herbert Morrison on What the London County Council does for London, in 1935, and the Ambassador of the United States of America in 1937.

When entertaining began again, in September 1951, even six years after war had ended the kitchens were not working, nor was the heating, but Ring & Brymer were reported as doing wonders and the abstemious Philip Unwin generously records that, fortunately, 'The Company's wine cellars had remained intact'.

The Company and Training

One notable success of the inter-war years had been education and training. From 1921 to 1939 the Hall was the centre for examinations in printing. The City and Guilds Grade II examinations had lost their way and in 1920 J.R. Riddell, the principal of the St Bride Foundation Institute, and also a Liveryman, persuaded the Court to set up the Stationers' Company and Printing Industry Technical Board. Students from the St Bride Printing School—which became the London School of Printing in 1922—came to the Hall to sit their examinations, receive certificates and awards, and to listen to lectures. In 1921, 372 students sat examinations in composing, cylinder machining, lithography and bookbinding; by 1936 the number of students had risen to 1590. After the war examining returned to the City and Guilds, which was by then in better order.

The Printing Industries Training Board also held six craft lectures in the Hall and these ran from 1922 to 1940. They took over the St Bride Trade Lectures which had started in 1917. The lecturers were seniors in the various trades of the Guild and the first lecture was given by Lord Riddell—no relation of J.R. Riddell—on *The Printing Business as a Career*.

The lecture given in 1929 was to have a remarkable, long-lasting and beneficial effect. The speaker was Dr G.L.Riddell, son of J.R., and a past pupil of the Stationers'

Company's School. His subject was *The Application of Science to Printing*. The lecture was so well received that Lord Riddell called together leading printers to meet at the Hall. A committee was formed from which grew the Printing Industry Research Association (PIRA) now Pira International.

PIRA's objects were to bring together and to publish research from all over the world, to be an information centre, and to carry out technical and scientific investigation for its members. Its first director of research was Dr Riddell, and its first offices were at the Hall and, while these offices were soon outgrown, the Stationers' connection with PIRA continues to this day through the Educational Charity's postgraduate research grants.

The craft lectures were not revived after the war and Philip Unwin describes this as 'an interesting opportunity lost for the Company to do more towards getting back into the trade'.[13]

The Hall as a Focal Point

In the 18th and 19th centuries the Company was important not only for education, but also for ceremonial and charity, with its Hall continuing to be popular for social and commemorative functions. It was as if the Hall conferred legitimacy upon a trade event, and this remains true to this day. In 1871 a charitable fund was organised by the London trade for Paris publishers, booksellers and assistants to help relieve their suffering from the Franco-Prussian War and its revolutionary aftermath. It was launched at the Hall and at the first meeting £500 was subscribed in the room. The fund ultimately reached £2,000.[14]

The Booksellers Association (it changed its name from Associated Booksellers in 1948) and the Publishers Association, both having grown out of meetings in the Hall, celebrated their centenaries—in 1995 and 1996 respectively—in the room in which they had been born. In 1897 the London Master Printers asked to use the Hall for an annual meeting, and this booking, with many more to be added, was taken up by its successor the British Federation of Master Printers. In 1912 the Booksellers Provident Institution took an office at the Hall and joined the Publishers Association and Associated Booksellers in being allowed to hold meetings there. The Papermakers Association was given permission to hold its meetings at the Hall in 1919. The Royal Literary Fund took an office in 1921, and continued its tenancy until 1956; it continued to hold its committee meetings in the ante-room until 1983.

Between July 1905 and October 1908 there were 98 meetings of Councils of members of the Publishers Association, Associated Booksellers, Wholesale Stationers, Master Printers and seven other organisations. This level of activity declined as their businesses grew and many found their own premises; but other organisations and other activities took their place.

---

13 Unwin, p.33.
14 *The Bookseller*, 1858, reprinted 3 May 1958, p.1530.

3. Menu for the first Ladies' Dinner at Stationers' Hall, 1893.

The Hall has been a natural venue for exhibitions and celebrations. In 1899 the Court placed the Hall and Stock Room at the disposal of the Publishers Association to host a Congress of the International Publishers Association. In 1904 there was an exhibition of antiquarian books demonstrating the history of the printed book, put on for the congress of International Antiquarian Booksellers. In 1908 a delegation of French book-sellers was entertained. In 1911 the Royal Colonial Institute hired the Hall to entertain the President of Tasmania. (This was a glimpse of the future. By the third quarter of the 20th century an important stream of income has come from letting the Hall, for meetings and events, to organisations which have little or no connection with any of the Company's traditional trades.)

Among numerous jollities held over the years was that of 19 November 1927 when the Publishers Association gave a dinner at Stationers' Hall to celebrate 'The Co-operative Spirit of the 1920s'. The President of the Associated Booksellers had pride of place at the top table. William Longman took the chair and among the distinguished guests were A.S. Eddington, Rudyard Kipling (who had been made an Honorary Freeman and Liveryman in 1925 along with Earl Balfour and Sir James Barrie, to a chorus of disapproval from traditionalists), Dean Inge and G.S. Gordon. There were long speeches and, surprisingly, sketches from comedians. R.J.L. Kingsford, in his *The Publishers Association 1896-1946* (Cambridge University Press, London, 1970), remembers Arthur Askey with particular affection. Askey was diminutive, wore huge hornrim spectacles, was famous for his playing of the Dame in pantomime, and his first words were always 'Hello, playmates!'. Perhaps he had a different persona for occasions in the City.

On Tuesday 23 October 1928, women were invited to a banquet in their own right. Among luminaries who entertained them were the Austen Leighs, Roy Truscott, J.R. Riddell and Sidney Hodgson. Among the guests Pippa Woodman (see pp.32, 33) and Beatrice Warde of the Monotype Corporation, were to be as famous as any of their hosts.

In 1926 the Society of Bookmen was founded, with Hugh Walpole its first President, as a ginger group to encourage the book trade to improve itself. When the Society became 50 years old, in 1976, it was taken for granted that its anniversary dinner would be at Stationers' Hall. In 1957 the Wynkyn de Worde Society was formed—the brainchild of James Moran, notable printing historian and first librarian of the Stationers' Company—as a luncheon club for printers and designers. It was natural that it should hold its meetings at the Hall, just as it was for the Bibliographical Society to hold its centenary celebrations there in 1992. In 1964 on the occasion of an International Printing Exhibition and World Book Fair, held at Earl's Court, the Master welcomed guests, many from overseas, at two receptions given by the Company.

And for matters of moment the Hall was an equally obvious venue. On 5 July 1940 Geoffrey Faber, then President of the Publishers Association, Stanley Unwin, Edmund Segrave the editor of *The Bookseller*, the by now knighted Hugh Walpole in the chair, J.B. Priestley, A.P. Herbert and the Archbishop of Canterbury were among those influential in the book trade or distinguished outside it who met at the Hall to form the National Book Committee. Its object was to protest against the proposal of the Chancellor of the Exchequer, Sir Kingsley Wood, to put Purchase Tax on books. A.P. Herbert, then the independent M.P. for Oxford University, subsequently made a speech of great power in the House of Commons. In the light of the enthusiasm and support for his speech, and the wide and sympathetic reporting of the meeting held at the Hall, the Chancellor reversed his decision. The National Book Committee grew into the National Book League, now called Book Trust.

Efforts to be 'More Useful'

But none of these useful, enjoyable or worthy activities made the Company any more central to the day-to-day business of its members. Efforts to change this began before the First World War had ended, and continued, intermittently, for the next 50 years before there was more than limited success. The Court Minutes for 8 January 1918 recall that it was moved by Mr Warden Layton and seconded by Sir Thomas Vezey Strong and resolved unanimously

> That a committee of the Court be formed, with power to invite not more than four representative members of the Livery to assist them, to prepare a scheme with a view to obtaining increased revenue, and under which the Company might be made more useful to the Livery and a desirable home or centre for co-operation for the various Societies connected with the trades from which the Livery is drawn and that the results obtained be submitted to the Court.

The committee met several times with the President and Vice President of the Federation of Master Printers, and of the London Master Printers Association. The joint committee—as it then termed itself—produced a printed report which was received by the Court at its meeting of 8 October 1918. Among the recommendations was that there should be 'an association of the Societies connected with the stationery, printing, publishing and cognate trades', with the tasks of representing the common interests of all but without interfering in any way with the constitution or particular work of any individual Society already working for them.

The joint committee listed as common interests:

> to take part in the important after war conferences which are anticipated with Cabinet Ministers, Masters and Labour; to watch projected legislation; to seek to improve the present laws and regulations of trade; to overlook technical education; to form benevolent funds; to promote social intercourse between members, and to hold exhibitions of their work.

The report may have thoroughly alarmed the Court when it also recommended that the new Society be accommodated in offices to be built over the garden and above the Hall and Court Room. The Federation of Master Printers had provided the services of its surveyor and offered to build the new accommodation, at an estimated cost of £25,000. It would have its own offices there. In addition it was to have use of the Company's premises on Monday, Wednesday and Friday and of the Hall twice a year for exhibitions, at a rent of £1,000 a year.

At a special meeting on 12 November 1918 the report was considered. But as the war had ended the day before, the consideration was brief. Most of the meeting was spent drafting a message of congratulation to the King, followed by a message to the Lord Mayor of London, a fellow Liveryman, congratulating him upon the auspicious opening of his year of office.

Herbert Jameson Waterlow moved

> That this Court while approving of the principle of making the Stationers' Company a centre of the printing, bookselling, paper and allied trades resolves that the report and suggestions of the committee ... be referred back to the committee for further consideration of the original reference of the 8th January 1918.

Although refined proposals were considered on 14 January 1919, and accepted, and a sub-committee authorised 'to pursue negotiations and make all enquiries on the basis of these suggestions subject to all such negotiations being finally approved by this Court', matters must have run into the sand and no more is heard. The Court Book does not say what kind of sand it was. Blagden comments, simply, 'It is easy to see where the fears lay'.[15]

The Livery Committee Tries its Hand

The Livery Committee was formed in 1920. It was, in part, a response by the Court to the perennial complaints made about how long it took to become a member of the Court, how old the Court was, and how out of touch with the working world lived in by many members of the Livery.

The Livery Committee saw itself, then, as a ginger group. Its objects were to represent to the Court the views and aspirations of Liverymen, to increase knowledge of and interest in the Company among Liverymen, and to foster interest in the Trades of the Guild.

On 4 March 1921 the minutes of the Livery Committee show it discussing the principle of direct representation of the Livery on the Court. At its Annual General Meeting of 22 June 1921 the Livery Committee 'Resolved that the Committee continue to press for direct representation of the Livery on the Court by election', and the Minutes record that 'several questions were asked in relation to the advantage of anyone becoming a member of the Company'.

In June 1926 the Court agreed that four Liverymen might be put forward, of whom the Court would choose two, to sit with it for one year only and not to be re-eligible except by seniority. R.A. Austen Leigh and J.R. Riddell were the first to go forward. The Clerk, Reginald Rivington, informed them that 'they would have to take steps to provide themselves with Livery gowns.' By March 1927 the Livery Committee had collected £32 3s. 6d. to provide two gowns, to be the property of the Livery. (These were to be lost in the Second World War, and in 1948 the War Damages Commission paid for new ones at £19 a garment.)

15 Blagden, p.279.

4. F.D. Bone's sketch, 1938, for a proposed club house and library to be built round the plane tree. (See Illustration 76, p.198.)

ELEVATION of PROPOSED LIBRARY

looking from Entrance Door in corner of Courtyard

At the Annual General Meeting of 1928-29 the Livery Committee reported that, at the request of the Court, it had sounded out the Livery about women members: 'Such a departure would not be acceptable to the majority of the Livery'. Ginger only went so far.[16]

In 1930 Liveryman Herbert A. Cox put forward some proposals to try to refresh the Court and to bring down from 20 years to 14 the number of years a Liveryman might expect to remain as a member of the Court. In 1932 the Livery Committee 'viewed with increasing concern the decreasing interest in the Company by those eligible ...', and wondered what the Court proposed to do about it.

In May 1939 G.L. Riddell, the secretary of the Livery Committee, asked for comments on the state of the Company. The Chairman of the Livery Committee wrote: 'I am sure when it is seen that it is possible to get on to the Court before one has to be wheeled

16 The admission of women into the Company is more fully dealt with in Chapter Two, pp.32-5.

there in a bath chair, that it will give a fillip to membership of the Company'. F.D. Bone, who was a newspaper maker member of the Livery Committee from December 1939 to 1946, wrote:

> I beg to offer suggestions and observations concerning matters in which the Newspaper
> Makers are interested. In general terms they would like the Company to take an active part
> in promoting the social and material welfare of people employed in the newspaper industry.
> Among such matters, I venture to cite the following ...[17]

He then asked for support for the Bill before Parliament requiring the registration of journalists, scholarships for youngsters, prizes for press stories and pictures of excellence, a bungalow around the tree in the courtyard to house a library and reading room, and a luncheon club in this 'garden pavilion'. Mr Bone produced drawings for the bungalow, which are still held in the library. War intervened before anything could be done.

In 1957, the war 12 years in the past and the kitchens back in order since 1954, the Committee arranged the first of what became annual Livery Lectures. The object was to promote the Company and to stimulate interest in it among potential members. Sir Lionel Heald spoke on Copyright in 1957, Sir William Haley on Television and the Press in 1958, Philip Unwin on Trends in Book Publishing in 1959, Sir Francis Meynell on the Typography of Advertising in 1960, Sir John Simpson on Her Majesty's Stationery Office in 1961, Philip Walker on the British Paper Industry in 1962, and Sir James Waterlow on Periodical Publishing in 1963. While there have been fluctuations in quality, generally the standard has continued to be high.

In 1960 Cyprian Blagden gave a talk on the past and future of the Company which led to a committee being set up in March 1961 to produce 'Proposals for making the Company more active in the printing and allied trades'. There were representatives of advertising, newspapers, book publishing, authors and printing. The report was forwarded to the Court early in 1962. In September 1962 it was reported that the Court had not yet had an opportunity to discuss it. Even Blagden's *imprimatur* could not cause a ripple on the Court's deep waters.

The Liverymen had another try in 1965 when Philip Unwin and Christopher Rivington circulated to members of the Court a memorandum called *Election of Liverymen to the Court of Assistants and Election of Master and Wardens*. As the election of representatives of the Livery to the Court had been on the agenda since 1921, some irritation might have been expected. However, with two such authors the paper was impeccably courteous.

Its essence was that most of the traditional activities of the Company were done by employers' associations and trade unions active within its traditional trades; that Liverymen would welcome more matters of trade interest to be held at the Hall such as exhibitions, lectures, discussion meetings, greater moral and financial support for

---

17 Livery Committee minutes.

training in the trades; that election to Master had too much in it of Buggins' turn; and that election to the Court should in some measure depend not just upon seniority but also excellence and current involvement in the trade.

The final recommendation was that the Court set up a combined committee of Assistants and Liverymen

> to examine procedures and customs for calling Liverymen into the Court and electing Master and Wardens ... in the light of present and future needs of the Company, and particularly with reference to the Company's aim of being more closely connected with its associated trades; and to recommend what changes, if any, should be made ...

The memorandum was circulated in January, the committee was appointed in October. In April 1966 the Court approved that in future it would be joined by five further Assistants elected from Liverymen, irrespective of seniority; that it be possible for Assistants to retire, or even to be retired, without penalty or loss of rights, and that a ballot be reintroduced for the election of the Under-Warden. The Under-Warden previously had progressed automatically to be Master, and had reached his position by seniority alone. The first Liveryman elected under the new dispensation was Leonard Kenyon, director of what was then the British Federation of Master Printers.

The Court Minutes[18] do not make a connection between the memorandum and the setting up in March 1967 of a publicity sub-committee to proclaim the Company as still active, and not just a traditional or historical association, but the timing is suggestive. The sub-committee was instructed that the interests of the Company were to be stated in this order: printing and allied trades, the City of London, and education and charity. Items of news interest about the Company's activities were to be communicated to the press.

In 1973 the Trades of the Guild Committee was set up under the chairmanship of Leonard Kenyon. This was more focused. In a time of increased political activity under, and frequently against, the governments of first Edward Heath (1970-74) and then Harold Wilson (second term 1974-76), it was felt that there would be benefit in regularly bringing together the presidents and chief executives of the larger trade associations. Thirteen associations were represented and Sir Derek Greenaway (Master, 1974) said, in his annual report, that they accounted for 6.7 per cent of Gross National Product.

For some years the increased liaison between senior members of the trade associations was of value and excellent seminars and lectures were also organised. In April 1985, the Hall was used for *Caxton '85*; 63 exhibitors lined the Stock Room and hall as part of an educational fund-raising event which made £16,000 for the Hall Preservation Fund. Two years later came *Excellence '87*, the brainchild of Master Allen Thompson, which aimed to show the high quality of British book production, printing, bookbinding and paper conservation. Liverymen took an active part, representing

18 Court Book n, 7 March 1967.

many companies and craftsmen in the trades of the guild. It was opened by the Duchess of York.

However, by the 1990s, a working party of the Trades of the Guild Committee, under its then chairman Roy Fullick, had to report (June 1992) that

> During the intervening years [from 1973] the duties of directors-general have grown more complex and demanding, particularly with the European Community dimension, while lay members of the Trades of the Guild Committee holding office in trade associations have progressively found it more difficult to spare time from running their own businesses to take part in further extra-mural activities such as the Trades of the Guild Committee.

The working party proposed that the Committee should in future be drawn only from members of the Company, and that it should continue to organise at least three events during the year: a lecture on a subject of major importance, a panel-led forum of equal significance, and an opportunity, with the Master as host, for directors-general of trade associations to meet informally at the Hall to discuss matters of mutual concern. The report was accepted.

In the same year (1992) the Trades of the Guild Committee recommended that eligible trades should include computerised typesetting and page planning, electronic image making, desk top publishing, photocopying, direct mailing, newspaper and periodical wholesaling, book wholesaling and distribution, film and video production and direction, and the manufacture or supply as a main activity of machinery or equipment for any of these trades. While the number of members of the Livery remained unchanged, the Company was in no other sense exclusive.

In 1994 the Committee changed its name to the Trade and Industry Forum. The chairman, by now Richard Harrison (Master 1999), wanted it to have a more modern emphasis. But its objectives continued to be the encouragement of cooperation between the trades of the Guild by consultation with and between trade associations, and to provide a place and platform for debate. The excellent Livery Lectures continued, as also the summer colloquium and the autumn event which, in 1997, for the first time had a commercial sponsor. And, with only that nod to modernity, the pattern of the Company's relations with its trades continued.

Would Blagden feel that it had become 'more useful' than when he published his strictures in 1960? The question cannot be answered. Perhaps it is enough to say that the Company remains, and that it is apparently permanent in a changing world. It stands ready when its traditional members want to make use of it, and it welcomes new recruits from younger disciplines. It provides a centre when its dispersed trades wish to re-establish their identities, and it lends its own dignity to their different occasions—lectures, dinners, seminars, debates—and provides a cheerful venue for their celebrations. It is there, when it is needed.

CHAPTER TWO

From Masters to Managing Directors

The Impact of Technology on the Membership of the Stationers' Company

MICHAEL BERLIN & ROBIN MYERS

The managing-director of the modern printing firm as a rule knew nothing of printing, and cared less; dividend was the thing he was after all the time. A century ago at least two employers were found writing technical books of instruction—and good books they were too; they have not lost their value yet; and it was recorded in Johnson that certain master printers met and discussed the merits of the printing machine.[1] But what was the position of the modern managing director? If a new machine was introduced he had to refer to his manager, and the manager before he could place the case before the director had to get the assistance of the counting house to put down in £ s. d. what the advantages were. The employer has no feeling of craftsmanship in his mind nowadays, whereas the old employer took pride in his craft.[2]

5. Apprentices being bound by the Master, Cuthbert Grasemann, at the Hall, 1956.

This pessimistic view, voiced at a trade lecture at Stationers' Hall in November 1927 by H.W. Killinback, a machine manager, must have been echoed by a generation of men who had been bound apprentice there. His nostalgia for a lost golden age when employers were all master craftsmen could have been expressed at any time after the mid-19th century. Over the two centuries covered by this volume the sort of men and women coming into the Stationers' Company has changed in the way that the composition of the Trades of its Guild, and the role of all the city livery companies as trade organisations and part of the public life of the City of London have changed. The Stationers' Company is unusual among livery companies in having kept its links with the trades it was founded to foster, but it was not immune from the forces breaking down the barriers of guild controls. For the first part of our period the English Stock, which still gave its partners good dividends, helped to keep the Company's strong links with its trades even though, as the 19th century advanced, it lost what remained of its once leading position as the voice of the printing and book trades.

At the beginning of the period the customs and conventions of the printing office were much as they had been from the time of Caxton, but by the end of the 19th century technological change and the concentration of businesses into fewer and fewer hands as the great family firms were bought out or absorbed into large-scale companies undermined the ordered system of master, journeyman and apprentice. Book printers,

---

1   John Johnson, *Typographia, or the printer's instructor; including an account of the history of printing*, 2 vols. (1824).
2   J.R. Riddell, *An address on apprenticeship together with the opinions of representatives of the printing and allied trades* (1927), p.27.

attracted by lower wages and cheaper rents, began to move out of London to provincial towns, loosening the trade bonds with its historic roots in the vicinity of Stationers' Hall and Fleet Street.

The abolition of Stamp Duty in 1852 paved the way for the growth of London-based mass circulation newspapers, which created a demand for semi-skilled and unskilled labour, as did the expansion of bulk supplies of, among other printed paper products, business stationery, packaging and advertisements. New technology did not widely affect working practices in the first half of the 19th century but from the 1880s the introduction of new machinery revolutionised the printing trade. The age of the jobbing printer and stationer gradually gave way to the modern conglomerate and the old intimacy of master and indoor apprentice as part of the household became a thing of the past.

Whereas in 1851 more than half the printing houses were still employing fewer than five men, towards the end of the century the scene altered radically;[3] firms with close ties with the Stationers' Company, such as Eyre & Spottiswoode, Harrison and Waterlow, began to expand and employ scores of journeymen, and to take many more 'out-door', that is living-out apprentices who lived at home in the care of parent or guardian, and were paid a wage. Outdoor apprentices were nothing new but by the end of the century the numbers were regularly so much greater and masters no longer took much responsibility for apprentice welfare.[4] Fewer and fewer were taken on to learn a trade, more and more were being exploited as a form of cheap labour.[5] In particular, the trade unions, in their complaints about the decline in apprentices' conditions, focused on the practice of paying them piece rates rather than a day wage.

During the decade 1870-80, at a time when technical education was being widely promoted, a total of 774 apprentices were bound at Stationers' Hall, rising to a high-point of 180 bound in one year, 1883.[6] The stationers', printers' and bookbinders' skills were still best acquired by traditional apprenticeship of seven years—which, after 1889, could be shortened to five. Most employers in the 19th-century book and allied trades were content to continue with practical training by apprenticeship and were slow to appreciate the importance of technical classes for apprentices. Legalisation of the payment of wages to apprentices, the shortening of working hours and the recognition of 'outdoor' apprentices—made the system more flexible than previously and encouraged its survival in the printing and associated industries of late 19th-century London.

What was the effect of all this on the composition of the Company? The formal structure, the ordered *cursus honorum* by which a man might progress to the freedom by servitude, patrimony or redemption, thence to the livery, to election to the Court after service as Renter Warden, and finally, Under Warden, Upper Warden and Master, did

---

3 Gareth Stedman Jones, *op. cit.* p.29 and appendix table 9.

4 In the late 18th and early 19th centuries, masters of the larger London printing houses, such as Hansard and Sons and John Nichols, had used them as a means of breaking combinations of journeymen.

5 Charles Booth, *Life and Labour of the People of London* (London, 1890), 2nd series, vol.3, p.236.

6 Copy of Clerk's affidavit, 11 February 1858, brown school box, unclassified.

Feb. 12. 1806.

Dear Sir,

I had great pleasure in your Note; I have pleasure in your correspondence.

Do me the favour to send the young men to me, and they shall be provided for.

I perceive they are for going ding-dong to Business; — bidding farewell to home on a Wednesday — coming to London on a Thursday — and "beginning work on Friday Morning."! — Towns! This

is Bonapartism altogether!

Softly, softly; let us shut the door.

Send them to me on Friday — I will send them to Market on Saturday — to Church on Sunday — & to my Chapel on Monday.

Believe me always truly Yours

Luke Hansard

J. Nichols, Esqr

not alter very much. But as redemption gradually replaced the established route to journeyman and master by servitude, and the larger commercial organisations ousted the old-style printers, small booksellers and stationers, so in the second half of the 20th century managing directors, frequently professional accountants or those trained in management skills, replaced the 'guvs' who had been bred to the trade.[7]

Entry by Servitude and the Effects of Mechanisation

The *Memorandum Books* at Stationers' Hall record father's occupation and place of origin, master's occupation and place of residence, length of service, size of premium or formerly, in the case of poor boys or orphans, payment of premium by a charity.[8] From the early 1850s the particular branch of trade is given as bookbinder, typefounder, compositor, engraver or law stationer and so on and, as printing became more and more specialised, the particular area of training as lithographer, lithographic draughts-

6. Letter, 12 February 1806, to John Nichols, from Luke Hansard offering to take on two young men. 'Send them to me on Friday—I will send them to Market on Saturday—to Church on Sunday—& to my Chapel on Monday' (from the Nichols family archive).

---

7 Gaps in the records make it impossible to give the precise number but a calculation based on annual average annual admission from 1800 would give a round figure of 7,000.

8 Such as that administered by the Worshipful Company of Drapers under the bequest of William Dixon.

man, machine printer or machine minder. Because apprenticeship was not insisted on to the same extent in the other trades of the Guild, most of the information about members of the Company relates to those bound as printers or bookbinders.

For most of the 19th century the number of boys and young men being bound was very buoyant and the yearly intake of apprentices for the first three-quarters of the century remained remarkably constant.[9] Although numbers had declined in the 1790s, owing, perhaps, to a demand for army and navy recruits during the Napoleonic wars, above all during the invasion scare of 1797 to 1799,[10] thereafter the annual figure never fell below 100 until 1842, and was at one time as high as 144.[11] The greatest variations took place at the very end of the century; in 1893 the number of apprentices went down to double figures and the 20th century saw the number of bindings spiralling ever downwards. There were over 1,200 between the end of Victoria's reign in 1902 and the General Strike of 1926, but numbers fell remorselessly thereafter.[12] The effect of the First World War is seen in the relatively small number freed in the post-war years. Of the thousand or more bound in the first 20 years of the century only 190 were freed between 1920 and 1939—a vivid if unproven indication of the disruption caused by the First War and the carnage of the trenches.

The Second World War did not have the same effect in decimating the male population and it was some years before changing circumstances affected apprentice numbers. 1957 was the peak post-war year for bindings, a great many being apprenticed to Harrisons, government and security printers; nine were bound at the January court and another nine in October. But the upturn was not sustained; the writing was on the wall even if, at the April 1959 Court, Sir Guy Harrison disregarded it in speaking 'of the intrinsic value and effect of the ceremony of binding apprentices at Stationers' Hall ... his company had made a practice of observing this traditional custom with considerable success'.[13] In the intervening 40 years never more than two or three in a year have taken their oath at the Hall.[14]

It should be borne in mind that there was always a number of apprentices who were the sons of 'guvs', often from families with strong patrilineal ties with the Company, who might come in either by servitude, if they were to have an apprentice training, or by patrimony if they were not. A somewhat extreme case is that of the sons of Cholmeley Austen-Leigh, M.A. (cloathed March 1878, died 1899), partner at the New Street premises of Spottiswoode Ballantyne and great-nephew of Jane Austen. The elder two took their apprentice oath as Eton schoolboys and spent the intervening years as Cambridge undergraduates before being freed.

9   Beadle's Book, p.72.
10   The numbers dropped to 67 to 78 per year in 1797-99.
11   Between 1825 and 1850 it was 119 but it dropped dramatically to average 87, rising slightly in the last quarter of the 19th century.
12   Between 1902 and 1929, there was an average of 60 per annum in spite of the effects of war. 674 boys were bound between the 1920s and the 1950s.
13   Court Book m, 7 April 1959.
14   Not more than 89 in total.

Table I shows that, at the beginning of the 19th century, boys came from almost every class; they also came from all over the country but, in the course of the next 200 years, fewer and fewer came from outside London:

TABLE I

Occupations of Fathers of Apprentices, 1800-1900

	1800-25	1825-50	1850-75	1875-1900
Print	96	102	73	102
Food and Drink	58	29	27	21
Metal and Glass	28	13	10	18
Furniture	14	6	3	8
Textile and Clothing	35	23	19	17
Agriculture	18	6	3	5
Transport	19	14	22	22
Building	21	7	16	28
Other manufacturing	2	2	6	10
Professional and military	13	8	4	5
Service and labourer	24	6	8	10
Commercial	9	4	11	17
Retail	8	10	0	2
Clerical and administrative	-	15	3	17
Gentry	34	22	1	1
Misc.	3	4	3	5

The table shows that early in the century the sons of skilled master craftsmen, goldsmiths, coach builders, cabinet makers and watch makers, were being bound alongside the sons of farmers, husbandmen, farm labourers, London gentlemen and 'esquires' (who disappear after 1850), lawyers, surveyors, auctioneers, and schoolmasters with a sprinkling of army and naval officers.[15] Commerce was well represented with large numbers of merchants, wholesalers and shopkeepers, and those in the victualling trades, a numerous group ranging from tavern keepers to butchers, all binding their sons at the hall.[16] Was a miner 'late of California' binding his son in the hope of putting the proceeds of one of the gold rushes to good use? It shows how disparate were the Company's apprentices in those years.[17]

15 It has to be taken into account that men often described themselves in a most haphazard way; one man might say he was a gentleman, another from the same stratum of society might not. The Austen-Leighs were certainly gentry but not so described.

16 Of the 1,129 names sampled out of the Memorandum Books (1800-1900) some 56 fathers are listed as 'gentlemen' or 'gentry', all but two being before 1850. For the reputation for respectability of printing as an occupation in this period see John Child, *Industrial Relations in the Printing Industry* (1967), p.97.

17 Apprentice Memorandum Book, 1877-1890, December 1889.

As the 19th century progressed a growing number were the sons of working printers, perhaps partly owing to increased specialisation.[18] There were also more sons of semi-skilled or unskilled men, dockers, porters and navvies with correspondingly fewer boys from the older skilled artisans' trades—this was part of the general pattern of London employment as workers in small-scale handicrafts such as clock and watch making and the furniture, clothing and textile trades, were being driven by provincial and overseas competition to find employment in less skilled trades; but contemporaries saw it as the degeneration of the apprenticeship system. As a writer in *The London Typographical Journal* for May 1906 put it:

> we seem to be getting the failures at school, the riff-raff of the streets, the rejects of other trades. I can remember when printing was an occupation to which the lower middle class and the upper lower class were glad to put their sons, when printers ranked a grade higher than the joiner, the bricksetter and the fitter.[19]

In addition to the fee for binding a boy at the Hall, payment of a premium to the master was common for most of the 19th century, which represented a substantial investment in a boy's future. Sums of £20 to £50 were not uncommon up to the 1850s, and might be as much as £200. The practice began to decline from the mid-century but as much as £90 was occasionally paid as late as the 1890s. By the beginning of the 20th century premiums were considered an archaic or even a dubious practice according to J.R. Riddell, Principal of the London College of Printing:

> Allow me to express in the strongest possible terms my contempt of a seeming revival of this old custom, which originated when apprentices lived with their masters. I consider premiums an undesirable method of securing money by mercenary people, who are usually quite incapable of teaching a boy his trade ... It cannot be too widely known that printing firms of repute do not require 'consideration money' when apprenticing boys.[20]

The downgrading of apprenticeship caused growing anxiety as the 19th century progressed. Henry Tompkins of the National Graphical Association put it bluntly in *The London Typographical Journal* in May 1901, 'it is clear that the system of apprenticeship is rapidly dying out'. The editorial pointed out:

> In days gone by, the master printer took a close personal interest in the welfare of his apprentices, whose position was usually safeguarded by a form of indenture which left no opportunity to the master or man to escape his responsibilities ... with the upswing of huge factories, however, the lad has lost the advantage of that personal supervision which is such a potent factor in the production of a finished craftsman. The impersonal limited liability company has taken the place of the master of old; and the apprentice has become part and

---

18 Marjorie Plant, *The English Book Trade* (London: George Allen & Unwin, 1974), pp.367-8.

19 L.A. Wallis, *The Devil's Background: A Preliminary Investigation into the History of Apprenticeship in the Print Trade* (London, 1991), p.13.

20 J.R. Riddell, *op. cit.*, p.13.

parcel of the 'economy of production'—ostensibly learning a trade, but really a 'servant of the company'.

By the end of the century printers were looking back nostalgically to the heyday of the indoor apprentice. Frederick J.E. Young, Chairman of the Printers' Pension Corporation,[21] had been bound to George Spottiswoode of No. 8 Little New Street, just off the bustle of Fleet Street, in 1853. Writing in the *Caxton Magazine* in 1901, he described an idyllic seven years spent learning his craft, his free time spent playing cricket in the shade of a tree said to have been planted by Dr Johnson in New Street Square:

> In those days the age was not so restless, and though the quiet life spent by us might appear monotonous to the present day indoor apprentice, surrounded by the attractions of cheap tram fares and greater facilities for getting about, to us life seemed satisfying, and its quietude gave one better scope for concentrating one's energies on the trade he had embraced ... it is a moot point whether the system of indoor apprentices can be so successfully carried on now that the joint stock companies are replacing old unlimited liability firms ... The idea of an apprentice living with his master at the end of the 19th century seems almost an anachronism. Yet at 'Number Eight', until the year I left the city, the old time custom was in vogue—and is so still.

In the 20th century things improved; fewer boys were bound but the promotion of technical education, in which the Stationers' Company played an important part, and a general rise in the standard of education and training meant that there were fewer from semi-skilled backgrounds than in the last years of the previous century. Apprenticeship began once more to be valued as a way of training, even if it was no longer the commonest way into the Company, and the Court began to see the need to promote it. In July 1909 they expressed support for the attempt of the Stationer Lord Mayor, Sir Thomas Vezey Strong, to revive apprenticeship in other trades. They praised the system of apprenticeship 'which has been continued in this hall for the last 500 years with great advantage to all employed in the printing and cognate trades'. They acknowledged the need for improvement but proposed no immediate action, although later in the year the award of a prize of £5 5s. and a silver medal for the apprentice with the highest marks in typography, bookbinding and lithography marked the Company's first tentative steps towards the provision of technical training (see Chapter Seven).[22] George Duke, a Freeman who had been apprenticed as a compositor to William Hugh Spottiswoode, was particularly assiduous in forging continued links between Eyre and Spottiswoode and the Company. Between 1913 and 1937 he was responsible for presenting 'upwards of 200' of Spottiswoode's apprentices for the Company Freedom. In March 1914 the Court recorded his 'splendid effort' and, in 1922, he was awarded the first Silver Medal for service to the Company and was also congratulated on forming a City of London Police

21 The Printers' Pension, Almshouse and Orphan Asylum Corporation.
22 Court Book g, 16 July 1910.

Reserve from amongst Freemen of the Company who had been Eyre and Spottiswoode apprentices.[23] In 1925 he presented two books of autographs of those he had brought into the Company.[24]

The Industrial Training Act of 1964 caused a sharp decline in bindings and the virtual collapse of the system.[25] Whereas 26 boys were bound at the Hall in 1963, the next year there were only 13, and thereafter they fluctuated between 14 and seven, falling away until, in 1984, they ceased altogether. Some liverymen still occasionally come forward, generally binding their sons or daughters out of sentiment—there were three between 1990 and 1995. But so rare is it today that when Liveryman Douglas East, a bookbinder and conservator at Westminster Abbey, wished to free his apprentice, the Beadle had to apply to the archivist to find out the form of words and procedure—a sad comment on the times.

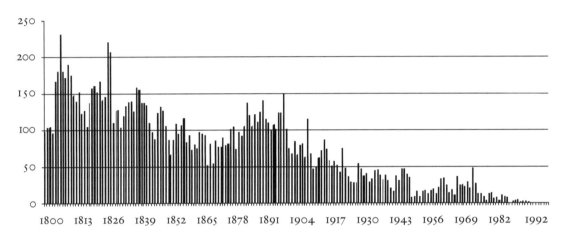

Graph showing Apprentices Bound at Stationers' Hall from 1800 to 1992[26]

The schemes for technical training and increased job security, at least until the upheavals of the 1980s, and the active recruitment by men such as Duke helped to keep apprenticeship going well into the 20th century. Youths from a broad cross section of the London working class, many with established family links in printing, began once more to be bound at the Hall. The non-printers' sons generally came from other London trades, electricians, builders, lorry and cab drivers, policemen, Post Office, railway and London underground workers or else from the other great sources of employment in London at that time, city firms and the docks. A century earlier as many as a quarter of all printing apprentices had come from the country, and a Reading

23 Court Book g, 29 July 1913, 13 March 1914.
24 He also presented a copy of the history of the City of London Police Reserve in 1921, an antique silver tipstaff engraved with the City arms in 1922.
25 The Act withdrew support for apprenticehip which was substituted by a system of waged training and sandwich courses.
26 Figures taken from Blagden, the *Memorandum Books* and the Beadle's Book.

'banker's son'[27] or a Bristol stationer was nothing to remark on, but by the 1890s the Apprentice Books show the overwhelming number hailing from a tightly defined area, from the working-class suburbs of Hackney, Islington, Hoxton, Shoreditch, Bethnal Green, Lambeth, Bermondsey and the Old Kent Road. This bears out the findings of Charles Booth, who wrote of a 'regular colony of printers' at Walworth and in the neighbourhood of the Caledonian Road, and found that a very high proportion of those in the London printing trade were born and bred in London.[28] At the end of Victoria's reign the skilled working classes began to disperse to the new working-class and lower-middle-class suburbs of north, east, south and to a lesser extent, west London. The Cheap Train Acts were a factor in the expansion of London to Wood Green, West Ham, Camberwell and Acton and farther afield. Booth noted that 'the cheap service of workmen's trains (of the Great Eastern Railway) has no doubt attracted many of the men, and accounts for the numbers of printers living at or near Walthamstow, Edmonton, Tottenham and other suburban stations on this line'.[29] The City had begun to lose its residential population as early as 1845 when the Town Clerk made a return in which he reported that there were only 161 householders in the City among the 1,045 Freemen.[30] This the governors of the Company's school discovered soon after it opened its doors in Bolt Court in 1858. Within thirty years there were so few local boys that in 1894 it had to move out to Hornsey (see Chapter Seven).

For the majority of apprentices a lifetime of drudgery in the printing house beckoned and very few saw the point in being freed.[31] Of the large numbers of those bound throughout the 19th century, only a small minority took the Freedom at Stationers' Hall, as Blagden's survey of bindings and freedoms from the Company's earliest years to 1959 shows.[32] Of the 110 boys bound in 1840, for example, only 22 were freed seven years later. Table II (overleaf) shows the marked decline in entry by servitude since the end of the Victorian period, and the corresponding expansion in the numbers of redemptioners. This has meant that the mix of social classes in the Company narrowed as those near the poverty line ceased to be members.

Entry by Redemption: New Members for Old

Many old links were severed by the decline of apprenticeship but the last hundred years has seen the Company's prosperity increase through an infusion of new blood which has drawn it into the modern world. Then, as now, a redemptioner was sponsored by two liverymen but sponsorship records were not kept and only in very few, mainly chance instances, are the sponsors known. So we do not know whose initiative led the

---

27 The term in use for bank employees in the 19th century.
28 Booth, *op. cit.*, vol. 2, p.229, figures were: printers (66 per cent), stationers (70 per cent), paper manufacturers (78 per cent) and bookbinders (81 per cent), for which see Stedman Jones, *op. cit.*, pp.136-7.
29 *Ibid.*, p.229.
30 Blagden, p.264.
31 Blagden, p.264.
32 Blagden, Appendix 1,* includes members of the Company of Newspaper Makers.

TABLE II

Modes of Entry into the Company 1800-1959

YEAR	APPRENTICES BOUND	FREE BY SERVITUDE	FREE BY PATRIMONY	FREE BY REDEMPTION	LIVERY	TOTAL FREE
1800-1819	2934	985	150	85	1220	273
1820-1839	3007	980	205	49	1234	215
1840-1859	1950	490	132	24	646	151
1860-1879	1799	390	105	63	558	152
1880-1899	1918	316	66	55	437	179
1900-1919	1088	567	63	156	786	195
1920-1939	691	190	29	358 ·	577	381
1940-1959	367	447	34	187	668	189

Company, well before the First World War, actively to seek out men of wealth and position in the modern 'cognate trades' and introduce them to the Company.

When the managing director of the Linotype Company applied to join the Livery in May 1902, the court amended the bylaws to offer new men immediate advancement to the Livery by the 'fast track'. It ruled that in future all 'principals actually employed in the business of limited and other companies carrying on the trades of Booksellers, Publishers, Printers, Typefounders, Papermakers, Engravers, Bookbinders and other cognate trades' would be eligible for admission to the Company.[33] In the decade before 1914 the new Freemen included advertising contractors, publishers' representatives and accountants, as well as those from the upper strata of the printing and allied trades. Newspaper proprietors and others associated with the mass circulation press were an important group; Cecil and Howard Harmsworth, founders of *The Daily Mail*, joined in 1911.

In the 1920s new members included managing directors of several large and medium sized publishing houses, printers, manufacturing and wholesale stationers, pulp wood and paper importers and paper merchants, among them the director of Newnes and Pearson, publishers of *Country Life* and *The News of the World* and Edward Fraser Stanford, cartographer and mapseller of Long Acre. There were also paper agents and suppliers in small and middle sized firms, publishers' accountants, fountain pen makers, cardboard manufacturers. The egregious George Alfred Isaacs, M.P. (1883-1979), later Minister of Labour and much else, who was involved in the world of print as General Secretary of NATSOPA, which originated with a strike at Eyre and Spottiswoode in 1889, was cloathed on 3 February 1931.

Counterbalance of Traditional Trades

The new men were counterbalanced by a variety of others from the Company's traditional trades. George Brimley Bowes (d.1946), admitted on 5 October 1920, was the son, later business partner of Robert Bowes (1863-1919), of the Cambridge booksellers,

33 Court Book e, 6 May 1902; Court Book f, 3 June 1902.

Bowes and Bowes, formerly Macmillan and Bowes, which traded on the site of the country's oldest bookshop.[34] William Foyle (1885-1963) who, with his brother, opened a bookshop in Charing Cross Road, which was later publicised as 'the world's largest bookshop', was admitted in 1933.

The Honorary Freedom and Livery

W.H. Smith M.P., founder of the firm which bears his name, was the Company's first Honorary Freeman and Liveryman in 1880. The honour has generally been very sparingly bestowed, except between 1923 and 1934 when the Company invested nine eminent men in various walks of life, perhaps as part of the drive to raise the Company's profile. They included Sir Israel Gollancz, the Shakespeare scholar, in 1923; in 1925 the Earl of Balfour, Prime Minister 1902-5 and architect of the Balfour Declaration which led to the foundation of the modern state of Israel; Rudyard Kipling, then at the height of his popularity, and Sir James Barrie; in 1927, Stanley Baldwin, later Prime Minister, and in 1929, the Archbishop of Canterbury, Lord Davidson of Lambeth. In 1933 Edward, then Prince of Wales, was given the Honorary Freedom and Livery prior to being elected Master of the Company, 1934 and 1935.

Arrival of the Company of Newspaper Makers

There were high hopes when, in 1933, the Newspaper Makers swelled the Company's ranks with 162 new Freemen taking the total of the Livery to 489. On one day, 16 October 1933, five senior Newspaper Makers and another 87 new members were formally admitted to the Livery (see pp.56-7). The influx provided a galaxy of new talent and persons of influence—six Aldermen, 11 members of the House of Lords and four of the Commons, as well as eminent men of letters such as H.G. Wells and George Bernard Shaw admitted the next year, 1934, chairmen, directors, managing directors, editors and journalists of several well known Fleet Street newspapers. R.D. Blumenfeld (1864-1948), the editor of the *Daily Mail* and first Master of the Company of Newspaper Makers, was freed and cloathed as a Stationer, 7 November 1933; the next year he deputised, with J.W. Davy, for the Prince of Wales when he was Master.

But there were misgivings among the older company members who feared a dilution of their ranks. The new arrivals had included some of the first practitioners of the modern arts of persuasion, directors of advertising firms, 'publicists' and advertising agents—young men such as John (later Sir John) Elliot (1896-1988), son of R.D. Blumenfeld, who changed his name during the wave of anti-German phobia generated by the First World War, in which he had served as a Guards officer: 'when I came out of the army and into Fleet Street in 1922, on the advice of Lord Beaverbrook, I dropped the surname by deed poll and took Elliot as surname'.[35]

---

34 He was part of the Macmillan dynasty through his grandmother, who had been Daniel and Alexander Macmillan's sister.
35 Letter to Robin Myers, 18 September 1986, accompanying a copy of his autobiography.

Sir John Elliot, as he eventually became, was one of the first persons in Britain to describe himself as a 'publicist' with the Southern Railway.[36] Amongst other advertising men was the head of publicity of Gaumont British Films, the director of Dorland Advertising and Sir Charles Frederick Higham, founder of the firm of Higham's, publicist and personal private secretary to no fewer than four Prime Ministers, whose mother company was the Gold and Silver Wyre Drawers, and whose outside responsibilities seemed to preclude his taking much part in the life of the Stationers' Company.

Admission of Women

Women had always been eligible for the Freedom (but not the Livery) but in practice most women freemen in times past were widows or daughters taking over a deceased husband's or father's business. They had the right to trade and bind apprentices at Stationers' Hall in their own name. A girl could be apprenticed to a member of the Company and in 1658 a bookseller's daughter was admitted by patrimony.

In the event, the admission of six women liverymen in 1933 proved to be the spearhead of the attack although it was another 43 years before, in 1977, the Company opened the Livery to women on equal terms; from the mid-1980s it has positively sought them. It can be imagined that when five women journalists and editors joined the Company, being members of the Newspaper Makers, they caused considerable upset among the Stationers' exclusively male old guard (see Chapter Three).[37] What would seem to have been a precedent was set with the admission in 1933 of Gertrude Violet 'Pippa' Woodman, a bookbinder, as the Stationers' token woman to counterbalance the five newspaper women whom the Stationers were reluctantly forced to accept in their midst. Pippa was still very young in 1933, but she had been managing director of the Fisher Bookbinding Company since her father's death in 1926; for many years she was on the council of the British Federation of Master Printers,[38] was for long the only woman steward of the Printers' Pension Corporation, and was president of the Bookbinders Cottage Homes and one of the first women members of the Institute of Directors. Unusually for a career woman of her day, she was married, being in private life Mrs Hunter, with two sons. She was personally popular with the Company but it was made clear that she was to be the sole Stationers' representative of her sex. As early as September 1929 the Livery Committee had discussed the admission of women but dismissed it as unacceptable. The Chairman canvassed the opinion of members and finally resolved that such a step 'would not be acceptable to the majority of the Liverymen'.[39] After the Second World War in 1949 the Company debated the question again, and once more decided against the admission of women; the six admitted into the Company at

36 See his autobiography, *On and Off the Rails* (1982).
37 As was usual in those years even with career women, the newcomers were freed and cloathed in their husband's names, single women were designated 'spinster'.
38 British Federation of Master Printers (BFMP), now the British Printing Industries Federation (BPIF).
39 Minutes of the Livery Committee, 1929-31 (unpaginated), 17 September 1929.

7. Pippa Woodman, the first woman Court Assistant, 1969, and first woman liveryman, 1933, posing beneath the portrait of J.M. Rivington.

the time of the amalgamation were to be 'the exception to this rule' and were not to set a precedent.⁴⁰

Yet the Stationers' Company was not unaffected by the quiet social revolution which has seen women enter all aspects of public life in this century. The first woman to be bound apprentice since the 18th century was presented at Stationers' Hall in 1974. From the early 1960s some forty women, though the Livery remained closed to them, were

40 Court Book l, 11 January 1949.

freed by patrimony, several being the daughters of Masters and Past Masters. In 1971 all four daughters of Sir Denis Truscott, Lord Mayor in 1957-8, joined the Company. A number of new women were pursuing careers in various branches of the trade, as freelance journalists, editors and managing directors of family printing and stationery firms. Among those admitted was Lady Georgina Coleridge, director of *Country Life* and Elizabeth Young, née Benn, editor of the women's page of *The Daily Telegraph*.[41]

In 1977 the rules and ordinances were amended to allow women to join the Livery and admission by patrimony was extended to apply to 'matri-heritage' (see glossary). At the cloathing ceremony the Master admits a woman with the words, 'Brother you are admitted to the Cloathing of this Company'. Ivy Sharp, editor of *The Fur Review*, freed in 1976, was the seventh woman to be cloathed in 1979. She made Company history in founding the first female Livery Company dynasty. In 1982 she sponsored her daughter, Mrs Elizabeth Wheatley for the Livery, and in 1999, her granddaughter, Diana Roach, was jointly sponsored by mother and grandmother.

Pippa Woodman, who had blazed the trail as the first woman Stationer to be admitted to the Livery, was also the first woman to be a Renter Warden and a Livery Representative on the Court and the first woman Court Assistant of any Livery Company (see p.32). She would, in due course, have been the first woman Master had she not transferred to the supernumerary list in 1976 after a bad accident, dying two years later in 1978. There have since been women Renter Wardens, and Livery Representatives on the Court. In 1999 there were some 45 women liverymen, and one woman, Elizabeth Benn (Mrs Young), on the Court. The presence of relatively large numbers of women is now taken for granted and is gradually changing the atmosphere of the Company, making it one of the more modern minded of the City livery companies.

The Freemen

Of the estimated 7,000 men (and since the 1930s, women) entering the Company between 1800 and 1990 fewer than a quarter took the Livery.[42] Few, until recent years, could afford the cost of a Livery gown, the payment of fines and fees or, in the 19th century, quarterage dues, unless there was some material advantage for them; but from time to time, a man took the Freedom and even the Livery, many years—even as many as thirty—after coming out of his time. There must have been a sentimental appeal in belonging to the Company when a man had got on in the world. Blagden calculated that in 1804 'the full tally of Freemen was probably about 1,500' while the Livery comprised 488.[43] In the middle of the 19th century the Clerk reported that there were about 800 Freemen working as journeymen or assistants in the printing, bookselling (which would also include publishing), stationery and bookbinding trades. This was the proportion of freemen to liverymen until the 1970s when the initiative of one Master, C.A. Rivington, coincided

41 Cloathed 1977 by her father, Glanvill Benn, then Master.
42 Court Book O, 11 April 1972.
43 Blagden, p.245n.

with social changes in Company and community and helped to bring about a radical transformation.

'After all,' he argued in his annual report as Master in 1970, 'nearly all of them qualified in one of our trades but for the last two hundred years the Company has for all practical purposes disregarded the freemen's existence ... it would strengthen the Company if we could keep in touch with them.'[44]

Four hundred letters were posted to those Freemen admitted in the past 25 years for whom the Company still had an address; 200 replied and were invited to a wine party, with a guest. The Master arranged for them to receive a copy of the recently inaugurated newsletter, *The Stationer and Newspaper Maker*, in a further attempt to encourage the Freemen to take more interest in the Company and to proceed to the Livery. A first Freemen's dinner was held for both sexes at which the custom was established that a woman would propose the principal toast. A Freemen's Association was founded which has flourished ever since and holds an AGM, dinner, summer reception and annual concert in the Hall. Old boys of the Stationers' School were made eligible for the Freedom, and in certain cases, the Livery; all this helped to dispel the age-old feeling among the Freemen, who were for the most part skilled craftsmen, that they were regarded as second-class citizens.

The Livery: Its Size and Composition

The size of the Livery and the ratio of Freemen to Liverymen has always been of intermittent concern to the Court. In 1809 the Court sought to reduce the size of the Livery by raising the fine to £50 the next year, 1810, but it reached an all-time high of 517, the largest number ever recorded.[45] Numbers gradually fell thereafter and for the next 40 years the number of Liverymen hovered between 400 and 500. From the early 1850s Livery numbers fell steadily to below 400, by the mid-1880s they were under 300, although the Stationers was still among the largest of the livery companies; in 1882 it had the fifth largest Livery. In the middle years of the century the Clerk reported that there were 385 liverymen; he calculated that 132 were stationers, 109 booksellers, 85 printers, 11 bookbinders, six engravers, four type-founders and 38 were not engaged in those trades, with few exceptions living in or near London.[46] In 1897 it fell to just 247. A Court order of March 1977 limited the Livery to 450 with the proviso that 'this figure may be varied by the court ... if in the future circumstances make it desirable to do so'.[47] In 1992, because a waiting list had built up, the limit was raised to 476 with the same provision for variation.[48] There still seems no difficulty, despite the size of the fee (in 1999, £420 for Freedom by redemption and £650 for the Livery), in keeping the full complement.

44 *A list of the livery and annual report for 1969-70*, pp.4-5.
45 *Ibid.*, p.253.
46 Clerk's affidavit, brown box School, unclassified.
47 Court Orders 1 March 1977 and *Rules, Ordinances and Established Customs* (1979), p.7 and notes.
48 Rules and Ordinances, 1992, p.13, 'Size of livery'.

The requirement of fining or serving as Renter Warden before being eligible for election to the Court may formerly have acted as a disincentive to those aspiring to office. It was affordable only by the better off and service meant time away from personal business. As time went on a body of Liverymen, as much as a third of the entire Livery, took no part in Company affairs for whatever reason and chose neither to fine nor serve. They came to be known as 'Rotten Row' and were destined to be passed over for election as Renter Warden and to stay in 'Rotten Row' all their lives. In 1984 the Court instituted a 'special list', later called the supernumerary list, which was ratified in the Rules and Ordinances, 1992, to which inactive members and those who declined to pay quarterage transferred, reverting to the status of Freemen, in order to make room for incoming entrants. There were some 30 supernumerary members in 1989, 59 in 1999.

The Company continued to require that only those working in the trades of the Guild were eligible to join by redemption or translation. Joseph Baker, a Court Assistant, told the 1834 Municipal Inquiry, 'the object of not admitting any one on the livery who does not belong to the trade is to keep the Trade as much as possible together. Several attempts have been made to evade this principle, but they have always failed.' He referred to the case of Mr R.G. Pead of Honey Lane, Cheapside, who was freed by servitude but rejected for admission to the livery on the grounds that he 'kept a ham and beef shop'. Later that year Pead wrote to *The Times* complaining that he had been traduced by Baker's evidence, that the Beadle had advised him to reply in the affirmative when asked by the Court whether or not he was carrying on the business of a Stationer but he refused to lie and challenged the Company: 'I would ask those gentlemen of the Court, some of whom are magistrates, what value they can set upon a man's oath whose first step to be initiated into their Company is to tell a deliberate lie?'.[49]

The Court might condone such hypocrisy but when it came to those who did not abide by the stern moral code and rules of social propriety which held sway in Victorian and Edwardian times it was another story—they were unlikely to make much progress up the Company's hierarchy. At this distance of time, the Beadle's Book, which documents some of the social failures with press cuttings and police reports, makes entertaining reading.

The Daily Telegraph report of the case of Henry Baynes is one such. He was admitted to the Livery in 1859, convicted of embezzling funds from his employer by selling under-priced stationery to the Imperial Fire Insurance Company, pleaded guilty and was sentenced to four months' hard labour. 'There was considerable audacity in this case by the prisoner's endeavouring to bring an action against his employer for illegal discharge', according to the report. In Alderman Sir Robert Carden's view, 'it was a melancholy thing to see a man in the prisoner's position in the dock'. Not surprisingly Baynes thereafter disappears from the Company records.

49 Beadle's Book, p.5.

Then there was the case of Augustus Frederick Miles, a member of one of the Company's more prominent dynasties, with a number of relations on the Court, two Company chaplains and four Masters between 1875 and 1967. Augustus Miles would seem to have been set for advancement; a solicitor and partner of the firm of Belfrage and Company, he was elected Renter Warden in 1884 and served as colour sergeant in the 7th Middlesex (London Scottish) Regiment; but in 1907 he was cited as co-respondent in a divorce case. The proceedings were recorded in the Beadle's Book. Letters from Miles to one Carrie Alta Gilling were read out in open court, including the words, 'I hope the bed was comfortable last night and did not break again. Perhaps next week its stability will be put to a greater test'. The revelation of these indiscretions led to his rapid downfall; in February 1908 he was declared bankrupt and his share of the English stock paid out in March the same year. The Beadle's Book records his death at the London Hospital in the East End on 29 January 1909.[50]

Less dire was the case of Thomas John Hunt, an account book manufacturer with premises in Garlick Hill in the City and a house in Leytonstone, who was admitted to the Livery in 1901. *The Echo* of July 1903 reported the contretemps in a second-class railway carriage when he was travelling with his two sons from Liverpool Street to Leytonstone and got into a dispute with a Mr George Payne travelling with his wife. Payne later charged Hunt with assault, alleging that Hunt kept making abusive remarks saying he was 'soft in the head' and that 'people like you ought to be in a third class carriage'. He then struck Payne on the mouth and hit him several times. Hunt pleaded self defence, saying that he had only spoken to Payne after the latter had put his feet on the seats when he said jokingly, 'if you were in a fourth class carriage you would see a notice: "Keep Your Feet off the Seats"'. The Court accepted Payne's testimony, found Hunt guilty of assault and 'extremely indiscreet conduct', and fined him 10s. plus costs. The incident may have cost him further advancement in the Company but his pugnacious character seems to have served him well in local politics for he was elected Mayor of Shoreditch in 1908.

Rather different was the disgrace of John Joseph Lawson, a printer on *The Times*, who was cloathed in 1831. His career in the Company seems to have been blighted because on 30 January 1839 he was jailed for a month for printing a libellous article on Sir John Conroy's purchase of an estate in Wales. The jury found him guilty of 'a certain misdemeanour in printing and publishing certain scandalous libels'; he was fined £200 'of lawful money of Great Britain' and imprisoned in the Marshalsea for 'a calendar month now next ensuing'. On his release he was presented with a silver snuffbox inscribed 'to J.J. Lawson Esq. on the day of his liberation from the Queen's bench prison, from a very sincere friend, 28 February 1839'. There is no further mention of him in the Company's records.[51]

---

50 Beadle's Book, p.391.
51 *The Stationer and Newspaper Maker* 76, May 1999, p.6, and *The Times* 8 February 1999, p.22, which records that a descendant had sold the snuffbox at auction.

On the other hand, Thomas Curson Hansard (1766-1833) escaped Company disapproval. He was the eldest son of Luke Hansard, founder in 1799 of one of the Company's 19th-century dynasties. T.C. Hansard junior (1813-91) was Master in 1886, aged 73. T.C. senior became very eminent in the trade and gave his name to the language by printing Cobbett's verbatim reports of Parliament; but in 1809 he printed an indignant article by Cobbett in the *Political Register* on how British soldiers who had mutinied for arrears of pay were flogged by German mercenaries at Ely. Cobbett was tried for seditious libel, sentenced to two years in gaol and fined £1,000; Hansard was gaoled for three months and fined £400. His father wrote of 'the heart-rending disgrace of Thomas's incarceration', but the Company took no action against him although he was never called into Court.[52]

Patrimony and the Company's Dynastic Families

A livery company is a long-term establishment. It doesn't live from hand to mouth.[53] The dominance of long-standing families in particular livery companies is a feature of City life re-enforced by the system of patrimony. The Stationers' Company, because of its continuing strong links with its trade, does not have, and has never had, as many entrants by patrimony as those companies which have abandoned trade associations; but it has always had a small number, generally non-trade members, who give the Company the advantage of their special expertise, as in the case of the various legal Rivingtons. In the last decades of the 20th century they can also come in by matri-heritage or family redemption (see *Glossary*).

The Rivingtons are the oldest, most numerous and most diverse of the Company's dynasties. The first Charles Rivington started bookselling in St Paul's Churchyard in 1718.[54] He bound his son, Charles Rivington II, to the eminent printer and novelist Samuel Richardson, and in 1753 he set up as a printer in Staining Lane; as late as 1905, then trading as Gilbert and Rivington, their stock of exotic sorts for bible and prayer book printing in foreign languages rivalled that of the Oxford University Press.[55] A second branch of publishing Rivingtons specialised in the publication of religious tracts and school books, while the legal Rivingtons were Clerks to the Company (1800-1957).[56] Their rivals in antiquity but no longer associated with the Company were the Longmans, booksellers from 1719. The Harrison family, which equals the Rivingtons in dynastic strength, stuck to its last as royal printer and printed the *London Gazette*. They were security printers and started printing Royal Mail stamps in 1911, they produced almost all the British stamps up to 1980 and continued to print a substantial proportion thereafter. Other 18th-century families have died out of the Company: the Nicholses, printers and publishers (1757-1939),

---

52 *The Autobiography of Luke Hansard*, ed. by Robin Myers (1991), pp.56-7.
53 Adapted from Harold Macmillan's words in 1931, 'A publishing house is a long-term business. It doesn't live from hand to mouth.' Charles Morgan, *The House of Macmillan* (1943), p.49.
54 Bookselling and publishing were more or less synonymous until the mid-19th century.
55 See L.W. Wallis, 'Legros and Grant; the typographical connection', *Journal of the Printing Historical Society* 28 (1999), pp.6-7.
56 There were some 11 Rivingtons on the Court between 1805 and 1962 and in the 1870s there were three Rivington Masters.

the Hansards (printers to the House of Commons, 1797-1880) and the Woodfalls, printers from 1719. Nineteenth-century printing families who have died out of the Company are Adlard, Austen-Leigh, Spottiswoode, Truscott and Unwin—the last named diversified into publishing after the First World War; the last Stationer of the family, Rayner Unwin (d.2000), transferred to the supernumerary list in 1987; but the names of Waterlow in printing (although no Waterlow has been Master since 1939), Murray and Whitaker in publishing continue to be found in the current Livery lists.[57] As old dynasties die out, new ones arise, the Benns in publishing, the Tollits and Rymans (though no longer associated with the firm which bears their name) in wholesale and retail stationery, and yet newer dynasties are forming as Liverymen continue to sponsor sons and daughters.

The Hodgsons, book auctioneers in Chancery Lane from 1807 to 1973, have continued in the Company since the early 19th century, with four Hodgson Masters since 1866, the last two, Sidney (1876-1973) and his son Wilfrid Becket Hodgson, Master 1979, deeply concerned with and benefactors to the archive and library. Sidney Hodgson joined the Company in 1907, was Stock Keeper in 1930, called into Court 7 October 1941, chairman of the School governors (1942-4) and the third Hodgson Master, in 1949 aged 70. (For his award of the Company's Silver Medal in 1969 see Appendix 2B p.181.)

The publishing family of Macmillan is a 20th-century dynasty. Sir Frederick Macmillan (1851-1936), architect of the Net Book Agreement and eldest son of the firm's co-founder, Daniel Macmillan, was cloathed 8 October 1897, Stock Keeper, 1918 and called into Court, 1933, but died before he could reach the chair. His nephews were members of the Company: Daniel Macmillan junior (1886-1965) was cloathed 7 July 1907; his even more distinguished brother, Harold (1894-1986), Prime Minister (1957-63), later Lord Stockton, worked in the firm for a number of years and never entirely abandoned publishing for politics. He was elected to the Honorary Freedom and Livery in 1956 and his portrait in extreme old age hangs in the Stock Room. His grandson, the present Lord Stockton, was called into Court in 1995 and transferred to Court Emeritus list, 2000.

The Beadle's Book lists several families who were trading from the same premises over three successive generations. Six generations of Harrisons were at 45 and 46 St Martin's Lane between 1840 and 1963; successive generations of Truscotts, including Francis W. Truscott, Lord Mayor, 1878-9, were in Suffolk Lane down to the 1920s. Two generations of Greenaways traded from premises in Camomile Street between 1905 and 1930, including Alderman Sir Percy Greenaway, Master and Lord Mayor in 1932-3. Ties of locality such as these served to re-enforce family connections with the Company, but do so no longer.

The changing nature of modern business and the rise of the business manager have undermined the old traditions, yet the continued presence of the Company's dynastic families, even if few of them are still associated with the firms that bear their name, gives a sense of stability and continuity in a changing world.

---

57 Although in 1896 the Court declined 'the proposed gift of a bust of the late Joseph Whitaker who was not a member of the Company', Court Book e, 5 May 1896.

Service on the Court: Under Warden, Upper Warden and Master

Not all the Company's ruling families are also household names in the trade; nor have all whose influence has been strong in the Company reached the chair—there has never been a Longman or a Murray Master, for example. Yet of the 190 Masters between 1800 and 1990, 47 have belonged to the families of Adlard, Evans, Greenaway, Harrison, Hodgson, Miles, Nichols, Rivington, Spottiswoode, Truscott, Unwin and Waterlow. The Harrisons have so far provided the Company with eight Masters since 1784. A Harrison was Master in 1900, another, Richard Harrison, was Master in the millennium year 1999-2000. He is the last of the printing Harrisons, entering the family firm in 1954 and read engineering at Cambridge. He directed the stamp printing office for several years before becoming Managing Director, leaving in 1979, the year the firm was acquired by Lonrho. Rivington Masters, 12 in all, 11 since 1800, outnumber the rest; the 11th, Charles Arthur Rivington, Master in 1969, was the last non-trade Master of the Company.[58]

For those who did not step out of line and who lived long enough, higher office was the crown of a working life. Death, bankruptcy and unwillingness to serve weeded out a substantial number of those called into Court. Of the 272 called from the Napoleonic period to the 1960s some 87 failed to make the final ascent to the chair. The Beadle's Book records those claimed by sudden death. In 1835 a Court Assistant was killed when his horse ran away from his gig; in 1840 another was shipwrecked and drowned off the coast of China; in 1848 another, a Whitaker, fell to his death from a train in New Zealand; in 1900 yet another died from enteric fever. One mid-19th-century Liveryman died in the office armchair at Stationers' Hall, while talking to the Clerk. Bankruptcy accounted for several being passed over. A considerable number chose to fine rather than serve as Warden or Master. Some 24 paid as much as £100 to be excused office; Thomas Longman III was called into Court in 1829 and paid £200 to avoid holding office and his son Thomas Longman IV also fined in 1879.

For those who stayed the course it was often decades before election to the Court, and ascent up the final slope could be tediously slow even for the prosperous and successful. The career of Henry Adlard (1799-1893), a member of one of the Company's dynastic families, exemplifies the slow progress by seniority in the early Victorian period. Freed by patrimony, 6 February 1821, at the age of 22, he set up as an engraver and printer in Duke Street. He was called into Court in 1863 aged 64. He served as Under Warden 1866-7, Upper Warden 1867-8 and Master 1868-9, aged 69. He was, unusually, Upper Warden for a second time 1873-4. He died in Hackney aged 94.[59] Another was William Will, General Manager of *The Graphic*, cloathed in 1912 at the age of 48 but not called into Court until July 1942. He was elected Master in 1953 in his 87th year, 41 years after joining the Livery. The career of Edward Chenevix Austen-Leigh (1865-1949), eldest

---

58 Three Waterlows served on the Court between 1864 and 1940, there were four Truscott Masters between 1879 and 1959, including Francis Truscott, Lord Mayor of London in 1879 and Sir Denis Truscott, Lord Mayor 1958-9.

59 Beadle's Book, p.99.

son of Cholmeley Austen-Leigh, was similarly long drawn-out. Admitted by patrimony in 1888, he served as Renter Warden aged 25 in 1892. In 1927, he was elected Livery Stock Keeper, aged 60, was called into Court in May 1929 and elected Master in 1939, aged 72.[60] His younger brother, Richard Arthur Austen-Leigh (1872-1961), had an even longer wait. Although he was active in the Company throughout his career, he was not called into Court until 1942 at the age of 70, and did not reach the chair until 1954, then in his 82nd year. After gaining a first in Classics at King's College, Cambridge, he became a clerk in the House of Commons (1897-1900) but resigned after the death of his father to join the family printing firm of Ballantine, later Ballantine, Spottiswoode, as a director. He took a lifelong interest in his school and college, wrote and published much on the history of Eton and King's and his firm were their printers for many years.[61] His younger brother died in 1901 at the age of 27, and the two elder brothers, Edward Chenevix and Richard Austen-Leigh were left to manage the firm which expanded and prospered under their direction. They were both active in the trade, as Presidents of the Federation of Master Printers, Richard in 1922, and, towards the end of their lives, Masters of the Stationers' Company. Richard was a tall, imposing figure, with a ready wit, a man of great charm and a skillful negotiator. He was president of the Printers' Pension

8. *Left, from left to right.* Charles Robert Rivington, Master 1921, with Herbert Fitch, Upper Warden, and Edward Unwin, Under Warden, Ash Wednesday, 1922.

9. *Right.* R.D. Blumenfeld, Master 1934, first Newspaper Maker Master of the Company, who deputised for Edward, Prince of Wales.

60 A third brother Charles Raymond (1876-1901) was bound, 1891, and admitted to the Livery in 1898. He died three years later, aged 25.

61 He published *Spottiswoode, the story of a printing house,* 1910, compiled and published the *Eton College Register (1699-1790),* edited and wrote much of *Etoniana* until his death, edited several of Jane Austen's novels and what was for many years the standard edition of her letters, and contributed papers to the Bibliographical Society's proceedings in 1923 and 1936.

10. *Left.* Sidney Hodgson, Master, 1949, book auctioneer, first Honorary Archivist.

11. *Centre.* Richard Arthur Austen-Leigh, Master, 1954, printer, first Chairman of the Livery Committee 1920.

12. *Right.* Victor Penman, Master 1957, brother of William Penman, who opposed the terms of winding up the English Stock, 1961.

Corporation in 1941, chairman of the Joint Industrial Council of the Printing Trade (1927-8) and founding chairman of the International Bureau of Federations of Master Printers (1933-49). At the beginning of the Second World War he organised the move of the federation's offices from Berlin to Paris. He was chairman of the Committee of Management of the National Benevolent Institute (1936-45): President of the Festival of the Printers' Pension Corporation (1941) and editor of the Master Printers' Annual from 1920 until his death. He was also president of the Huguenot Society (1934-47) and the first of three Stationer presidents of the Bibliographical Society (1934-36). As founding chairman of the Livery Committee (1920-7), he pressed for publication of the early records (see pp. 187, 188). On the other hand, the illustrious Sir Sydney Waterlow rose rapidly through the Company.[62] Elected Alderman aged 41, he was invited to join the Court of Assistants. Knighted in 1867, he was elected Lord Mayor and Master in 1872 at the age of 50. He subsequently entered Parliament and was MP for Maidstone between 1874 and 1880.

The length of time between cloathing and reaching the chair—in the 19th and early 20th centuries the Master was almost always in his '70s or '80s—became a matter of growing concern to the Company. In a tactful letter to the Court in 1921, J.R. Riddell, 'in no way actuated by revolutionary motives'[63] as Honorary Secretary of the newly formed Livery Committee, petitioned for the inclusion of two Liverymen on the Court.

62 For further details of Waterlow's career *see* Chapter Ten.
63 Court Book h, 21 July 1921.

The Livery hoped to keep the Assistants in touch with developments in the various trades of the Guild and to have a voice on the governing body. In 1926 two Liverymen were provisionally accepted on the Court and in 1929 their term of service was extended to two years. Forty years later, in January 1965, Christopher Rivington, one of the Livery Representatives on the Court (1965-66) and Court Assistant Philip Unwin, wrote a confidential memorandum on 'Election of Liverymen to the Court of Assistants and Election of Master and Wardens' (see p.17). They pointed out that 'a liveryman was rarely called into court until thirty-five years from joining and might become Master after about forty-five years in all'. They suggested that the Company follow the example of some other livery companies and elect 'a sprinkling of younger men and of those still active in corporate work for their trades'.[64] The old guard, led by Past Master John Betts, who was in his mid eighties, were set against any change, but with the backing of Past Master J.M. Rivington, the Treasurer, a man of great charm and of considerable influence on the Court, it was finally agreed by a narrow majority in April 1966 that in future five out of the 30 assistants be elected out of seniority, 'on merit' as it was then called. In order to make room for the younger men, a Court supernumerary list was introduced, re-named Court emeritus list in 1997, to which elderly or infirm assistants might transfer without the penalty of a fine—previously a stumbling block to voluntary retirement. In May 1978 transfer at 75 was made obligatory, with an age limit for election to the Court.

13. *Left.* John Mylne Rivington, Master 1963, barrister, who negotiated the final settlement of the English Stock, 1961.

14. *Centre.* Donald Kellie, Master, 1966, one of the few craft bookbinders to be Master since Samuel Mearne, 1679.

15. *Right.* Charles Arthur Rivington, Master 1969, who drew up Library Trust deed, was Chairman and Hon. Librarian 1974-84.

64 Livery Committee minutes quoted by Philip Unwin, *The Stationers' Company 1918-1977: A Livery Company in the Modern World* (1978), pp.93-4.

16. *Left.* Philip Unwin, Master 1971, author of *The Stationers' Company 1918-77.*

17. *Centre.* George Riddell, Master 1972, founder of the Printing Industries Research Association and its Library and promoter of technical training for printing.

18. *Right.* Sir Derek Greenaway, Bt., Master 1974, who negotiated the sale of the school land, 1983-4, and the new Educational Trust.

By a Court Order of 1 June 1999 only those under 62 are eligible for election, effectively abolishing seniority as a qualification and the necessity of serving or fining as Renter Warden.[65] In 1990, there were 16 on the Court emeritus list, 18 in 1999.

Some indication of the variations in the social structure of the Company over the past two centuries and its relation to the printing and other trades of the Guild is given by the occupation of the Masters. Between 1800 and 1899, 65 Masters gave their trade as stationer but since 1900 the printers have been supreme with no fewer than 42 Masters. Almost all of the 27 bookseller or publisher Masters (in the early 19th century the terms were still interchangeable) occupied the chair between 1800 and 1910.

Conclusion: The Last Fifty Years

The job descriptions of today's Stationers would be incomprehensible to the Masters of Luke Hansard's day, yet the Company has managed to keep its traditional trade links through a period of bewildering and ever-accelerating change during which the managerial classes have come to dominate the Company. More and more managing directors, general managers, sales directors, chartered accountants come from a variety of large and small concerns involved in one way or another with the whole of the industry; book, newspaper and periodical publishers and printers, bookbinders, ink manufacturers, type founders, business and law stationers, newsagents, advertising agents, graphic designers, paper importers, pulp mill owners, manufacturing and wholesale stationers and business equipment manufacturers.

65 Court Book r, 1 June 1999.

The technological and commercial revolution which has affected the way that members of the Company make their living in the post-war years has made the term 'trade' more and more of an anachronism. Large conglomerates have absorbed the older independent publishers. The revolution in book production which began with the first Penguin paperbacks in 1935, to which there was so much resistance from the old guard, expanded rapidly in the 1950s and since the 1970s non-print forms have become a vast communications industry. Offices have become automated; a whole new area is concerned with sophisticated office machines. Paper production and packaging have become multi-million pound global industries of which book papers are now a minute part. There has been an explosion in scientific and technical periodicals to meet the scientific advances in new fields and here online publication will soon be in serious competition with the conventional paper format. Computers and the growth of the internet have capped a half century of intense change in the ways in which information is disseminated.

Amid so much novelty, the traditional trades are still represented. Quite at the other end of the scale is a development of the last few years, that of very small firms; in the printing trade, men or women computer-setting from home; or craft bookbinders and conservators working on their own; and the rare book trade, in contrast to new bookselling which is become a large-scale business requiring vast resources, has frequently shrunk to a one-man or one-woman operation generally selling books by catalogue and working from a private address; fewer and fewer antiquarian bookshops still employ assistants.

19. *Left*. Edward Glanvill Benn, Master 1977, whose daughter and son are on the Court at the time of writing.

20. *Centre*. Allen Thompson, Master 1986, Chairman of the Library Trust, 1984-7; he organised the trades' Excellence '87 exhibition in the Hall.

21. *Right*. George Thomas Mandl, Master 1992, Chairman of the Library Trust, 1992-7, who proposed a new history of the Company's later years.

In 1989 the Court ruled that librarians and archivists be included in the categories of 'qualifying occupations'.[66] Librarians had occasionally circumvented the rules—Arthur Oliver Mudie (died 1936) of Mudie's Circulating Library (but perhaps a commercial concern was acceptable) was admitted as a 'Librarian', 3 October 1882; in recent years the public librarian, Brian Baumfield (admitted 1970). Rather different were those from university and special libraries who joined the Company under the new rules in the early 1990s, and had become interested in the Company through its archives. They were the deputy librarian of the University Library Cambridge, David Hall, the librarians of the House of Commons and the House of Lords, David Menhennet and David Jones, the Bodleian Library's head of conservation, Michael Turner, and the librarian of the London College of Printing, Patricia Batley. The Company's own archivist was admitted as a bookseller, which she had once or twice unsuccessfully and briefly been, before the rules were changed. So far no other archivist has been cloathed.[67]

New Liverymen had come from firms with some of the most familiar names in post-war British publishing, Cecil Arthur Franklin of Routledge & Kegan Paul, John Allan White, chairman of Methuen, Alexander Frere, chairman and managing director of William Heinemann, Isaac James Pitman of Sir Isaac Pitman & Sons Ltd., Walter Godfrey Harrap and the Company's historian Cyprian Blagden (1906-62) who joined the Company in 1952. A bishop's son, a schoolmaster and school inspector before joining Longmans Green at the beginning of the war, he ran its Indian office during the war and became a director on his return (see Chapter Nine). Geoffrey (later Sir Geoffrey) Faber (1889-1961) was admitted in 1945. He came from a scholarly and clerical background and was a Fellow of All Souls, Oxford. In 1923 he founded the publishing house of Faber and Gwyer (later Faber and Faber), which he steered through the slump years, with T.S. Eliot and the designer Berthold Wolpe as co-directors, to become one of the most original and distinguished publishing houses of its day. From a very different milieu was Ellic Howe (1910-91) (cloathed 1945), the orphan grandson of a tobacco manufacturer whose wealth he inherited as a schoolboy. A typographer and typographical historian, during the war he was in charge of the government's 'Black Propaganda Unit' which, among other assignments, faked German documents for men and women dropped behind enemy lines. At Stationers' Hall he was a protégé of Sidney Hodgson who may have sponsored him for the Livery and with whom he worked energetically to put the Company's archive on the map (see Chapter Nine). At the end of his life he fell on hard times and died sadly in an old age home, in receipt of a Company pension.[68]

The association with newspaper and periodical publishing, established formally in 1933, has had less of an impact on the past fifty years than might be expected or the

66 The rules and ordinances of 1992 speak of 'book archivists', a term unknown in the archive world.
67 She was the sixth woman to be admitted, sponsored by the Master and Immediate Past Master in 1979, 'all fines and fees paid by the Company'.
68 Obituary in *The Daily Telegraph*, 23 October 1991.

22. The Court
saluting the
Company flag,
1985.

Company hoped, although both 'Fleet Street' and the provincial press have filled the
Livery with general managers, advertising and circulation managers, editors and
journalists from *The Daily Telegraph*, *The Daily Herald*, *The Daily News*, *The Western Daily
Mail*, *The Times*, *The Observer*, *The Guardian*, *The Kent Messenger* and *The Surrey Advertiser*.
The deputy vice-chairman of Times Newspapers, Sir Edward Pickering, was made an
Honorary Freeman and Liveryman in 1985 and takes an active part in the Company.
Several editors and journalists of periodical publication include those from *The British
Medical Journal*, *The Builder*, and *Wisden's Cricketers' Almanack*.

Whereas from 1800 to the 1920s there were more than twenty bookseller Masters, in
the last eighty years there have been none; equally, booksellers in the Livery have been
few and far between—Sir Basil Blackwell (1894-1984), head of Blackwell's of Oxford,
known affectionately in old age as 'the gaffer', elected an Honorary Freeman in 1972;
already mentioned, George Brimley Bowes of Bowes & Bowes, and the last head of
Heffers' of Cambridge, Nicholas Heffer. Benjamin and Uriah Maggs (died 1955), major
antiquarian booksellers, were admitted 4 March 1924.[69] Another was Philip Robinson

---

69 Their firm, Maggs Brothers, was at 34 and 35 Conduit Street; in 1939 they moved to 50 Berkeley Square. In 1932
they presented a broadside proclamation relating to printing of 11 March 1680 (Court Book j, 25 April 1932).

(1902-91), famous in the trade for the fortune he and his brother, Lionel, who did not join the Livery, made in 1944 by buying the residue of the vast assemblage of books and manuscripts collected by Sir Thomas Phillipps (1792-1872) from the Phillipps trustees. He was a native of Newcastle whose university library he endowed and he was also a benefactor to the company's archive and library. Other rare book dealers have been John Lawson, President of the International League of Antiquarian Booksellers in the 1980s, who transferred to the supernumerary list in 1991, and the Company's honorary librarian Keith Fletcher, a third-generation antiquarian bookseller and past president of the Antiquarian Booksellers Association.

The older and the recent additions to the allied trades rub shoulders—those from printing, typefounding, bookbinding, publishing including microform publishing—Sir Charles Chadwyck-Healey who published the microfilm edition of the Company's records in 1986, was cloathed in 1988—book designers and typographers, printing ink makers, paper makers, wood pulp and cellulose importers, paper making machine manufacturers, carton and envelope manufacturers together with those from entirely new industries; manufacturers and suppliers of office equipment, typewriter manufacturers, photocopy firms, computer manufacturers, design consultants.

As the 19th century advanced, as London expanded, and the trade moved away from the City, as each branch of the trade formed its own association and pressure group, the Company's hold seemed to weaken because there ceased to be a material advantage in being a Citizen and Stationer. No longer, at whichever end of the spectrum, is there a professional necessity for those engaged in the multifarious branches of the book and allied trades to belong to the Stationers' Company. Nevertheless, sentiment or conviviality may play a part and members of 'the trade' continue to join whether they are leading figures looking to combine commercial success with an active part in civic life, or craftsmen and women working in isolation and seeking a sense of belonging. Continuity is fostered by those entering by patrimony, or, since 1977, by matri-heritage, some from families with long-standing ties with the Company, others with a relatively recent family connection.

The rise of the present-day manager, not bred to the trade but an accountant or graduate of business school, and the growth of larger companies have accelerated the demise of the family firm. More and more, the Company's senior ranks come from this background although they work in a branch of 'the trade'; of the 476 Liverymen in the Company in 1995, 100 described themselves as publishers and booksellers, 141 printers, 54 paper manufacturers, and 18 newspaper makers. As Charles Rivington commented in his 1979 revision of the Company's rules and ordinances, 'An order of Court, made 4 May 1880, stated: "the ancient custom of electing to the Court only gentlemen who have been connected with the trade and carried on business on their own account shall be adhered to". This has not been adhered to for many years and has been omitted.'[70] Yet most

---

70 Explanatory note to accompany the draft abstract of the Rules, Ordinances and Established Customs of the Company, inserted in the printed rules, 1979.

members of the Stationers' Company, whatever their professional expertise, are still employed in the trades which its members have historically pursued but in a vastly different world.

CHAPTER THREE

The Newspaper Makers and the Stationers

Michael Harris

The history of the Stationers' Company is partly a tribute to consistent principle. Against all the odds, the Company held the line for nearly four hundred years against any decision to change the composition of its membership. However, in 1933 a sudden shift occurred through the incorporation of a group of people whose background and interest, though rooted in print, lay outside the sphere of book publication. Identified by the slightly whimsical term of 'newspaper makers' they appeared more alien than was in fact the case. The questions of how they came to be located outside the Stationers' Company, how they were brought into the membership and who they were, will provide the subject for this chapter.

English newspapers have a complex and largely uncharted history. They emerged in London in the 1620s and from the first were produced as a commercial product by printers and booksellers working in related areas of publication. Under the licensing system the newspaper experienced an erratic half-life which after control lapsed in 1695 changed dramatically. Through the 18th century the number of London and local papers in publication followed a steady upward line both in the number of titles and of copies.[1] London remained the base for newspaper production and in London the ownership of all the main publications was organised among the principal booksellers in shareholding cartels. This enabled the core members of the London trade, grouped within the Stationers' Company, to control and use this form of serialised print for their own advantage. The advantage lay in the combination of a modest but increasing income from sales and, more importantly, from the mixed benefits of advertising.[2]

For the first two hundred years the newspaper remained part of the infrastructure of the trade in print which included books of all sorts and was dominated by the interest of the London book trade. From about 1800 this began to change. By the early 19th century the demand for, and output of, the established combination of news and advertising was beginning to accelerate. The character of the serial product made it look increasingly inappropriate alongside the conventional, culturally constructed output of the booksellers. At the same time the scale of production, as well as the increasing

23. View of Fleet Street, *c*.1925.

---

1 The expansion of the newspaper press during the 18th century can be followed through: G.A. Cranfield, *The Development of the Provincial Newspaper*, 1700-1760 (Oxford: Clarendon Press, 1962); R.M. Wiles, *Freshest Advices: Early Provincial Newspapers in England* (Ohio: Ohio State University Press, 1957); Michael Harris, *London Newspapers in the Age of Walpole* (London and Toronto: Associated University Presses, 1987).
2 Harris, *Newspapers*, Chapter Four.

diversification of content, made it harder to accommodate the newspaper within the slow-motion schedules of book-centred production and publication. It began to look like a juggernaut which was running away from the traditional intervention of shareholding booksellers. Through the first half of the 19th century the newspaper emerged as a distinct, printer-driven form of material whose production was located at the cutting edge of a constantly diversifying technology.

The repeal of the taxes on advertising (1853), newsprint (1855) and paper (1861), the 'taxes on knowledge', pushed things forward even faster. Cheaper newspapers with steeply rising circulations, produced in their own purpose-built premises centred on the burgeoning newspaper district in and around Fleet Street, ceased to have direct links with the trade in books.

In fact, the newspaper as well as establishing its own pragmatic, information-based functions was also developing its own forms of internal and external organisation. None of the main personnel, owners, editors and journalists, fitted into the recognisable patterns of the literary *beau monde*. The individuals concerned were closer to the centres of commerce and politics than to those represented by the book trade and the Stationers' Company. Advertising was setting the tone of its primary medium—the newspaper press. Within their own self-contained production centres and exclusive networks of wholesale and retail distribution the London dailies had left the leisurely slopes of book publication far behind.

The sense of the newspaper as a raffish product of a starkly populist and market-led system was given a boost in the late 19th and early 20th centuries with the introduction of a new approach to the construction and presentation of news. This was based on the application of a range of techniques, applying to format as well as content and based on sometimes sensational American models, which became known as 'the new journalism'. The *Daily Mail* which appeared in 1896 was an archetypal product of the new approach and was the first paper to reach a circulation of a million copies per issue.

Allied to this process of forward momentum, involving ever higher levels of investment, was the emergence of individuals, prowling around the environs of Fleet Street within striking distance of Stationers' Hall, described rather uneasily as the press barons. Alfred Harmsworth (Lord Northcliffe) and Max Aitken (Lord Beaverbrook) came to stand, during the early 20th century, for a particular phase in the history of newspaper publication as the form began to cater for what was becoming a mass readership.[3]

This brisk account of a long historical process leading from the 17th to the 20th centuries, during which the newspaper changed from a single-sheet, bookseller product to a multi-page mass-market publication produced within its own industrial environment, is intended to suggest that what the Stationers' Company began to undertake in the 1930s

---

3 A listing of the printed works through which the history of the newspaper can be tracked is provided in David Linton and Ray Boston, *The Newspaper Press in Britain: an Annotated Bibliography* (London and New York: Mansell, 1987); David Linton, *The Twentieth-Century Newspaper Press in Britain* (London and New York: Mansell, 1994), and Dennis Griffiths, *The Encyclopaedia of the British Press, 1422-1992* (1992).

was a far from simple matter. It was certainly true that the newspaper never lost its underlying sense of social benefit. The liberal mid-Victorian notion of the press as 'the fourth estate' lingered on and, as the newspaper developed its own internal institutions, journalists could be represented as legitimate, even valuable, members of society. It was partly the wish to emphasise the element of respectability and social status that prompted the emergence of the strangely archaic Newspaper Makers' Company in 1931.

Meantime, how were the Stationers doing? In 1918 the Company emerged from the war in straitened circumstances. Membership was static and ageing. References to the 'dear old men' on many of the Company's ruling bodies suggested a general problem. At the same time, the Stationers' finances were at a low ebb and the ending of official registration had deprived the Company of both a source of income and its primary cultural justification. In the immediate post-war period, the Stationers made a concerted effort to locate themselves at the centre of the organisation of the English book trade. Even before the war, the Company had adopted a policy of providing access to the Hall for groups involved in the trade. In a survey of lettings from July 1905 to October 1906 it was found that 98 meetings had been held in the Hall and that the organisations involved included the Publishers' Association, the Associated Booksellers, the Wholesale Stationers' Association, the Master Printers and Allied Trade Association and seven others. The Publishers' Association had taken up semi-permanent occupation on the premises with the Beadle acting as Assistant Secretary.[4] (See p.5.)

By the 1930s the number and range of the personnel earning a living from the English press had been greatly extended. Outside the core activities of production and distribution, agencies for news, advertising and public relations were jockeying for position in the national and international market. At the same time, organisations centred on specific functions or particular geographical sectors had continued to proliferate from the early 19th century. Unions, associations and societies whose membership consisted of proprietors, journalists, printers, members of the provincial trade, as well as such low-key functionaries as newsagents, formed a complex network of print-centred interest.

The latest to emerge from the noisy background of the English newspaper press was the Newspaper Makers' Company. Based on an organisation called the Newspaper Club, it adopted all the traditional trappings of the ancient companies. Its structure of Master, Deputy Master, Wardens, Clerk and Court of Assistants was entirely compatible with, for example, the Stationers' Company. Founded in March 1931, it was intended to provide an umbrella organisation for anyone involved in the newspaper business—'people of technical, organising and commercial ability, publicists and journalists'. The inaugural dinner was held at the Mansion House on Friday, 26 February 1932 with the Prince of Wales as the principal guest and main speaker.[5]

4 Court Book f, 5 February 1907. The Royal Literary Fund continued to have a base at the Hall until 1956.
5 *The Times* 46,068, Saturday, 27 February 1932.

24. Grant of Arms
to the Worshipful
Company of
Stationers and
Newspaper Makers,
1951.

25. The Court Orders for 16 October 1933, when 87 new liverymen were admitted.

During the evening, as reported in *The Times*, the objectives of the new Company were identified. It was intended to promote close working alliances within the trade, to increase 'the prestige of the calling' and to engage in benevolent and educational activities. These included the award of the Gordon Selfridge award for meritorious journalistic work. In all respects the overlap with the Stationers' Company was striking. Even in December 1931 public reference had been made to the possibility of a merger, though it was said that the limited accommodation at the Stationers' premises might prevent it. After all, the Hall could only seat 200 at a dinner at most.[6] In March 1932 the Newspaper Makers moved to Ludgate House in Fleet Street and in July 1933 they finally received a Royal Charter.[7]

The stages by which the organisation merged with the Stationers are unclear. The membership of the Newspaper Makers consisted of 32 honorary or life members and 130 annual subscribers, and consequently in this respect as in most others the Stationers'

6   *The Times* 46,009, Friday, 18 December 1931.
7   *The Times* 46,482, Wednesday, 28 June 1933. It was stated that during its first year the Newspaper Makers had distributed £5,000 for the relief of unemployed journalists and other causes.

Company was clearly the senior partner.[8] Even so, the Stationers had an urgent need for new members and the presence of a number of wealthy and high status individuals among the Newspaper Makers offered its own benefit. Major the Honourable J.J. Astor, in 1933 Chairman of the Times Publishing Company, and Lord Illiffe of *The Daily Telegraph* would have been hard to refuse. At the same time, the Stationers had never been unwilling to cooperate with individuals or groups based in the newspaper industry. This was partly a matter of letting the Hall to the British International Association of Journalists (1909 and 1927) or occasionally admitting someone with a newspaper background to the membership. Before 1914 Cecil and Howard Harmsworth, founders of the *Daily Mail*, had been admitted by redemption and advanced to the Livery, while in 1923 John Akerman, manager of *The Times*, was also granted the Freedom.[9] It seems from the outcome that negotiations between the Master of the Newspaper Makers, the American R.D. Blumenfeld, who was Chairman of Express Newspapers, and the Stationers followed a straightforward course. It certainly offered the Newspaper Makers a favoured position in the modified organisation and even Philip Unwin noted some dissatisfaction at the limited financial benefit to the Company, a modest £4,000 from fees.[10]

The means by which the two organisations were to be integrated were ratified at a Special Court held on Monday, 22 May 1933. The Master, Sir Percy Greenaway, who was also Lord Mayor and who was described by Philip Unwin as a 'Pickwickian figure' with impeccable manners, was to be re-elected in July. In January 1934 he would stand down for an elected Newspaper Maker—presumably Blumenfeld. A similar sort of rotatation was to extend through the upper echelons of the Company and representation on the Court was to be gradually extended up to 1951. A very detailed schedule of fees was laid out for the new intake and among other issues the transfer of the Newspaper Makers' modest library and action on their now redundant charter were discussed.[11] (See Chapter Nine.)

Through the Stationers' records it is possible to obtain a detailed view of the new members. In October Blumenfeld and the officers of the Newspaper Makers were admitted to the Freedom and the Livery.[12] They were followed by a long list of ordinary members whose admission occupied successive Courts until December. True to its founding principles, the Newspaper Makers contained a mixed bag of individuals. Almost every aspect of the newspaper business was represented. Proprietors, editors, journalists, advertisers and public relations people were included in the list, representing both the London and the local press. Editors and managers of *The Daily Telegraph*, *News of the World* and *Financial Times* rubbed shoulders with representatives from *Berrows Worcester Journal*, *Surrey Comet* and *Hornsey Journal*. Most areas of the internal organisation of newspaper

---

8   The numbers are given in Court Book j (Special Meeting), 22 May 1933.
9   Court Book h, 6 November 1923. He was sponsored by Sir Frederick Bowater.
10 Unwin, *Stationers*, p.37.
11 Court Book j (Special Meeting), 22 May 1933. The library was valued at £600-700.
12 In one day, 16 October 1933, five senior Newspaper Makers and some 87 new members were formally admitted as liverymen.

work were represented. The advertising managers of a string of London dailies including *The Daily Telegraph* (Captain G.P. Swan), the *Star* (F. Simonis), and the *News Chronicle* (W.E. Tomlin), appeared on the list, as did the cartoonists from *London Evening News* (P.H. Fearon, 'Roy'), and *Daily Express* (Sidney Strube). Express Newspapers supplied several members, while among the directors of a wide range of newspaper companies and advertising agencies were at least four directors of the *Amalgamated Press*.

The five women Newspaper Makers who joined the Stationers' Company at this time included Dorothy Secker, a journalist with *Daily Express*, Dorothy Hughes, editor of *Journal of Careers*, Bessie Arram, who received the general designation of journalist and author, as well as Emilie Peacocke who was woman's editor of *The Daily Telegraph*. Women have since then become an integral part of the membership and, to some extent, this can be credited to the dynamic admissions of 1933.[13]

26. Betty Ross, journalist and the first woman Newspaper Maker to be admitted to the Livery, 16 October 1933.

Several of those entered were already members of City companies. Lord Iliffe of the Coach and Harness Makers, C. Grasemann of the Fruiterers and J.A. Le Brasseur described as Woolman. C.C. Wakefield, an officer of the Newspaper Makers, appeared as oil manufacturer, citizen and Haberdasher, while others on the list represented the Barbers, Needlemakers, and Gold and Silver Wyre Drawers. A few individuals were associated with the print trade: C.H. Gee, who as well as being managing director of his own firm was also president of the Midland Alliance of the Federation of Master Printers, and E.W. Whitworth, managing director of the firm of Crusha and Sons Ltd. which owned a number of local newspapers in the London region. The list also included a few individuals concerned with news agencies. Reuters, the National Press Agency and the Australian News Cable Service were all represented.

The members of the Newspaper Makers were clearly a respectable group representing, for the most part, the managerial side of the various businesses. There was a scattering of military and aristocratic titles and names such as Waldorf Astor and John Walter were redolent of money and history. H.G. Wells, described simply as 'Man of Letters', must have provided an added reassurance of cultural probity to the Stationers.

13 In 1971 all four daughters of Sir Denis Truscott (Lord Mayor in 1957-8) joined the Company. They pursued careers in various branches of the trade, working as freelance journalists, editors and managing directors of the family printing and stationery firms.

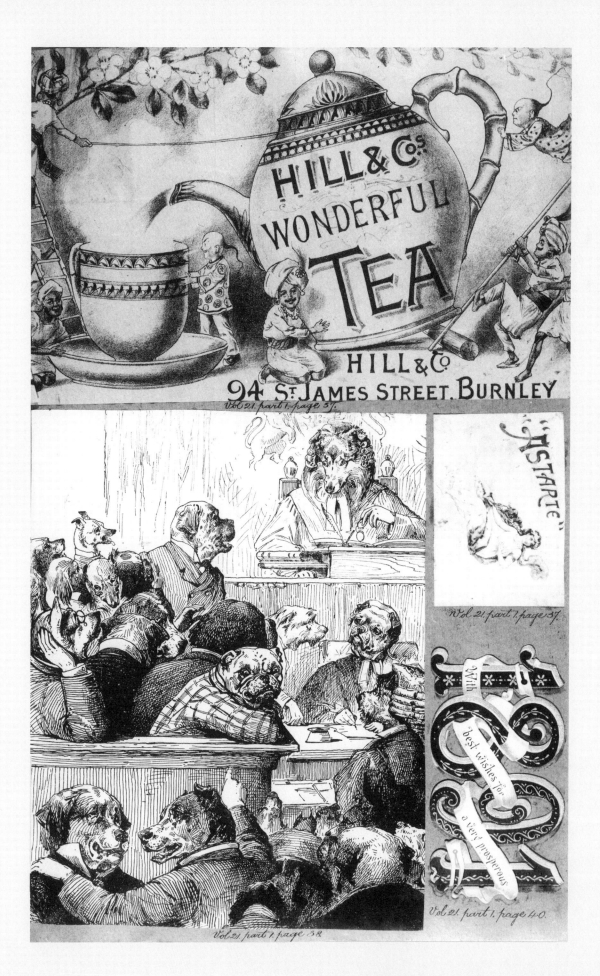

HILL & Cos WONDERFUL TEA

HILL & Co

94 St JAMES STREET, BURNLEY

Vol 21. part 1. page 37.

"ASTARTE"

Vol 21. part 1. page 37.

With best wishes for a very prosperous

Vol 21. part 1. page 40.

Vol 21. part 1. page 38.

CHAPTER FOUR

The Registering Office and the Administration of Legal Deposit

DAVID WHITAKER

Although it would be a gross exaggeration to claim that copyright protection grew out of literary censorship, it is a fact that historically the two notions developed side by side, having a common origin in the growth of printing, and that ordinances and Acts of Parliament designed to protect society against the abuses of the press frequently achieved, as a concomitant, the protection of authors and publishers against infringement of their rights.[1]

This ambivalence was acknowledged by the Court itself. Its minutes for March 1842 note that 'the Books of the Company of Stationers contain a fund of Literary Information at once curious and interesting and more especially in relation to Printing and the restraints, obstructions and penalties interposed by all parties in the State against Bookselling, Bookbinding, Letter founding and Printing from an early period after the invention of the latter most important Art down to the reign of Queen Anne'.[2]

The licence to which the Court minute referred was the Licensing Act of 1662 which, after a number of temporary renewals, expired in 1695. It was in some sense the successor to the Star Chamber decree of 1637 forbidding the publication of books without a licence. Its protectionist clauses suited the trade and the Company well enough, but the requirement to deposit at Stationers' Hall a copy of every book published to be forwarded to the Bodleian Library at Oxford, did not; the deposit clause in the 1662 Act added the libraries of the University in Cambridge and of the Royal Library in London to the Bodleian. Legal deposit was there to stay.[3]

The first law recognisably relating to copyright, rather than to state licensing, was the Copyright Act of Queen Anne of 1710.[4] 'It is quite clear,' according to John Feather, 'that the initiative for legislation ... came from the inner circles of the London book trade ... with the active support of the Stationers' Company.'[5] It stated that actions for infringement of copyright could be brought only for titles which had been entered in the Register of the Stationers' Company. Thereafter, however, during the passage of the Bill through the

1 Ian Parsons, 'Copyright and Society', in *Essays in the History of Publishing*, ed. Asa Briggs (1974).
2 Court Book V, May 1842.
3 For a full discussion of the Licensing Act and its eventual expiry, see Raymond Astbury, 'The Renewal of the Licensing Act in 1693 and its lapse in 1695', *The Library*, 1978, and Michael Treadwell, '1695-1995: Some Tercentenary Thoughts on the Freedom of the Press', *Harvard Library Bulletin*, 1996.
4 The Act of 8 Anne C.19, entitled 'An Act for the Encouragement of Learning', paid lip service, if no more, to the rights of authors. It obtained the Royal Assent 6 April 1710.
5 John Feather, *Publishing, Piracy and Politics, an Historical Study of Copyright in Britain* (1994), p.28.

Houses of Parliament, legal deposit requirements, which had gone out with the Licensing Act, were revived and made more onerous. A fourth copy, for Sion College, was added in 1706. In 1707, to mark the Act of Union, the Faculty of Advocates' Library in Edinburgh was added too, and Scottish peers—with a patriotism and generosity made simpler by being at the expense of others—then added four Scottish universities.

Penalties were incurred by a printer who failed to deliver the legal deposit copies to the Stationers' Company warehouse keeper, and by the warehouse keeper if he failed to deliver them to the libraries on demand; but any action at law for the recovery of these penalties by the libraries had to be brought within three months. The Act specified no penalty for failure to enter a title in the Register. The booksellers therefore argued that registration was not obligatory and that they need enter and so deposit only those books for which they wished to obtain copyright protection.

John Oates describes the state of affairs in the early 19th century, 'and so they commonly neglected to enter large and learned works, such as the universities in particular wanted, and entered only such potential bestsellers as might attract piratical publication, these being for the most part books of dubious usefulness to academics; and being understandably reluctant to give away nine copies of a multivolume work even when they wished to protect it, they would sometimes register the first volume only and decline to deposit the remainder or even to sell them to the privileged libraries unless they paid for the whole set. Against obstruction such as this the libraries found themselves with no remedy, since it proved in practice impossible to bring a prosecution within the statutory limit of three months.'[6]

The privileged libraries got little of the output, and little of that was of significance. Poetry, sermons and pamphlets predominated. R.C. Barrington Partridge records that in the first 14 years of the Act Sion College got, on average, just over one publication a week. In 1724 the Sion College librarian estimated the value of the legal deposit privilege at £5 a year.[7]

In 1798 the case of Beckford v Hood, heard in the Court of King's Bench, reversed the general opinion that a proprietor had no copyright in a work unless it was registered at Stationers' Hall. Registrations fell again. In 1797 there had been 651, by 1812 they were down to 271.[8] As publishers claimed that the privileged libraries had no right to unregistered books, and Beckford v Hood established copyright in unregistered books, there was a positive disincentive to registration unless an action for infringement was to be brought. No action could begin without the Company's certificate of registration.

In 1801 the law of copyright was extended to Ireland,[9] which had become a centre of piracy. Again the book trade was expected to pay a price: the Trinity College and King's Inn libraries, in Dublin, were added to the list of recipients of free copies. The impost

---

6 J.C.T. Oates, 'Cambridge University and the Reform of the Copyright Act 1805 13', *The Library*, December 1972.
7 R.C. Barrington Partridge, *The History of the Legal Deposit of Books throughout the British Empire* (Library Association, 1938).
8 Barrington Partridge, p.43.
9 41 Geo.3.C.107.

of Anne's Copyright Act, of nine copies, had become 11 copies. However, from the point of view of the supposedly privileged libraries, a situation which was already bad simply· became worse. The Stationers were in the position of being both the taxed and the tax collector, which did not make for enthusiastic enforcement. According to B. Montague, writing in 1805, in 1803 only 22 out of 391 London publications were received by Cambridge, and in 1804 only 25 out of 400.[10]

The dissatisfaction felt by Montague was felt also by Edward Christian, Downing Professor of Law, whose early brilliance was marred by a later obduracy which caused a contemporary to write of him that at Cambridge 'his society was avoided by everyone whose time was of any value'.[11] But it was perhaps this obduracy which persuaded the University in 1812 to sue a printer called Bryers in the Court of King's Bench[12] where it was decided that 11 copies had to be delivered to Stationers' Hall for the use of the privileged libraries, whether or not the work was registered. Richard Bell, writing in the *Law Librarian*, comments that 'This decision destroyed a construction of the Act which had been accepted by most lawyers, successive Parliaments, the publishing trade and the libraries themselves, for more than 100 years'.[13] Naturally enough, the trade complained bitterly and publicly about the result of the Bryers case.

Oates records that on 16 December 1812 Davies Giddy, the Member of Parliament for Bodmin and the owner of a private press, presented to the Commons a petition from the booksellers and publishers of London and Westminster complaining that the new interpretation of the law would 'subject the petitioners to great expense, and operate very seriously to discourage literature' by killing the production of expensive books in small editions. Various examples were quoted, among them the financial burden involved in the compulsory deposit of 11 copies of such books as Daniel's *Oriental Scenery* (£2,310) and *Lord Valentia's Travels* (£577). This brought a rejoinder in January 1813 from Glasgow University, which wrote that expensive books such as these were precisely those which it needed most and could least afford. They were essential for instruction and gave a university, in the eyes of its students and of the public, that 'dignity and respectability so essential to its real usefulness'.[14] This was not an argument which found much sympathy among the Stationers. In March the printers of London and Westminster petitioned at the House, and Giddy introduced a motion to appoint a committee to examine and report upon the Copyright Acts.

By this time, as Oates writes, 'The champions on either side were hard at work'. He quotes Sharon Turner who stressed that the deposit laws were an invasion of the sacred rights of property 'as completely as if it were to be enacted that a silversmith should give to these public bodies 11 silver candlesticks'. J.G. Cochrane, a partner in the publishing house of White, Cochrane & Company, pointed out that all of the libraries sold or

10   B. Montague, *Enquiries and Observations respecting the University Library* (1805).
11   Gunning, *Reminiscences* (1854).
12   Cambridge Univ. v Bryers, 16 East, 317.
13   Richard Bell, 'Legal Deposit in Britain', the *Law Librarian*, 1977, vol. 8 nos. 1 and 2.
14   Barrington Partridge, p.127.

destroyed as useless many of the books which they received. Only St Andrew's University felt itself in a strong enough position to deny this. When the Committee made its recommendations the trade was both astonished and infuriated to read that the Committee recommended the existing 11 privileged libraries go on receiving their copies as this would 'tend to the advancement of learning and diffusion of knowledge'.[15]

The 1814 Copyright Act sought to clarify the situation.[16] The British Museum—the recipient from George II in 1753 of the old Royal Library, together with its legal deposit privileges—was to get a copy on the best paper, on registration.[17] It was the duty of the warehouse keeper at Stationers' Hall to send a list of all titles registered to the other 10 libraries which were still to receive copies should they wish for them. These were to be demanded from the publishers within 12 months of the registration. Delivery might be either via Stationers' Hall or direct. While the number of registrations increased—from 580 in 1814 to 1166 in 1815 and this annual total was more or less maintained until 1842—the librarian at Sion College estimated that, despite the increase in registrations, only one publication in eight was actually delivered.

Publishers and their sympathisers continued to be vociferous in their efforts to have the law changed. Sir Egerton Brydges, Member of Parliament for Maidstone and owner of the Lee Priory Press, wrote that before 1814 the books sent to the Bodleian which were not thought worthy of a place in that collection were either heaped together in a small room as lumber, or disposed of by the curators at their periodical visits as they thought fit.[18] In 1818 a Select Committee of the House of Commons was brought together to examine all of the then current Acts relating to copyright and all the old complaints of 1813 were again rehearsed.[19] The Committee proposed that the obligation to give 11 free copies be repealed and in future one free copy only was to be provided to the British Museum. The other recipients were to get an annual sum in lieu or, failing that, the committee recommended that other free copies should go only to Oxford, Cambridge, Edinburgh and Dublin.

In his evidence to the Select Committee the Company's warehouse keeper, George Greenhill, said that between April 1814 and April 1818 there had been 4,353 entries for books and music in the register, at a fee of two shillings per entry as laid down in the Act. Between 1811 and 1814 the total of entries had been 1,530 only.[20] In his evidence William Longman said that only one or two per cent of Longman books were registered and this was 'almost invariably' *after* publication and was prompted by the threat of infringement and that, therefore, it was possible that Longman might have to take a case

15   House of Commons Parliamentary Papers 1812-13, vol. ix.
16   54 Geo.3.C.156.
17   It was rumoured that he wanted the space to make room for his mistresses; George III regretted this and with the help of Dr Johnson put together another library. In due course this too went to the British Museum and is known as the King's Library.
18   *A summary statement of the great grievance imposed on authors and publishers* (London, 1818), p.14.
19   Parliamentary Papers 1818, vol. ix.
20   George Greenhill was Treasurer of the English Stock and warehouse keeper, with which was combined the duty of Registering Officer from 1793 to 1849 when he was succeeded by his son Joseph.

28. Copyright register for 19 March 1842 showing George Greenhill's signature.

to court. Interestingly, he maintained that all Longman books were sent for distribution to the copyright libraries.

Nothing came of the Select Committee report until 1836 when a new Copyright Act was introduced by James Silk Buckingham.[21] In its original form it proposed that the privileges of 10 of the 11 libraries to receive free books be abolished, and that the British Museum be required to buy a copy of every book published, these to be supplied at cost price. The 10 disenfranchised libraries were to be paid annual compensation from the consolidated fund. Amendments to the Bill during its passage into law reinstated the privileges of the British Museum, Bodleian, Cambridge, Edinburgh and Dublin libraries. The rights of the other six libraries were bought out. The International Copyright Act of 1838 gave protection to foreign works published in the British Empire and to the

21 6 and 7 Will.4.c.110.

works of British authors published in foreign countries provided that the works were registered at Stationers' Hall and one copy deposited, to be sent on to the British Museum within one month of publication.

The privileges of the five libraries were reaffirmed in the Imperial Copyright Act of 1842 which attempted to regulate Copyright legislation throughout the Empire.[22] The British Museum was to receive its copy upon publication, and other copies were to be rendered up to Stationers' Hall within one month of a written demand by an officer of the Stationers' Company or by the privileged libraries or their agents, within 12 months of publication. The Act confirmed, however, that Copyright existed whether or not a book was registered. Copies continued not to be delivered, whether automatically to the British Museum, or on demand.

In May 1850 the situation began to change dramatically. In that month the power to administer the Act of 1842 was transferred from the Secretary of the British Museum to the Keeper of Printed Books, Mr Antonio (later Sir Anthony) Panizzi. The Keeper was a dedicated man. He travelled throughout England, and into Scotland and Wales, enforcing the law upon recalcitrant publishers. From May 1850 to July 1876 the trustees of the British Museum instituted proceedings against no fewer than 158 of them.[23] Taking advantage of the decision of a Master of the Rolls in 1806 Panizzi also enforced the library's right to claim a copy of any book in print which had not already been delivered.

Panizzi's effect was remarkable. In 1859 the *Publisher's Circular* recorded a book title output of 4,258 for the year; *The Bookseller*, its rival in recording the book trade's title output, listed 5,490 titles; the registry book at Stationers' Hall contained only 1,135. The British Museum's Copyright receipt book recorded a whopping 28,808 items. While it must be noted that this latter total is not only of books, but included parts of periodicals, pieces of music, maps and atlases. Still, the discrepancies are huge.

Panizzi's actions encouraged the other privileged libraries. The Court Book for 1859 records that a letter had been received from the Bodleian Library: 'Having observed that for some years past the collection of books to which they were entitled under the Copyright Act was remiss and deficient ... determined with three other libraries which enjoy the same privileges to appoint an Agent of their own to demand and receive their books.[24] It was further proposed that Joseph Greenhill—warehouse keeper since 1849— should be invited to cooperate with their Agent, for which service he was to be paid an annual gratuity of £100 from the libraries.' To which Greenhill had responded, 'no official of the Stationers' Company could possibly act with any Agent in the way suggested'. He was wrong.

The Court ordered (10 January 1860) that Greenhill obtain monthly lists from the British Museum of all publications delivered there, that he check for titles not delivered

22 5 and 6 Vict.C.45.
23 Parliamentary Papers 1878, vol. 24, C.2036-I.
24 Court Book Y, 6 December 1859.

to Stationers' Hall, and that he demand them from their publishers. He was also to start a Libraries Receiving Book for 'entering books delivered at the Hall for the use of the Libraries'. This new set of record books began in April 1860.

The onslaught of Panizzi upon recalcitrant publishers, the efforts of the other privileged libraries and cooperation between the Stationers' Hall and the British Museum transformed the situation. The table below shows the numbers of books registered at Stationers' Hall in three years in the 1870s, the number of publications recorded in the trade press, and the number received by the Bodleian.[25]

YEAR	STATIONERS' HALL	THE BOOKSELLER	PUBLISHERS CIRCULAR	BODLEIAN
1874	2392	5493	4312	4405
1875	2731	5997	4903	4773
1876	2036	5765	4888	5112

All of the entries are for titles rather than volumes, and those for the Bodleian include vocal and instrumental parts of sheet music as well as, for 1876, maps. The Bodleian figures do not include parts of periodicals, which so hugely inflate the British Museum figures.

Publishers were restive. *The Bookseller* for January 1871 had reported Panizzi's activities in this way: 'By Act of Parliament the library of the British Museum is entitled to a copy of every book published in the United Kingdom; it should be sent without asking. If by any oversight it be not sent, the polite custom of the national institution is to purchase a copy at full retail price, and then summon the publisher for the amount, and the magistrate thereupon delivers a homily upon the unpardonable sin, and fines the delinquent the value of the book, and adds a sum of 50s also for costs.' Much lobbying took place which was to result in a Royal Commission in 1878.[26]

Those who lobbied, however, were not necessarily active in the Company, nor concerned for its interests. Indeed, the editor of *The Bookseller*, quoted above, who was particularly good at demonising Panizzi, was not a Stationer. Other publishers were dissatisfied with the Company for what they saw as its high fees for registration, although the fees were not set by the Company but by the Act of 1842. Members of the public who sought to consult its registers also became hostile and some became voluble.

The Company really was in an impossible position. Its registers had started in the 16th century as instruments of government control. The Company had seen them as a way of 'scotching infringements of copyrights and restricting trade to its own advantage'.[27] They had become, over the years, a useful record of who owned what, and whether wholly or in part; a place where transfers of ownership were registered without the need to pay legal fees and, because of the way the law was phrased, a source for the certificates necessary before a case for breach of copyright could begin.

25 Figures supplied by the Bodleian Library.
26 Parliamentary Papers 1878, vol. 24, C-2036-I.
27 *Myers*, p.17.

They were not registers of all publications. Once, under the Star Chamber and under its various spiritual heirs, that had been the intention but it had never been the reality. The Company's registers were never intended to be bibliographies; nor were they meant to show what books had been received for the privileged libraries, although sometimes they did so. And, by the 19th century, the Company was being made a convenience of. It had no power of dismissal of the Registrar who had, as the 1878 Commission was to find, 'for all practical purposes ... a life appointment'. The fees for registration and search went to the Registrar, and the Stationers' Company was paid nothing from them.

The work had also extended far beyond the registration of books. The International Copyright Act provided for protection in Britain for any book, dramatic piece, musical composition, print or sculpture first presented in a foreign country provided that that work was registered at Stationers' Hall and, for the printed materials, a copy deposited for sending to the British Museum.[28] The Fine Art Copyright Act of 1862 gave the Registering Office an additional task, and income.[29] The task was the maintenance of the Register of Copyright in paintings, drawings and photographs. In an age when fortunes were being made from newly mass-produced goods sold by the new means of mass advertising, the passing off of products and the piracy of images were widespread. In the registers at the Hall were images which ranged from labels to photographs of music hall stars.[30]

The table below shows the numbers of entries, assignments recorded, certificates issued, foreign works entered, and searches charged for from 1871 to 1875.

YEAR	ENTRIES	ASSIGNMENTS RECORDED	CERTIFICATES ISSUED	FOREIGN WORKS ENTERED	SEARCHES CHARGED FOR
1871	3231	156	325	845	612
1872	3247	140	399	1686	674
1873	2249	111	286	1967	727
1874	2440	154	369	2411	708
1875	2756	159	485	2568	730

The fee for an entry was 5s., for an assignment 5s., for a certificate 5s., for a foreign entry 1s. and for a search 1s. Thus, in 1875, the income to the Registering Officer, Joseph Greenhill, was £1,014 9s. From the fees the Registering Officer paid for two assistants. The Company paid for a porter, rent, repairs, coal, gas and water. Bearing in mind the criticism that the Company received for the way the Registry was managed, and its limited control over that management, one may reasonably wonder why it was not anxious to get rid of it. But clearly it was not. On 7 June 1864, for example, the Clerk

28 7 and 8 Vict.C.12.
29 25 and 26 Vict.C.68.
30 For a full description of various sequences of registers opened between 1662 and 1883, see Simon Eliot's article on '"Mr Greenhill, whom you cannot get rid of": Copyright, Legal Deposit and the Stationers' Company in the 19th century', in *Libraries and the Book Trade*, ed. Robin Myers, Michael Harris and Giles Mandelbrote (2000).

had been instructed to watch Mr Blake's Copyright Bill 'now pending in the House of Commons', and if any proposal to remove the Copyright Registers from the Hall was put forward, he was to bring this to the notice of the Court 'calling a special Court of Assistants if necessary'.

In 1866 Warden Hodges had pointed out that the registers, now going back some 300 years, were both valuable and vulnerable.[31] The Court ordered a fireproof safe and the Registering Officer took possession of the key. It may be presumed that he also took it home, because on 10 January 1871 the Court 'resolved that the Registering Officer be required to make arrangements at his own expense for the attendance of some trustworthy and competent person whenever the Registering Officer may be absent from the office ...'.[32] The Court ordered that the person appointed was to be able to open the safe.

This may have reflected an event in December 1870. C.H. Purday, researching for his *Copyright: A sketch of its rise and progress* (1877), was refused permission to inspect the records of 1826 upon demand. He made an official complaint to the Board of Trade about this, and about being asked to pay a fee. Note of his complaint, and the orders for a keyholder to be always on the premises follow on in the Court Book. On 4 July 1871 the General Purposes Committee recommended that a special room be provided in which members of the public might search the Registers 'conveniently and without interference with the Company's business'.[33]

Whether the room for the use of the public was in response to Purday's complaint to the Board of Trade, or to an anonymous 1871 publication *Entered at Stationers' Hall*, is unclear.[34] Purday has been suggested as the author of this 32-page pamphlet, but so also has Joseph Whitaker whose *Almanack* was first published in 1868 and was in competition with the quality end of the annual publications of the English Stock. A large part of *Entered at Stationers' Hall* is a ferocious attack upon the Company as almanack publisher but it also attacks the running of its registering office. The room and its processes are described in this way:

> The author ... will find himself in a narrow box like room, the part of which assigned to the public not above a dozen feet in length and breadth. A counter runs all around the sides, and behind the counter sit a couple of lads of 17, or 18, whose look suffices to show that they deem themselves very important personages. 'You come to register a book', asks the younger of the lads. 'Yes, if you please,' replies the meek author. 'Then pay first!' orders the little man: '5s. for registration and a penny more for the printed form.' And the youth turns round contemptuously, seeing that the money is not put down immediately.
>
> He seems cowed a little, the poor author, yet summons courage to say, 'I have not quite settled on the title of my work; that is to say, I do not know whether the title I have chosen is

---

31 Court Book Z, 6 February 1856.
32 Court Book a, 16 January 1871.
33 Court Book a, 4 July 1871.
34 Printed by M. Thomas, Franklin Press, Hanley Road, London, and sold by E. Truelove, 256 High Holborn, London.

one already taken by some former writer on the same object. May I ask you, therefore, kindly to let me look at the index of the books standing in the registers of the Stationers' Company.' The lad behind the counter drops his pen in astonishment. 'What does he mean by "the index", Jim?' he whispers to his slightly elder colleague. The latter thereupon rises grandly from his three-legged stool. 'We keep no index, Sir!', he informs, with a severe reproachful frown at the too inquisitive maker of books. It is now the turn of the author to be surprised, but he is too humble a man to exhibit signs of astonishment, and contents himself therefore to ask, in all meekness, the favour of looking over the registers of Stationers' Hall. For all reply, the two lads commence grinning, their grimaces saying plainly that the enquirer must be a fool. To search the registers of the Stationers' Company for any purpose of discovery? What an idea? You had better first search a London fog for sunlight.

When the eldest of the boys has done grinning, he addresses the stranger, saying sternly, 'Our charge is 1s. for examining any single entry, and it is for you to give the title and date of the entry you wish to see.' He feels amazed, the poor author; but there is no more time given to him for entering into conversation with the authoritative youngsters, for he is hustled away by others who come into the narrow box anxious to 'register', and to pay down their money. Recrossing the courtyard he hears the sound of festive music and clinking of glasses from the upper windows of the book registration office. The members of the registering brotherhood are dining together. Stationers' Hall, if it has no library, has a splendid cellar of wines.

All good knock-about stuff, but there is about it a sense of direct observation. Whether because of these, or of other strictures, in June 1873 the Court received a report from a committee which it had appointed to look into the Company's role in the workings of the Copyright Act.[35] The Court ruled that the rubrics which appeared on the Registering Officer's forms—'Parties must attend in person or agent'; 'No correspondence entered into'; 'Stamps not taken as fees'; 'Forms one penny each'—were to be omitted and the forms prescribed by the Act strictly adhered to. All entries were to be made not more than 24 hours after a properly completed and paid for application had been made. Certificates of entries were to be supplied on demand when practical. Separate books were to be kept for the registering of books and drama. Personal attendance was no longer to be necessary. Entries were to be numbered and the same number put on the application form and on the receipt.

The Registering Office, like many monopolies before and since, had become an organisation which put its own convenience before that of its customers. The Court was trying to tighten up. The French composer Gounod was one of the first to benefit. Greenhill had refused to enter his dramatic work *Jeanne d'Arc* and, following his own previous rule of 'No correspondence entered into', had not answered any letters either. On 1 January 1874 the Court ordered Greenhill to write an extended letter of apology which included the regret 'that I did not at the time read your written explanation'.[36] The

35   Court Book a, 16 June 1873.
36   Court Book a, 13 January 1874.

librarian at Trinity College, Dublin, had also complained.[37] His agent, he wrote to the Court, had been used to his porter collecting his books twice a week; now books accumulated 10 to 14 days before being given to the porter. On 20 January—less than three weeks after his Gounod climb down—Greenhill was ordered by the Court that all books were to be handed over the day but one following receipt. A record was to be kept of the title of each book delivered with its date of receipt and the signature of the person to whom it was delivered, and for which library.

The Court was more active in its overseeing of the registry in the 1870s than in any decade before it. But it could not escape the fact that while it might once have seemed an appropriate agent for the legal task required of it, this was no longer so. Many of the witnesses before the 1878 Royal Commission were hostile, as were some of the Commissioners, and the final report was damning. Even the evidence of the John Murray of the day, who was a senior Stationer, was not helpful: 'At present the fees are rather exorbitant: 5s is the sum paid, and as registration is not compulsory the result is that very few books are registered.'

Joseph Greenhill was more extensively interrogated by the Commission than was any other witness. He explained the workings of his office, the fees paid, his relationship with the Company and something of the Acts which governed his work. The Commission was much exercised (its questioning takes up five columns in the report) that Greenhill gave the porters who brought in the forms from the publishing houses—there could be many of these at a time—only a receipt for the money they handed over, not a dozen or more, as it might be, instantly completed registration forms. Greenhill explained that properly completed forms took some time to write out and, anyway, were seldom needed and that, if they were handed over at once, more staff would need to be employed otherwise 'it would frequently keep so many persons waiting'.

Anthony Trollope the author, who was also a civil servant, was one of the commissioners. He was worried about the possibility of registering books that did not exist, or books which were dummies. Why, he wanted to know, did the Registering Officer not see the books themselves? Greenhill's belief that there was little point that he could see in paying 5s. to register non-existing books, or non-eligible books (blotting books was an example that he gave) was obviously not shared by the pedantic civil service mind which Trollope chose to display. In fact he was only quieted by being reminded that the Act stated that to supply false evidence to the registry book was an indictable misdemeanour.

In his evidence, Mr Chappell, the music publisher, said, 'The register at Stationers' Hall is very badly kept; it is imperfect, it is irregular, and it is bad in many respects ... I can give the strongest possible instance ... an opera of our own which happens to be the most valuable one that we possess ... *Faust*. When we were told by a fellow publisher that we had no copyright in it, because it had never been entered at Stationers' Hall, I was thunderstruck.'

37 Court Book a, 3 February 1874.

Chappell continued that his brother 'went down to Stationers' Hall and with some difficulty persuaded Mr Greenhill to allow him to look over the day book of about the time when I knew it would be. The entry was found at last, but it had never been posted. Consequently, if we had not by an accident discovered it, we should have lost a property worth £5,000 simply from the negligence of some clerk at Stationers' Hall.' Mr Greenhill's reply was, 'With respect to that it is very improbable ... I turned to the index myself, looking back to the year 1859, and found the original entry of Monsieur Gounod's copyright of *Faust*, and also in the register of assignments Monsieur Gounod's transfer of the same to Emily Chappell and Thomas Patey Chappell, on 22nd June. There was no appearance of irregularity on either register, or index, or day book.'

The Commission continued to shake this one like a terrier with a rat, but Mr Greenhill was not to be moved. Mr Trollope asked, finally, 'Is it equally clear that it has been entered in due order in the index without any interlineation?'. To which Greenhill replied, 'Yes, I have brought certificates of the two entries referred to'.

Only the librarians, oddly in view of history, had no complaint. Trollope asked J. Winter Jones, principal librarian at the British Museum, 'I dare say you are not aware that not one in 20 of the books published is registered?'. Mr Winter Jones explained that the British Museum had circumvented the Stationers' Company; 'From 1850 to 1878 the British Museum took proceedings in 158 cases ... we soon got about three times as many books as were procured before ... I find no record of the Museum losing a case.' He believed, he added, that the Museum was getting most of the books that were published. The Bodleian librarian said, 'The books not sent are comparatively few', and Dublin and Edinburgh wrote similarly. They might have added that they, like the British Library, had largely circumvented the Company. Edinburgh appointed its own agent in 1860, and the Bodleian at Oxford, and the libraries at Cambridge and Dublin had all done so by 1864.[38]

Charles Robert Rivington, Clerk to the Company, also gave evidence. In it he said, 'The main use which the registry is at present is a means of transferring copyright from author to publisher, or publisher to publisher, without payment of any stamp duty, and without any necessity of any legal document whatever except the simple form of assignment. Then the other use of the registry is that, if a work is pirated, the owner of the copyright must go to Stationers' Hall and leave the form and pay 5s. before he can ground his proceedings for suppressing the piracy.' He went on to report to the commissioners that a committee of the Court of the Company suggested that fees be reduced, that a copy of every book published be produced at the Hall to be stamped, that a list of entries be published which would be a record of all works in which Copyright obtained, and persons not registering within a certain time should lose their Copyright. The offices should be modernised and made as useful as possible not only to publishers but to the general public.

---

38 David McKitterick, *Cambridge University Library: A History*, vol. II (1986), p.570.

In its report the Commission found that '... registration under the present system is practically useless, if not deceptive ... by the mode in which the register is kept ... we do not desire to express any censure upon the gentleman who holds the office of Registrar. Our censure is intended to apply to the system in force ... Moreover, in our opinion the fees are unnecessarily high.' It also made the point that '... as so few books are registered ... it is impossible to know when copyright commenced and when it will end.' The Commission ignored all of the Company's proposals for change. As an additional blow it recommended that the British Museum—which it proposed should be the only library to retain the privilege of a free copy—should take on the task of registration. However, as so often in matters of Copyright, nothing happened.

Despite the criticism it had suffered from the public and from the Royal Commission, still the Company did not want to rid itself of the Registry. The Court Minutes for 5 November 1878 resolved, 'That the Court is desirous to retain and preserve the rights and privileges which have hitherto appertained to the Stationers Company in respect of the registration of books and other articles and things and the copyright therein.'[39] When Parliament debated Copyright in 1891 the Company sent its 'Humble Petition to the Lords Spiritual and Temporal' which told their lordships, 'That your Petitioners in fact originated the system of registration of copyrights', and asked for the registers not to be taken away.

In 1883 Joseph Greenhill retired, and Charles Robert Rivington, the Clerk, took over responsibility for the registry. Registrations steadily increased as the number of titles published went up. From the proceeds Joseph Greenhill was paid a pension of £500 a year for his long tenure as Registering Officer. On 31 January 1903 C.R. Rivington reviewed his 20 years' responsibility in a letter to the Master, which is copied into the Court Book: 'At the time of taking over the Registry in 1883 the staff consisted of two clerks and the business was conducted in a small office under great disadvantages and few facilities were offered to correspondents from the Country or to persons desiring to search the registers.

> Attention was first directed to providing applicants with precise instructions as to the mode and effect of registration and to encourage registration by persons resident in the Country through the posts. This was promoted by printing on the back of all forms full instructions and circulating them throughout the Country and it is now well known that information as to registration can be obtained upon application to Stationers' Hall.
>
> The usefulness of the register being mainly dependent upon its contents being readily accessible much time and labour have been expended on compiling and maintaining an index ...

Staff were increased from two to five with two casuals and occasional help from the Beadle and porter. He went on,

39   Court Book b, 5 November 1878.

... these are also supplemented (as occasion arises) by additional assistants in order to carry out the rule laid down by the Registrar that all applications for entry on the register must be entered on the register within 24 hours after the terms of the Act have been complied with.[40]

In 1884 the salaries had amounted to £422 15s.; in 1902 they totalled £1,070. The Head Clerk got £300 a year. Income in 1902 was £2,589. The Registrar took £250. Mr Rivington said that the pecuniary benefit to the Company over the 21 years had been £8,591. This was very different from Greenhill's day when all the income had gone to the Registrar, but still could not be said to have been anything that was going to make the Company rich. Regardless of that, the Court clung on. On 7 July 1903 it was informed that the Publishers' Association had agreed to its request, and had written to the President of the Board of Trade supporting the continuance of registration of Copyright at Stationers' Hall.

The end, however, was in sight and came in 1911. The Copyright Act of that year confirmed that each publication in the United Kingdom must be delivered within a month of publication to the British Museum; and to all or any of the other privileged libraries on written demand which must be within 12 months of publication, with delivery to be within one month of the receipt of the demand.[41] To add insult to what publishers saw as continued injury, the University of Wales was added to the recipients of their unwilling largesse. The libraries were to have their own Agent, so that the Company's historic if unsatisfactory role in legal deposit was ended and, as a final blow, the legal status of the registers in Great Britain was to go.

The new Act came into force on 1 July 1912. The clerks who looked after registration were compensated by the Board of Trade for the loss of their livelihoods. After 44 years of service Mr Jobbins—who must have been one of the two 'important personages' of 1870—got £300. The Company did not have even that modest compensation. The Act was not fully in force throughout the Empire, until Canada ratified it in 1923. The next year, 1924, the Court decided that it would continue with a voluntary register in the office, which until very recently continued to be called 'registry'. It was administered by the Beadle or, when there was one, the Assistant Clerk. In April 2000 the Court ruled that it was not economic and should be abolished. Sentiment no longer played a part.

The Greenhills

The Greenhills, father George and then son Joseph, were Treasurers of the English Stock, Warehouse Keepers, and Registering Officers at Stationers' Hall from August 1797 to February 1883, a total of 86 years. They were at the heart of the Company, but one can glean very little about them as people from the almost always colourless entries in the Court Books, and the slender and occasional evidence elsewhere.

40 Court Book f, 2 March 1903, Election Court.
41 1 and 2 Geo.5.C.46.

These forms can be obtained at Stationers' Hall, price 3d. each.

For Office Use

TO THE REGISTRAR, STATIONERS' HALL, LONDON, E.C. 4.

Ch 14

I/We *Geoffrey Hall* of *24, George Street, Manchester, 1.*

do hereby certify, That ~~I am~~ ~~we are~~ the proprietor(s) of the Copyright of a Book, entitled *"New Nursery Rhymes for Old"*

; and I/we hereby require you to make an entry in the Register Book at Stationers' Hall

of ~~my~~ ~~our~~ Proprietorship of such Copyright, according to the particulars underwritten, and I/we hereby acknowledge that such Register

Book is not kept in pursuance of any Statute and that the entries made therein are for the purpose of record only.

ALL NAMES TO BE WRITTEN IN FULL.

Received   3 0 NOV 1949

No.   15764

Title of Book	Name of Publisher, and Place of Publication	Name and Place of Abode of the Proprietor of the Copyright	Actual Date of First Publication
	(If unpublished leave blank)		(If unpublished in "Unpublished")
New Nursery Rhymes for Old	*True Aim 24, George St., Manchester, 1.*	*Geoffrey Hall. 24, George Street, Manchester, 1.*	*May 6th, 1.*

Dated this *twenty-ninth* day of *November* 19 *49*.

(Signed) *G. Hall*

N.B.—In filling up the above form special care must be taken to insert the full and correct title of the Book, the name of the *first publisher*, with the place and of publication, if published. All communications to be addressed "**The Registrar, Stationers' Hall, London, E.C.4.**"

George was the son of Thomas Greenhill, a London bookseller who was in a good way of business in Mansion House Street and later in Gracechurch Street, both in the City. He was Master of the Company in 1787. George was bound to his father, freed in 1795 and in August 1797 was elected Treasurer of the English Stock and Warehouse Keeper, with which was combined the duty of Registering Officer.[42] In his evidence to the 1818 Select Committee of the House of Commons[43] to examine all the then Acts relating to Copyright, his evidence was simple and factual. He gave details of the numbers of registrations, and the fees received. He did not play a major part in the battle between the universities, notably Cambridge, seeking their free copies, and the authors and publishers who were anxious not to give them. The committee members did not show any of the animus toward him that some of the Commissioners of 1878 were to show towards his son Joseph.

George Greenhill resigned in July 1849 giving as his reasons 'the infirmities of advanced age', which the Court accepted with regret and recorded its satisfaction with the way he had filled the post of Treasurer for nearly 52 years.[44]

29. Registration certificate for *New Nursery Rhymes for Old*, published by True Aim, 6 May 1949.

42 Court Book P, 28 August 1797.
43 Parliamentary Papers 1818, vol. ix.
44 Court Book X, 3 July 1849.

The Treasurer then had a house adjoining the Hall and there George's son Joseph had been born in 1803. After he had completed his schooling, in 1819, Joseph joined his father as his assistant. He became a Liveryman in 1824. In 1849 he applied to succeed his father as Treasurer.[45] The post was advertised within the Company, an election was held and, at a special meeting in August 1849, he was elected. He was also appointed to be Registering Officer under the 1842 Copyright Act and instructed to lay before the Court immediately after the first of April every year a return in writing of the fees and emoluments received, under the provisions of the Act. The appointment was 'during the pleasure of this Court and subject to such regulations (if any) as the Courts may hereafter think to make with respect to this office'.[46]

It would seem that by 1855 Joseph had forgotten about the 'return in writing', for in 1859 he applied for an extra £100 a year[47] so that he might employ an assistant, but had this approved only after providing a return of his income for the previous four years.[48] In July 1871 the General Purposes Committee wondered if the fees from registrations, and his other emoluments, would not provide the Treasurer with adequate remuneration for his services, 'provided always that his income each year amounts to a certain sum to be approved by the Court'.[49] Nothing more is heard of this, but in August 1872 the General Purposes Committee did succeed in getting the Court to agree that its resolution of 2 October 1849 be acted upon and 'all expenses of carrying the Act into effect be defrayed by him out of the fees'. Joseph's extra £100 a year for an assistant was taken away.

Joseph Greenhill also looked after the buying of wine, and here he seems to have won his encounter with the General Purposes Committee.[50] In June 1872 the Committee was asked by the Court to '... ascertain and report on the system hitherto adopted with regard to the wine purchased by the Company with full particulars of the wine stock now in the Company's cellars.' This charge to the Committee came not long after the publication of *Entered at Stationers' Hall*, with its acerbic reference to the absence of a library at the Hall, but the presence of 'a splendid cellar of wine'. The anonymous author of *Entered at Stationers' Hall* turned out to be in this, as perhaps in other matters, nearly but not wholly accurate. The Company did *not* have a fine cellar of wine, but the English Stock did. In August 1872 the General Purposes Committee reported that the custom had been for Mr Greenhill 'for economy and convenience' to buy wines out of the floating capital of the English Stock;[51] all bills for wine were laid before its Board and cheques in payment were signed by the Master and Wardens.

The method of selecting wines was for Mr Greenhill to call together some junior members of the English Stock for what would now be called a 'blind tasting', of different

45 Court Book X, 28 August 1849.
46 Court Book X, 2 October 1849.
47 Court Book Y, 5 July 1859.
48 Court Book Y, 2 August 1859.
49 Court Book a, 4 July 1871.
50 Court Book a, 4 July 1871.
51 Court Book a, 6 August 1872.

wines at different prices from various merchants. Only Mr Greenhill knew which wines were which, and from whom, and he did the ordering. No records of the meetings were kept. The stock, in dozens, was 410 of port, 32 of Madeira, 11 of claret, 15 of Moselle, 110 of sherry, and two of champagne.

The Court resolved that in future there should be a Wine Committee made up of the Master and Wardens and two members of the Court, and that in any one year no more wine be ordered than had been drunk in the previous year. Which was all very right so far as it went, but that may not have been very far for, in March 1873, the General Purposes Committee was asked to ascertain the value of the wine in the cellars, belonging to the English Stock, and to consider and report whether '... the stock be purchased by the Corporation and at what price'.[52] No more is heard for ten years.

Joseph Greenhill retired as Treasurer of the English Stock in February 1883. The tribute to him in the Court Book notes that he had entered the service of the Company 64 years before and that he had been a Liveryman for upward of 59 years.[53] He was granted a pension of £300 a year for having been Treasurer, and of £550 a year for having been Registering Officer. The office of Treasurer was allowed to lapse and, in future, the wine cellar was to be in the care of the Wine Committee. In March the Court offered to 'Joseph Greenhill Esq. their hearty thanks for his long and faithful service ... and hope that he will be spared for many years to assist them with his advice and experience.'[54] In April the Court resolved that the Clerk have the key to the wine cellar, and the cellar book be laid on the table at each meeting of the Wine Committee.[55] After a decade the General Purposes Committee appears to have won. But Mr Greenhill had to retire first.

Those few bare bones do not provide a fleshed out life, and anything more must be supposition. However, as Joseph was born at the Hall, and worked there for much of the 19th century, he must have known everyone of any significance in the various trades of the Guild. Indeed, he must have watched the coming to maturity of many of those Liverymen whose 'respect and esteem' was to be recorded in the Court Book at the time of his death in 1892 at the age of 89.

From 1818 to 1883 he was associated with the English Stock and with the Registering Office, being Treasurer of the one and in charge of the other for 34 of those 64 years. As Treasurer he would have become familiar with the bookselling community and, however much the Registering Office was run, day to day, by his clerks, it would have made him familiar with the output and the fortunes of all of the publishing houses of his time. Few if any of his contemporaries would have had such a good view, and probably none for so long a time, of the businesses of bookseller and publisher members of the Company.

His attitude to the deposit libraries might well have been formed in 1818, when he was 15 years old, and his father was giving evidence to the Select Committee. It had been

52 Court Book a, 4 March 1873.
53 Court Book c, 6 February 1883.
54 Court Book c, 6 March 1883.
55 Court Book c, 3 April 1883.

30. Joseph
Greenhill in his
middle years.

called into being as a result of pressure from publishers, most of whom would have been members of the Company, protesting at the impost of 11 free copies to be given to the privileged libraries. The irritation of publishers with this tax in kind, unique to their trade, continued throughout that century, the one which followed it, and continues today. Often it has soured relations between the two parties. If Joseph Greenhill was less than enthusiastic about his role as claimer, receiver and passer on of legal deposit copies he was, in that, in tune with the trade he served, and with his Company.

There must have been those within the Company who were jealous of him. By the third quarter of the century his income was substantial. And he was in charge of the wine cellar. Those wine tastings must have been jolly occasions, much envied by those not included, and to be in charge of ordering would have brought many Christmas hampers from merchants as tokens of appreciation.

The Royal Commission of 1878 sought, to coin a phrase, to throw the book at him, but he defended himself ably enough, and if the Commissioners found that the job he did could be better done elsewhere, it made plain that its criticisms were not of him, but of the system he was there to oversee. And it is noteworthy that the proposals of the Court, relayed to the Commission by the Clerk, were wholly ignored.

Greenhill's notices, 'No correspondence entered into' and the like in the Registering Office, indicate all the impatience of a man who has no intention of serving his public in any way other than that which he has decided upon. But, apart from Mr Chappell whose indictment is harsh, but may not be accurate, Mr Purday, who came to the Hall when Greenhill and the key were absent, and was not given the respect his researches called for, and the anonymous author of *Entered at Stationers' Hall*, there does not seem to have been much complaint. The publishers themselves seemed happy enough for they, as the Clerk said in his evidence to the Royal Commission, used the Registry mainly as a means of transferring rights without paying lawyers, which was an obviously laudable aim.

On 4 November 1890, following the death of the Master James Adlard, Joseph Greenhill achieved what may have been his highest ambition and was elected Master for the remainder of his predecessor's term of office. Sadly, he presided over one Court only, and for all the others until his term expired in July 1891, Sir Francis Wyatt Truscott stood in for him. He died in July 1892. The Court recorded their sense of the '... unswerving integrity and ability of their late friend ... who won the affectionate regard of his colleagues on this Court ... and the respect and esteem of the Liverymen of this Company.'[56]

In February 1892, a few months before Joseph's death, his son, the Reverend Henry Joseph Greenhill, had been appointed Honorary Chaplain to the Company.[57] He died in 1907, ending his family's intimate connection with the Company which had begun with his grandfather over a century before.[58]

56 Court Book d, 5 May 1892.
57 Court Book d, 2 February 1892.
58 Court Book f, 1 March 1892.

CHAPTER FIVE

The English Stock and the Stationers' Company

The Final Years

RICHARD BOWDEN

At noon on 8 April 1959 George P. Simon, Master for 1958-9, opened the envelopes containing the final offers for the Ludgate Hill/Ave Maria Lane corner site. Through the English Stock the Company had gradually acquired the freehold of the whole of this site and less than a month earlier it had been put on the market. The asking price was £285,000. No less than 11 offers were received at this price or more, and the bidders were then invited to make a second offer with exchange of contracts within 24 hours. The highest offer, from the Colonial Mutual Life Assurance Society Ltd., was for the extraordinary and totally unforeseen amount of £663,000. This was a colossal sum at that time and was in a sense the English Stock's final legacy to the Company.

Just what was the English Stock? It began in 1603 as a separate joint stock publishing house within the Stationers' Company, with a monopoly in a small group of popular, best-selling works which included psalters, primers and almanacks. It rapidly developed into an extremely profitable business and the shareholders, or partners as they were usually called, were paid generous dividends. Some of the profits were invested in property and in 1611 Abergavenny House, site of the present Stationers' Hall (see p.152), was purchased for the Company for £3,500 out of the profits of the English Stock.

By 1800 the English Stock still operated in much the same way as it had done nearly two hundred years earlier. Fewer titles were being published but almanack sales were still growing; they peaked in the mid-1830s after the abolition of government stamp duty in 1834. It is in fact no exaggeration to say that the fortunes of the Stationers' Company in the 19th century depended on the circulation of Dr Francis Moore's almanack, *Vox Stellarum*, better known as *Old Moore*. In the second half of the century, however, almanack sales fell rapidly, although the Company's investments were still relatively successful and its income from rents continued at a healthy level. It was in 1902 that the clerk, C.R. Rivington, circulated an internal report, speculating for the first time how the English Stock could be wound up.[1] Rivington pointed out that this would require widespread discussion within the Company and legal advice at the highest level, and he warned of the difficulties of bringing such an unusual 300-year-old institution to an end. He warned that proceedings were unlikely to be initiated without a strong incentive.

---

1   *A Concise Account of the Origin and Present Position of the English Stock of the Stationers' Company* (1902).

32. Dividend book—£30 payment, midsummer, 1871, to the Court and widows.

41

A Dividend made on the 6th day of June 1871 for the half year ending Midsummer 1871

Stationer's Hall

Mr Henry George Brown	Master			
Mr William Tyler	Wardens			
Sir Sydney H. Waterlow ald.				
Mr Charles Adlard	Assistants			
Mr William Henry barden	Livery			
Mr William Rivington				
Mr Frederick Miles	Yeomanry			
Mr Charles Grinivade				
Mr Robert Fra. Cooke				

Share	N?	Name	Dividend			Address
£400	1	Mr Charles Adlard	30			45 Barbara Street West, Holloway.
		less quarterage	-	2	8	
			29	17	4	
"	2	Mr Richard Bentley	29	17	4	41 St John's Wood Park.
"	3	Mr James Smith	29	17	4	Watford
"	4	Mr Charles Whittingham	29	17	4	4 Hampton Grove, Maple Road, Surbiton, Livery
"	5	Mr Thomas Jones	29	17	4	Hensworth, near Dunstaple, Hertfordshire
"	6	Mr Edmund Hodgson	29	17	4	115 Chancery Lane
"	7	Mr Henry Adlard	29	17	4	42 Hatton Garden
"	8	Mr Henry Good	29	17	4	60 Moorgate Street.
"	9	Mr Henry George Brown	29	17	4	Higham House, Shooters Hill Road, Blackheath
"	10	Mr William Tyler	29	17	4	17 Queenhithe
"	11	Mr William Young	29	17	4	Kent villa, Avenue Road, Acton
		Widows				
"	12	Mrs Mary Walter	29	17	4	Chilwell Hall, near Nottingham
"	13	Mrs Mary Ann Newman	29	17	4	72 Lincoln Street. Mile End.

The annuitants' scheme is today the last tangible reminder of the English Stock, but from 1800 to 1961, perhaps even more than during the first two centuries of its existence, the Stock played a vital role in the life of the Stationers' Company. (For the part played by the warehouse keepers, George and Joseph Greenhill, during the years 1793-1883, see pp.72-7.) The Stock lingered on, partly by default, for more than fifty years after Rivington's report. In fact it was not until 1958, when a decision on the future of the Ludgate Hill site became urgent, that any active steps were taken. After the sale the Court sought counsel's opinion, with dramatic result. There followed two years of intense activity and also, at times, bitter internal dispute before the Parliamentary Bill which terminated the English Stock became law in July 1961. Nearly forty years have elapsed since then and it is time to look at the full story of the sale of the Ludgate Hill site, the way in which the winding up was achieved and William Penman's subsequent opposition to the Company.

The Origins of the English Stock

The English Stock was unique among the City livery companies. Its formal creation by letters patent of James I in 1603 was the culmination of many years of development, giving the Company a monopoly over certain types of publication in addition to the powerful printing privileges it had acquired through the 1557 Charter.[2]

Built on such well-laid foundations, it is not surprising that the English Stock lasted for over 350 years. As well as the main elements in the 1603 letters patent—the monopolies and the partnership system—£200 a year was paid out of the profits to the poor of the Company. This was a factor three hundred years later when the English Stock was being wound up. The earliest use of the term English Stock was in 1617, distinguishing this main company from the short-lived Latin and Irish Stocks, which were introduced as separate additional companies at that time, the 1603 letters patent having specified that several of the new rights were for books written in English.

The capital of the new company was set at £9,000, the shares being equally divided among Court Assistants, Liverymen and Yeomanry (see *Glossary*): there were 15 Court shares, 30 Livery shares and 60 Yeomanry shares. The capital was increased to £14,400 in 1614 and the shares were worth £320, £160 and £80 each respectively, changing hands at these values. As with any company, the English Stock's success can be measured by the demand for its shares and with a normal dividend of 12½ per cent the incentive to be a shareholder, or partner, was always considerable. Shares became available when a partner died or was elected to a higher category; they could not be assigned but they could be inherited by a partner's widow (and widows were quite a high proportion of the shareholders) and inherited by her heir. If she remarried she was repaid the value of her share, and it became available to another member of the Company.

Under the 1603 letters patent the value of the shares could not change but because of the demand for shares the number of partners was increased by dividing some of the Yeomanry shares into half-shares. During the 18th century, with the English Stock's continuing prosperity, the number of partners was further increased in each of the three groups, though the proportions between the groups remained the same, so that by 1803 there were 318 partners, holding 36 Court shares, 72 Livery shares, 78 full Yeomanry shares and 132 Yeomanry half-shares, compared with 105 in 1603. In 1803 the value of the English Stock's capital was £34,560 and the total payment made on its annual 12½ per cent

---

2   Blagden, p.92. This account of the grant of the letters patent in 1603 and the events leading up to it are based on details in his article 'The English Stock of the Stationers' Company; an account of its origins', *The Library*, 5th ser., 10, 1955, and chapters 4 and 6 of *The Stationers' Company; a history, 1403-1959*.

dividend was £4,320. All these figures were to rise further—for much of the 19th century the total dividend payment was £6,192—and then to drop right back.

The English Stock's business was conducted by the Stock Board, which met every month and consisted of the Treasurer and the stock keepers, who by the 19th century had increased in number to six.[3] Although nominally subject to the control of the Court the powers and responsibilities of the Stock Board itself were considerable. One 18th-century minute book, 1755-66, survives and then there are no more until 1869-80, then another gap until 1889, after which they are continuous until the end of the Stock in 1962. They show that the creative thinking and all the important decisions about the English Stock did indeed come from the Stock Board. Sometimes major items had to be referred to the Court for a final decision but it was rare for the Court to do other than confirm the views of the Stock Board. The Court's relative lack of involvement and somewhat blinkered vision was also a fundamental weakness which contributed to the Stock's eventual downfall.

The Importance of Almanacks to the English Stock

The huge scale of the almanack publishing operation meant that it had to be separately managed and run. Charles Knight's description of what happened at Stationers' Hall every year on Almanack Day towards the end of November, when the distribution of next year's almanacks began, sets the scene well:

> All over the long tables that extend through the Hall, which is of considerable size, and piled up in tall heaps on the floor, are canvas bags or bales innumerable. This is the 22nd of November. The doors are locked as yet, but will be opened presently for a novel scene. The clock strikes, wide asunder start the gates, and in they come, a whole army of porters; darting hither and thither and seizing the said bags, in many instances as big as themselves. Before we can well understand what is the matter, men and bags alike have vanished—the Hall is clear; another hour or two, and the contents of the latter will be flying along railways east, west, north, and south; yet another day and they will be dispersed through every city and town, and parish, and hamlet of England; the curate will be glancing over the pages of his little book to see what promotions have taken place in the church, and sigh as he thinks of rectories, and deaneries, and bishoprics; the sailor will be deep in the mysteries of tides and new moons that are learnedly expatiated upon in the pages of his; the believer in the stars will be finding new draughts made upon that Bank of Faith impossible to be broken or made bankrupt—his superstition, as he turns over the pages of his Moore—but we have let out our secret. Yes, they are all almanacks—those bags contained nothing but almanacks.[4]

Another witness to Almanack Day a few years earlier was T.F. Dibdin who took note of the particular publishers collecting their almanacks:

3   They dined together until 1847.
4   Charles Knight, *London*, 6 vols. (London: Charles Knight, 1841-44), vi, pp.211-12.

33. Almanack Day at Stationers' Hall (from Robert Chambers' *Book of Days*, 1869).

Meeting a partner in the Row, as he was threading his way towards Stationers' Hall, I was induced by him to come and witness the disperson of the *Almanacks* for the ensuing year—it happened to be the last Monday in the month. As we approached the Hall, I saw a crowd of merry scramblers, some hatted, some paper-capped, and more without either hat or cap, pressing the large outer folding doors of the Hall—and joyously clamourous for admissions. My guide obtained me an entrance by means of a private door, and mounting one of the tables of the Hall, I saw piles and pyramids of these Almanacks—ticketted according to their respective owners—and to be carried away by the many applicants without. The clock of the Hall struck three; the folding doors gradually expanded—and in rushed the importunate claimants running in all directions—zig-zag, straight forward, and oblique—pouncing upon the bundles of their respective masters. All was laughter and good humour. Within three minutes, I saw an eight-feet cubical pile of these annual lucubrations—belonging to the house of Messrs Longman & Co.—disposed of, and taken home; and was informed, by one of the partners, that, before St Paul's clock would strike eight, every country bookseller's order would be despatched to him by the coach! On further enquiries, I learnt that in this article alone, *one* house (I think it was that of Messrs. Simpkin and Marshall) paid £4,500 for the amount of its traffic. It was also, I learnt, within the same house that the *monthly publications* were chiefly collected for dispersion—when a scene of equal bustle and good humour might be witnessed.[5]

VOX STELLARUM;

OR, A LOYAL

ALMANACK

FOR THE YEAR OF HUMAN REDEMPTION

1837,

BEING THE FIRST YEAR AFTER BISSEXTILE ; AND THE
EIGHTH OF THE REIGN OF HIS PRESENT MAJESTY:

CONTAINING,

AMONGST A GREAT VARIETY OF USEFUL MATTER,

THE RISING AND SETTING OF THE SUN AND MOON ;

THE MOON'S CHANGES, SOUTHING, AND AGE ;

THE EQUATION OF TIME FOR SETTING CLOCKS AND WATCHES ; THE RISING
AND SETTING OF THE PLANETS ; OCCULTATIONS ; MUTUAL ASPECTS, ETC.

AND

𝔄 correct 𝔗ide 𝔗able.

ALSO,

A TABLE OF THE LAW TERMS;

A NEW AND CORRECT TABLE OF KINGS' REIGNS;

AN ACCOUNT OF THE ECLIPSES;

WITH ASTROLOGICAL OBSERVATIONS ON THE FOUR QUARTERS
OF THE YEAR ; AND

A HIEROGLYPHIC ADAPTED TO THE TIMES.

BY

FRANCIS MOORE,

PHYSICIAN.

LONDON:

PRINTED FOR THE COMPANY OF STATIONERS,

BY GEORGE WOODFALL, ANGEL COURT, SKINNER STREET;

AND SOLD BY GEORGE GREENHILL, AT THEIR HALL,
LUDGATE STREET.

34. Dr Francis Moore's *Vox Stellarum* ('*Old Moore*') for 1837, the peak year for sales. (Original page size is 6½ in. x 4 in.)

Details of the English Stock's almanack sales survive for much of the 19th century. In 1800 a total of 571,350 almanacks were printed of which 55,525 remained unsold—less than 10 per cent. *Old Moore*, with 353,000 copies, accounted for no less than 62 per cent of this total, only 13,250 of its copies being left unsold—less than 4 per cent of the number printed.

The surprisingly wide range of 24 titles included *Old Moore* and one sheet almanack—as the name implies a sheet almanack looked like a calendar while an ordinary almanack was in the form of a small booklet. The gross profit made by almanacks in 1800 was £3,876, about half the English Stock's total annual turnover, but within less than twenty years this figure had almost doubled. There was a slight dip for a year or two either side of 1830 but apart from that it remained close to this level until 1840. After that, a long, gradual decline began in both sales and profits.

The English Stock's income came from three main sources: investments, rent and the profit from its publications. As the century progressed and its turnover rose and then fell the relative importance of each of these changed. The only one of them to increase was the income from rents. The success or lack of success of the almanacks had a twin effect on the accounts: when they flourished, as well as the dividend's being paid, more investments could be made, but when they began to fail, as well as losing income from their sales substantial sums might have to be borrowed from the investments in order to pay the dividend. From a practical point of view therefore, almanacks played a crucial part in the English Stock's continuing success, this in turn affecting wider Company affairs.

The peak years were between 1837 and 1839. In 1837 the number of almanacks sold reached an all-time high of 636,553, giving a remarkable gross annual profit figure of £7,989. By comparison the net annual profit on almanacks, a more widely used statistic, was £6,148 in 1837, reaching its all-time high of £6,150 in 1838. The overall turnover of the English Stock went up to its highest point, £12,401, in 1839, the year when the largest number of almanacks was printed, 694,000. The dividend also went up, leap-frogging from its usual level of 12 per cent to 15 per cent in 1838 and then to 17 per cent in 1839. In 1840 a request for it to be raised even further to 20 per cent was rejected, but it stayed at 17 per cent for eight years until 1847.

The main reason for these exceptional figures was that in 1834 the Government abolished stamp duty on almanacks. This meant that the price of the almanacks published by the Stationers' Company could be considerably reduced—the price of *Old Moore* dropped from 2s. 3d. to 1s.—enabling them to compete at last on more equal terms with the illegal but very widespread 'unstamped' almanacks which had been a source of irritation to the Company for many years.

5   T.F. Dibdin, *Bibliophobia* (1832), pp.33-5. I am indebted to Marc Vaulbert de Chantilly for drawing my attention to this passage.

The Background to Almanacks

The closest modern equivalent to an almanack is a pocket diary on the one hand, or a year book such as *Whitaker's Almanack*, on the other. Almanacks did of course contain other things besides astrological predictions. The calendar itself came first with the days of the week, the date, the phases of the moon and church festivals and saints' days. This was followed by a section of general information such as the dates of markets and fairs, a list of the main roads from London, a summary of historical events in Britain, recipes, gardening tips and forecasts of the weather for the year ahead. The contents of this section varied from one almanack title to another. As well as long-established titles like *Old Moore*, *Poor Robin* and *Wing* there were the county titles and a group of titles indicating occupations or subjects, such as the *Freemasons*, *Clerical*, *Ladies* and *Medical* almanacks. Later on, when sales began to fall and some almanacks had to be discontinued, the Stock Board published a number of new titles targeting different groups of people (a fundamental 20th-century marketing technique). Most of them were only short-lived but they helped to stem the general decline.

Some of the almanacks included the picture of zodiac man, which showed how each part of the human body was controlled by one of the 12 signs of the zodiac. This was to help people to decide on the best (and worst) times for medical treatment each month during the moon's passage through all the signs; tastes change, however, and both the picture and the concept of zodiac man were considered too indelicate for the 19th century.

In the 1820s the Company was accused of deliberately setting out to exploit the superstitious tendencies of the uneducated. This was a valid criticism but nevertheless an over-simplification. For a start many almanacks contained no astrology at all. Nineteenth-century almanacks have been taken seriously and examined in detail for the first time in a recent book by Maureen Perkins.[6] In the first chapter of the book, entitled 'Almanacs, Astrology and the Stationers' Company', she describes many of the almanacks which the Company published from 1800 onwards and shows that several of the most popular and best-selling titles, including the *Gentleman's Diary*, the *Ladies' Diary* and *Goldsmith's* did not in fact contain any astrological information—it was by no means an essential ingredient.

The members of the Stock Board regarded almanack publishing simply as a business operation which provided the Company with the income it needed; any interruption to this process had to be robustly opposed and in this connection the Carnan dispute of 1775 needs to be mentioned. At the beginning of the 19th century this was still within the memory of many of the Company's Liverymen. All sorts of unpleasant issues to do with almanack publishing had been raised—it was the first time the Company had been publicly criticised—and the English Stock's stability had been seriously threatened. In order to survive it became even more determined for its publications to succeed, and this determination was certainly one of the reasons why they lasted so long.

6   Maureen Perkins, *Visions of the Future: Almanacs, Time and Cultural Change 1775-1870* (Oxford: Oxford University Press, 1996).

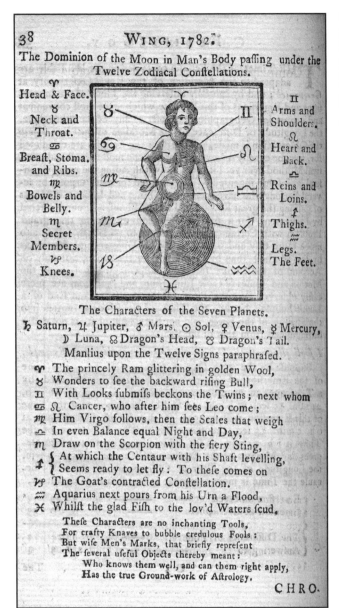

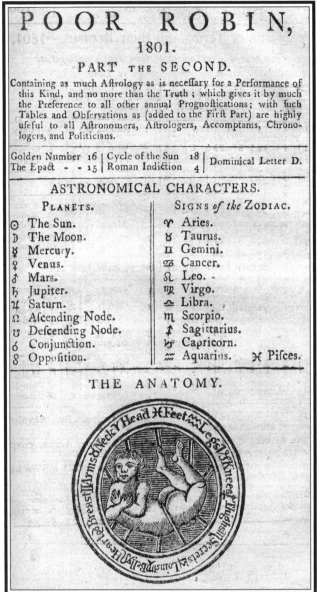

The Carnan Dispute and Charles Knight's Attack

The bookseller Thomas Carnan challenged the Stationers' almanack monopoly—and he won.[7] In November 1773 the Company took out an injunction against Reuben Burrow's *A Diary for the Year of Our Lord 1774* which had been published by Carnan, claiming that it was in effect an almanack. Three months later the House of Lords made its historic judgement over a pirated edition of Thomson's *Seasons*, overturning the concept of perpetual copyright, and in May 1775 the Court of Common Pleas, influenced by this verdict, ruled that the Crown had not been entitled to grant the Stationers' Company its perpetual monopoly in almanacks. Carnan was jubilant—he had had a longstanding

35. 'The Zodiac Man' from *Wing's Almanac* for 1782, and *Poor Robin* for 1801. (Original page sizes 6½ in. by 4 in.)

7 Blagden, pp.234-42.

grudge against the Company. As an experienced publisher he was fully able to benefit from his victory, and by 1777 he was producing 31 almanack titles. For the next ten years his impact on the English Stock's almanack sales was considerable and the Company was able to save the situation only in 1788, when, just three weeks after his death, it bought up all his almanacks.

The ending of the monopoly brought other competitors besides Thomas Carnan but the Government raised the level of Stamp Duty so much that after Carnan's death only the Stationers' Company could afford to pay it and continue to publish almanacks legally. That still left the illegal, unstamped almanacks, and they are thought to have numbered almost as many again as those published by the English Stock.[8]

Illegal copies of almanacks had always been produced. Before 1775 offenders had regularly been prosecuted by the Company, but when its monopoly came to an end so did its prosecutions. The Government was simply unable to cope with the flood of unstamped almanacks in spite of the revenue it was losing—in 1833 Stamp Duty was bringing in £30,000 a year, three-quarters of it paid by the Stationers' Company, so the potential amount of lost revenue must have been of some concern to the Treasury.[9] A street seller of almanacks interviewed by Henry Mayhew around 1850, after Stamp Duty had been abolished, gave this account of what used to happen:

> It was a capital trade once, before the duty was taken off—capital! The duty wasn't in our way so much as in the shop-keepers', though *they* did a good deal on the sly in unstamped almanacks. Why of a night in October I've many a time cleared 5s. and more by selling in the public-houses almanacks at 2d. and 3d. a-piece (they cost me 1s. and 1s. 2d. a dozen at that time). Anything that way, when Government's done, has a ready sale; people enjoys it; and I suppose no man, as ever was, thinks it much harm to do a tax-gatherer! I don't pay the income tax myself (laughing). One evening I sold, just by Blackfriars-bridge, fourteen dozen of diamond almanacks to fit into hat-crowns. I was liable, in course, and ran a risk. I sold them mostly at 1d. a piece, but sometimes got 6d. for three. I cleared between 6s. and 7s. The 'diamonds' cost me 8d. a dozen.[10]

These were the sort of prices the Stationers' almanacks were competing with before 1834. Mayhew was told that by the time he was writing, around 1850, the street trade in almanacks 'had become a mere nothing'. With no monopoly and no stamp duty, competition really was open to all and eventually this meant that the English Stock would be forced to abandon its almanack publishing. But we are anticipating.

Another attack on almanacks came in 1828, from Charles Knight. Anonymous articles in the *Athenaeum*[11] and the *London Magazine*[12] are generally thought to have been written

---

8   Perkins, p.14.
9   Court Book U, 6 July 1833.
10 Henry Mayhew, *London Labour and the London Poor* (London, 1851), vol. 1, p.271.
11 *Athenaeum*, 2 January 1828.
12 *London Magazine* 2, Series 3, December 1828.

by Knight, who was later a generous member of the Company (for his benefaction to the Company's school). Knight, as the publisher of the Society for the Diffusion of Useful Knowledge (the SDUK), was a vigorous campaigner for universal education and the articles accuse the Stationers' Company in forthright terms of failing to meet its responsibilities to the newly-literate.[13] He objects most of all to the astrology but he was also concerned with the wider damaging effect of these almanacks. He ignored their sheer entertainment value, particularly for sections of society with few other sources of amusement. The SDUK published material for the people for whom the Mechanics' Institutes had been founded—intelligent working-class people, who wanted to take hold of the opportunity to acquire an education; Knight claimed that they were vulnerable and impressionable. Was he right? There may have been an element of truth in what he said but, as Maureen Perkins shows, he overstated his case, ignoring the fact that many of the Stationers' almanacks contained no astrology.

During his first few months with the SDUK in 1827 Knight decided to start a new almanack of his own, the *British Almanack and Companion,* which was published for the first time in 1828. It contained several new sections of practical information and of course no astrology. Knight also denounced one of the Stationers' almanacks, *Poor Robin,* for its 'obscenity', citing Lord Erskine's attack on it in the House of Lords in 1779, when he was opposing the reintroduction of the monopoly and described it (with a certain amount of poetic licence) as suitable reading for a brothel; he refrained from quoting from it, he said, only out of respect for the House.

The Stationers reacted quickly to Charles Knight's remarks and this in itself is an indication of the force of his criticism. In 1829 they launched a new title, the *Englishman,* to compete directly with Knight's *British Companion.* They also removed zodiac man for ever from English almanacks by withdrawing the controversial *Poor Robin*—a gesture, but not too great a sacrifice as it had been making a loss for many years.[14]

The English Stock's profits were noticeably affected by the *British Companion.* In 1833 Knight again took the initiative by actively investigating the problem of unstamped almanacks. Just how strongly he felt can be judged from his autobiography, written more than thirty years later, where he informs us that 'the low-priced and illegal almanack trade was conducted with more regard to the morals and intellect of the people than the impostures and indecencies of the Stationers' Company'.[15] Like anyone campaigning for a cause he believes in, Knight had a tendency to exaggerate, sometimes in colourful terms. The Company's main preoccupation in selling its almanacks was to maintain a healthy income. It had certainly been shaken by the Carnan dispute, and following that had been forced to make some readjustments. Knight's attack had made the Stock Board think about its almanacks again; but his accusation of their having sinister motives was not only unfair but ridiculous.

---

13 Perkins, pp.23 and 75.
14 Perkins, p.16.
15 Charles Knight, *Passages of a Working Life*, 3 vols. (London, 1865), II, p.65.

The Court Books have little to say about the Stock Board at this period but they contain a revealing account of an incident in 1833 when the problem of unstamped almanacks seems to have been at its worst. The Stock Board had followed up a visit to the Commissioners of Stamps and Taxes in December 1832 to complain about this 'evil' by sending a delegation to see the Chancellor of the Exchequer, Lord Althorp, at 11 Downing Street, in July 1833. The Stationers wanted the power to arrest anyone purchasing or possessing unstamped almanacks, like excisemen pursuing smugglers. Lord Althorp was not prepared to consider extending the law any further but he did tell his visitors that the repeal of Stamp Duty was on the way.

As the months passed and nothing more was heard the Stationers could contain themselves no longer. The Court minutes of November 1833 give the full text of a letter of protest dated 19 October and signed by the Clerk, Charles Rivington, which was sent to the Commissioner of Stamps and Taxes: they had discovered unstamped almanacks for 1834 being 'daily hawked for sale in the most public thoroughfares in London' six weeks before their own publication date ... They had hoped in vain for a new Act,

> ... As they had to pay a much larger sum in stamp duty than its cost on every almanack they sold they could not compete with these 'lawbreakers' ... They were prepared to go on publishing almanacks and helping the Revenue provided the Government protected them ...

The letter finishes with the Company actually threatening that if nothing is done they will pull out of publishing almanacks altogether!

It is doubtful whether this extraordinary threat would ever have been carried out but the fact that it was committed to paper shows the level of indignation the Company felt about the situation: the problem of unstamped almanacks, the Government's lack of support and the constant interference from Charles Knight which even challenged the morality of their almanacks.

In 1834 Stamp Duty finally was removed, the almanack market became completely free and, as we have seen, the English Stock could at last bring its prices down and compete more fairly with everyone else. True, it was no longer able to make the grand claim that the Company was playing an important part in raising revenue for the Government, as implied in the letter to the Commissioner of Stamps and Taxes of October 1833, but with the extra profits its almanacks were now making, this argument was perhaps no longer relevant.

The End of the English Stock's Publications

The new impetus that was given to the almanack trade when Stamp Duty was repealed did not last, as can be seen from the graph on the next page.

The Company's net annual profit on almanacks had been £3,867 in 1834 before all the increases occurred; by 1852 this figure was back to the same level again and this time it continued to fall. The detailed records of almanack sales which survive for this period end in 1869, so one cannot continue this particular table beyond that date.

Net annual profit on almanacks 1801-69.

In 1847 the dividend was reduced from 17½ per cent to 15 per cent and the annual dinner for the English Stock's customers was discontinued—they were to be invited to ordinary dinners instead. In 1850 the first of a whole series of reports that would be produced on the English Stock over the next seventy years was presented to the Court. It dealt with the way its shares operated, but it also noted the separation of the English Stock from the main body of the Company and looked back at its origins, commenting that they appeared to be 'involved in obscurity'. The report concluded by saying that any change in the English Stock's constitution would need to go to 'the highest legal authorities'—unwittingly looking a hundred years into the future.

With no Stamp Duty to pay and the price of paper having fallen, the Stock's subscribed capital was larger than it needed to be but in 1853 a proposal to repay half of it to the shareholders was rejected. Meanwhile its funded capital, swollen by new investments for similar reasons, stood at £76,459 in 1859. A sub-committee which was reporting on the 'expediency' of dividing some of these riches among the shareholders came up with the straightforward if bold suggestion of issuing a bonus of 150 per cent. After debate this was also rejected. In view of the next round of public criticism the Company was to receive it was probably just as well.

At this stage the English Stock's almanacks were still very much in business. There was a curious reversal of fortune in 1869. It was the year that *Whitaker's Almanack* started and this may have induced Charles Knight, then aged 78, to give up the *British Almanack and Companion*. He had to a certain extent hauled down the flag in 1855 when he sold the copyright to the Stationers' Company, and now the Stock Board bought the remaining rights from him for £750. *The Englishman*, which the Stock had started in 1829 to compete with Knight's almanack, had been struggling for some time and was now promptly withdrawn, leaving the field clear for the *British Almanack and Companion* which, with a healthy circulation of around 7,000 copies went on for another 45 years.

There was probably no way in which the Stationers' Company could have stemmed the downward path in almanack sales. But while Knight's charge that the Company was exploiting the ignorance of the masses probably went too far in one direction, it would be equally wrong to accuse the Stock Board of taking too much of a *laissez-faire* attitude towards its publications, for they kept careful records of their sales figures and responded to them.

Old Moore certainly dominated the sales figures (see p.94), but it should not be forgotten that the English Stock went on publishing more than twenty other almanacks every year until the 1870s. Several of them dated from the 18th century and one or two from even earlier. There were also some ten titles aimed at specific counties—these were among the almanacks bought from Carnan in 1788—and in addition to these two groups there was another fluctuating group of newer almanacks initiated by the Stock Board itself. Many of them did not last more than a few years but they show how fully involved the Stock Board was as a publisher. They are listed here in chronological order of starting date, together with their terminal dates:

CLERICAL	1810-1878
CLERGYMAN	1820-1896
IMPERIAL	1822-1826
ENGLISHMAN	1829-1869
TRADESMAN'S	1830-1835
MEDICAL	1835-1843
EVANGELICAL	1835-1837
FAMILY	1835-1842
LADY'S AND GENTLEMAN'S DIARY	1841-1871
VESTRY	1842-1872
FARMER'S	1843-1848
GARDENER'S	1844-1867

No new titles appear to have been started after 1844 perhaps because the Stock Board felt they no longer had a great enough chance of success.

By 1871 the total number of almanacks sold annually by the English Stock had fallen to 250,000 from the all-time high of nearly 640,000 in 1837. There may have been fewer almanacks in circulation but they were certainly still controversial, for an anonymous pamphlet appeared that year attacking the Stationers' Company as never before, much of the attack being against its almanacks.[16]

The author of *Entered at Stationers' Hall* has not been identified but the pamphlet may well be linked to a complaint the previous year from someone who had been using the copyright registry, Charles H. Purday, who claimed that he had not been allowed proper

16   *Entered at Stationers' Hall: a sketch of the history and privileges of the Company of Stationers with notes on Francis Moore, John Partridge and other distinguished personages.* (London: printed by M. Thomas and sold by E. Truelove, 1871), 32 pages.

44   MOORE, 1800.

THE HIEROGLYPHIC.

Of the Brumal Ingreſs, or Winter Quarter.

THIS Quarter commences on *Saturday* the 21ſt Day of *December* 1799, at 33 Minutes paſt 6 o'Clock at Night, when 9 Degrees of ♈ culminate, and 3 Degrees of ♌ aſcend; the *Moon* is in the 4th Houſe, departing from the * of ♄, and □ of ☿, and her next Application is to the △ of ♃. And in this Scheme ♂ and ♃ are within Orbs of a Zodiacal ☍ from the 5th and 11th Houſes; ♂ is at the ſame Time haſtening to a Zodiacal △ Aſpect of ♄; *Saturn* in the Aſcendant ℞, and *Mars* ſtrong and potent in his own Dignities in the Sign *Scorpio*. From the Poſitions of the Planets at this Ingreſs, we may ſtill expect ſome more than ordinary Affairs to be in Agitation; there are ſeveral Cabals, and private Negotiations, going on in ſeveral Courts of Europe; and a Spirit of a religious Frenzy ſeems to poſſeſs the Heads of many Men, eſpecially of the Eccleſiaſtics, in all or moſt of the *Popiſh* Countries; and they ſeem to be very zealous of a new Project as yet in Embrio; but as the *Popiſh* Power is near its Exit, they will ſoon find their mighty expected

Aſtrological Predictions.   45

expected Birth to prove an Abortion.—The *French* Nation is much perplexed with Fears and Jealouſies, and not without great Cauſe; they (with other Connections) are preparing Strength againſt the formidable combined Powers; there will be warm Debates in their Councils, and the People are all in a Hurry; ſome are for preparing Preliminaries for ſome Treaty, whilſt others are more violent.—The Affairs of the *German* Princes and States, nay even all *Europe*, are now in a violent Ferment and convulſed State.

Of the Vernal, or Spring Quarter.

Here follows a Scheme of the grand RADIX of the Year's Revolution, or the SUN's Ingreſs into the Equinoctial Sign of ARIES.

SUN's INGRESS into ARIES.

SUN in ARIES,
March, 1800.
D. H. M. } at Night,
20 .8 .3 } App. T.
Latitude 51° 31′
☽ ab ☌ ♂ ad ☍ ♄
et ☌ ♀.

THIS Quarter begins when the SUN apparently touches the firſt Point of the Equinoctial Sign *Aries*; which happens this Year upon *Thurſday* the 20th of *March*,

access (see pp. 67, 77). He felt so strongly about the matter that he took it up with the Committee of the Privy Council for Trade, who then wrote to the Clerk to the Stationers' Company politely suggesting that the keys to the registry should be available via the Beadle at any time during the day.[17] Judging by the reaction at Stationers' Hall an error of some significance had occurred.

The Court had as it happens been asking questions about the English Stock's accounts just before Charles Purday's complaint but during 1871 it suddenly became very much more involved with the Stock's affairs than usual. The anonymous pamphlet is of course never mentioned in the minutes but one senses that a belated attempt was being made to close the stable door.

The pamphlet's attack extends to much more than the copyright registry. The jibe, 'authors must pay that Stationers may dine', echoes Pope's 'and wretches hang that jurymen may dine' in *The Rape of the Lock*. The writer goes on to describe the 'political

36. The hieroglyphic from *Old Moore* for 1800.

17   Court Book a, 6 December 1870.

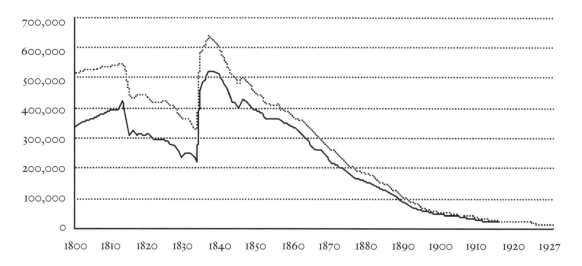

Almanacks sold 1800-1927.   ▬▬▬ Old Moore   ▪▪▪▪▪▪ Total

villainy and religious hypocrisy' surrounding the Company's origins in the 16th century and compares its 'degrading task of gagging the press' to the Spanish Inquisition. He accuses them of 'doing all in their power for two centuries to spread superstition and perpetuate ignorance' by the astrological predictions in their almanacks and there are acid comments about their purchase of Knight's *British Companion*. The pamphlet is on the whole a powerful and accomplished piece of invective and a reprint of it later in 1871 includes extracts from a number of sympathetic reviews. One cannot help feeling that some of this must have hurt, particularly from what followed.

In January 1871 the Court recommended that the registering officer should appoint a deputy at his own expense (see p.67). In March, following the discovery of several serious errors in the almanacks, a special sub-committee was set up, chaired by the Master, to ensure their editorial supervision. The editor was sacked and a new one appointed. By May the sub-committee was talking in terms of using 'modern commercial principles' to find the right way forward for the English Stock's almanacks.[18] *Partridge*, the oldest of the Company's almanacks, dating back to the 17th century, was discontinued as was the *Lady's and Gentleman's Diary*, and four pages of astrological predictions were removed from *Old Moore* and replaced with popular scientific informa-tion. In July a separate room for consulting the copyright registers was suggested and a year later the (considerable) building work that this involved was carried out. The author of *Entered at Stationers' Hall* would have had every reason for self-congratulation.

Yet in spite of the efforts of the new sub-committee and the Stock Board itself, almanack sales continued to fall. The Education Act had been passed in 1870 and public

18   Stock Board minutes, May 1871.

37. Henry Adlard's election certificate for a Court Assistant's share, 18 January 1899.

Stationers' Hall, E.C.,

Jany 18   18 99

Sir,

I am desired to acquaint you, that at a Court of Assistants, held on the _10_ day of _January_ inst., you were elected to a Share of £ _40_ : — : ___ in the English Stock of this Company; and to request you will be good enough to forward me not later than the _7_ day of _February next_ inst., the sum of £ _46_ : — : _6_ in payment for same. You will please to make your draft payable to my Order, and cross it " Barclay & Co., Ltd."

I am, Sir,

Your obedient Servant,

Chas. Robert Rivington,

Clerk.

H. F. Adlard Esq

*** In the event of the money not being paid by the time stated, the Share will be disposed of at the following Court.

opinion was changing but the almanack writers lacked the imagination to respond. A report on the English Stock in 1887 noted that the annual profit on publications, £4,000 in 1850, was down to £2,000 in 1880 and was still falling; the only possible remedy, not really a remedy at all, was reducing the number of shares. Attention was also beginning to turn to the development of the Company's estate in Ave Maria Lane, where Messrs. Simpkin Marshall had recently opened a warehouse.

W.S.B. Woolhouse, the compiler of *Old Moore* and several other almanacks since 1841, died in 1893. This was in a sense a turning-point for in the same year the Government, one of the English Stock's best customers, announced that it was cancelling its almanack order. This meant the end for *Wing*, a sheet almanack dating from the 18th century, and for the eight remaining county titles. In 1895 another report was made to the Court, this time specifically on the English Stock's publications, giving details of the disastrous almanack figures. The annual sales of *Old Moore*, which in 1885 had still been over 100,000, had fallen below 50,000 after only ten years and the equivalent figure for the other six remaining titles, which had sold 15,000 copies in 1885, was now under 7,000.

Almanack sales for the whole period from 1800 to 1927 are summarised in the graph on page 94. From 1870 onwards the figures used are from the Stock Board minutes. The difference between the numbers of almanacks printed and sold was usually around five per cent and, where the minutes give only the number of almanacks printed, five per cent has been subtracted to reach a close approximation for the number sold. Exact figures for sales are given after 1900.

It is remarkable that at this point the English Stock did not abandon its almanack business altogether. A change was made but almanacks remained, though to a lesser degree, part of the picture for another thirty years.

To begin with they were published by Charles Letts with a six per cent royalty being paid to the Stationers' Company. Under the terms of the 1896 agreement with him no 'unreasonable or capricious' criticism by the Stock Board was permitted and no advertisements were allowed 'of an objectionable character, such as would not be admissable in *The Times* or a good quality magazine'. Only five almanacks were left now—*Old Moore,* the *British Almanack and Companion,* the *Clergyman, Goldsmith's* and the *Stationers'* but Charles Letts was unable to make a success of them. In 1902 he tried to end the contract but was persuaded to carry on for another five years.

The Court's report on the English Stock of 1902 looked more broadly at its problems. Paying the dividend was a particular difficulty. This report finally put an end to the continued selling off of stocks in order to meet the requirements of the dividend payment, insisting that instead the number of shares must be reduced to a more realistic level. The report accepted that the English Stock's publishing business was now finished, investments having replaced publishing profits; the time may have come, it said, for it to be wound up and advice should be sought from the High Court.[19] However, at this point, this was too big a step for the Company to take.

In 1907 a new agreement replacing the one with Charles Letts was signed with Cassell and this lasted for another twenty years. By now the Company's almanacks were fighting a losing battle against *Whitaker's Almanack* (first published in 1869), the *Daily Mail Year Book* and other similar publications, and only *Old Moore* and the *Stationers'*—a sheet almanack—survived the First World War. In 1927 when *Old Moore* was selling only 15,000 copies a year and actually running at a loss the Stock Board handed it over completely to Cassell. The reason given for the final parting was that 'in its present form it does

19   Court Book f, 5 May 1903.

not enhance the reputation or dignity of the Company'—the conclusion reached by the author of *Entered at Stationers' Hall* 56 years earlier and by Charles Knight 99 years earlier.

Just a few vestiges of the English Stock's publishing legacy remained even now. In the 17th and 18th centuries, as well as the almanacks a long list of books had been published from Stationers' Hall. By 1830 only five of these were still being sold and a hundred years later just one of them was left, Carey's *Gradus ad Parnassum,* a well-known Latin grammar.[20] It remained in print right up to the 1960s. The sheet almanack, the *Stationers',* together with the Diary and Year Book, a new venture, was published for the Company after 1927 first by de la Rue and from 1929 again by Charles Letts. The sheet almanack was discontinued in 1941 after the second air raid on Stationers' Hall, but the Diary and Year Book, though it never sold in large numbers, continued to 1988, in its last years published by the Company, having long outlived the English Stock itself.

Property Replaces Publications

Property had been one of the Stationers' Company's interests from the beginning—we have seen how Abergavenny House itself was acquired with English Stock funds in 1611. In 1875 the Pellipar estate in Londonderry (see p.116), which had been similarly acquired in 1614, was sold. The proceeds of £40,000 were partly reinvested and partly used to prop up the dividend. As the almanack business began to decrease the Stock Board again became more interested in property, concentrating in particular on the area around Stationers' Hall. Beyond acting for the general good of the Company it probably had no clear strategy until the 1950s, when the strength of its position suddenly became apparent. Even then no one could possibly have predicted what would happen in 1959.

The relative importance of the three main elements in the English Stock's income—almanacks, rents and investments—changed considerably during the 19th century. Figures quoted by Blagden in his history of the Company have been used to compile the pie chart (p.98), where this steady change can readily be seen. In 1866 almanacks still accounted for 34 per cent of its income but by 1900 their share was down to five per cent.

Rents were becoming increasingly important. The original Abergavenny House site included the area to the east of the Hall facing on to Ave Maria Lane, but did not extend as far south as Ludgate Hill; none of the houses along the north side of Ludgate Hill, therefore, belonged to the Company and gaining control of them would be a useful move.

Some of the five properties between St Martin's church and Stationers' Hall Court (originally known as Cock Alley) belonged to the Merchant Taylors' Company and, although for a while the Stationers had an interest in two of them, it was the six properties on the other side of the narrow alley that became the focus of attention, 18-28 Ludgate Hill. These properties were part of the same block as the large group of

20   Blagden, p.242.

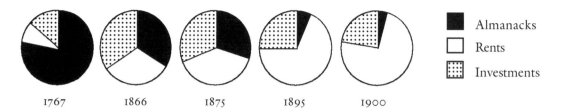

English Stock income.

warehouses behind them which the Stock Board had leased to Messrs. Simpkin Marshall, the Oxford University Press and the Cambridge University Press from the early part of the 19th century onwards.

No. 22 was the first of these properties to be acquired in 1900; it was demolished, rebuilt and let to Simpkin Marshall. No. 20 was next in 1930; it cost £13,000. Three years later the Stock Board was offered no. 26 for £12,000 but the price was considered too high and in 1939 it also decided against buying no. 28; at this stage there was evidently no real pressure to acquire this group of properties.

After the war the Company was desperately short of capital funds. The Ludgate Hill site was considered too risky for any development to be attempted but when 24-28 Ludgate Hill and 1-2 Stationers' Hall Court came on to the market together in 1949 the temptation was too great; somehow the £17,000 was found that was needed to buy the whole of this group of properties—little more than an empty site because of the war.[21] This left only no. 18. In order to have any say in developing the site as a whole the Company had to acquire this last property. With some difficulty it located the owner. During the summer of 1952 the Company turned down offers from him of a 30-year lease and then a 33-year lease, but in November they finally accepted an 80-year lease for £11,550. After completion in June 1953 the entire corner site was theirs and discussion began on what was to be done with it.

For planning purposes all the buildings on the west side of Ave Maria Lane, including the Stationers' corner site, were part of the Paternoster Square development and this meant that the Company by no means had a free hand. There was in fact a delay of five years while the future of this important area was being decided but this gave the Company time to think about whether they should sell the site outright, lease it for development or develop it themselves. The second of these solutions was the one favoured by a building committee set up in 1955. It was chaired by William Penman, who was then serving on the Stock Board; he was Upper Warden at the time and by profession an actuary. In 1957 the Company's surveyors, Daniel Watney, Eiloart, Inman and Nunn, drew up a full-scale development plan for the site so that an application could be made to the London County Council for outline planning permission, but the

21 Stock Board minutes, November 1950.

planners were in the process of making a decision about the whole Paternoster Square development and did not want to make any pronouncement about Ave Maria Lane until after that. At this stage everything depended on planning consent being granted. It came only at the end of 1958 after the Company had successfully appealed to the Minister and its plans had been approved by Sir William Holford and the City's own planning committee. In October it acquired a final lease that was still outstanding on one of the corner site properties and was at last free to take action. Not surprisingly, however, so much time had passed that there was now disagreement about what should be done with the site.

The Court left this decision, or a recommendation as to what it should be, to a special meeting of the Stock Board on 15 December 1958. By now, after that of the corner site, the question of the English Stock's future was the one uppermost in everybody's mind and it was entirely appropriate that the Stock Board itself should take this crucial decision, which was so closely linked to its own future. At the last moment G.W. Matthews of Daniel Watney, Eiloart, Inman and Nunn recommended what had been debated before, namely that the Company should develop the site itself. The attractions of the Company's creating its own splendid new building were very great but the costs of such a development were felt to be too high.[22] Mr Matthews' revised figures did not carry quite enough weight and the Stock Board overturned the original 1955 plan, and recommended selling outright. This was endorsed by a meeting of the Court in January 1959 which went through all the arguments again and finally voted 15-5 in favour of the Stock Board's recommendation.[23] Most unusually a memorandum of 31 October 1958 by William Penman, who had become Treasurer in 1957, outlining the first three possible courses, is pasted into the Court Minutes together with the one from G.W. Matthews with his recommendation.

Even now there was uncertainty; the Stock Board suddenly decided that it wanted to retain part of the site for the Company and there was concern that the planners would change the line of Ave Maria Lane—earlier this had been a possibility. These last minute doubts were firmly dealt with by a new working committee consisting of George P. Simon, Master for 1958-59, William Penman, his brother Victor, and Sir George Wilkinson; they overruled the suggestion that the Company should keep part of the site and on 12 March set the price at £285,000. Less than a month later it was sold. The final figure of £663,000 was the equivalent of £1,750,000 an acre, easily a record at that time.

The 1961 Act

The realisation that time was running out for the English Stock seems to have dawned on the Company only gradually. It was an awkward issue and, understandably, the Court delayed taking action for as long as possible.

22 Unwin, pp.68-71.
23 Court Book m, 3 February 1959.

The 1902 report had solved the immediate problem of paying the dividend by recommending a reduction in the numbers of shares. A further reduction had to be made in 1911 when copyright registration was abolished. It had become another useful source of income after the Clerk took over the running of it from the Greenhills in 1883 (see p.75). Two more reports on the English Stock's finances followed, in 1911 and 1918, but they produced no new ideas and the Stock Board carried on in the usual way in spite of the virtual ending of the almanack business in 1927. It was a small, exclusive and powerful body; at this stage it still had another thirty years ahead of it.

One of the more unexpected features of the English Stock was the secrecy that surrounded its accounting processes. Its Treasurer seems to have started the practice of presenting its accounts to the Court every year only in 1837 and before the changes of 1870 it had no annual balance sheet. (When the English Stock accounts for 1869-70 were shown to the Court, the first to be presented by this method, the 'large excess' of the balance was actually queried and the Treasurer was requested to report on it to the Finance Committee.)[24] In 1930 the Livery Committee came up with the very reasonable proposal that at their annual meeting the English Stock's partners should be circulated with copies of its accounts. The Stock Board's reaction was first to postpone any decision about the matter for two years and then simply to refuse to make any change; it felt that no change was needed, even though the dividend had by then fallen below 12½ per cent for the first time.

The dividend remained in single figures up to the outbreak of war. With the war, of course, came further disaster—the destruction by enemy action of all the English Stock's property, and the loss of all its income from rents. No dividend payments were made for eight years and when they resumed in 1949 it was at the modest level of 2½ per cent.

Change was now essential. Herbert A. Cox, Treasurer of the Company, produced a report on the English Stock in 1943 which suggested amalgamating its accounts with those of the Company but overlooked the fact that under the terms of the 17th century by-laws the partners in the English Stock had special rights—he called them merely loan creditors of the Company. The 1902 report had acknowledged these rights and also drawn attention to the large number of partners' widows; at that time 65 out of the 276 shares were held by partners' widows. For them the income from the English Stock shares was an appreciable part of their livelihood; any changes to the English Stock would have to take special account of their situation and when the time came this did indeed happen.

Events gradually moved forward after 1953, during the long period of waiting for planning permission for the Ave Maria Lane site, and they started to pick up speed when William Penman as Treasurer presented a full review of the Company's accounts in January 1958. In the course of this he took the important step of recommending that the English Stock should now be acquired for the Company. His recommendation was

24   Court Book a, 7 February 1871.

accepted by the Court and a special committee was set up to look into this in more detail. Having contributed so much to the difficult first stage of winding up the English Stock it is, of course, doubly unfortunate that William Penman should have disagreed so bitterly with the Company later on.

In April 1958, as Company Treasurer, he circulated a memorandum to the stockholders with details about the English Stock's historical background, proposing that the Company should purchase 90 per cent of its shares from the present holders. This way the English Stock would still be left in existence and the legal difficulties of dismantling it would be avoided, though he was well aware that legal advice would eventually be needed. It is significant that this first attempt at a solution was accompanied by a note from the Clerk, Patrick Wells, inviting replies from the stockholders—far from forcing a decision on them this was the beginning of a process of consultation.

By October, 136 replies had been received to William Penman's memorandum; 126 in favour and eight against though the opposition did include some experienced figures like Sir George Wilkinson, who had been Treasurer of the English Stock since 1944 and Company Treasurer from 1953 to 1957. However, the success of the sale changed everything and his scheme was abandoned in April 1959. In October after a summer full of disagreement about what to do next, a new constitutional committee recommended seeking counsel's opinion over the problem of the English Stock.

This was urgently needed after the disquieting advice that had been received in July from Mr Edward Iwis, the barrister who had been consulted over William Penman's 1958 scheme. In his view, because of the way in which the English Stock was constituted, the proceeds of the sale did not belong to the Company at all but to the stockholders!

The next 18 months were probably among the most difficult in the Company's history; with so much at stake there was also a real threat of a split within the livery. The joint opinion of Sir Milner Holland and Mr L.A. Wolfe, which was delivered in December, was less categorical than Mr Iwis. It suggested that the stockholders' rights were limited but that if things were left as they were the proceeds of the sale really would have to be divided among them. The by-laws of 1681 which still governed the English Stock were entirely clear about its obligations to make regular charitable payments and for dividends to be fixed by the Court and paid to the stockholders; the problem arose from the section where they allowed the Court to expend such sums from the English Stock's profits as they thought fit 'for the necessary use and occasions of the Company'. This phrase would always be difficult to interpret but in the light of the £663,000 its meaning did need to be further defined. The only way this could be done was by private Act of Parliament.

The Court formally agreed to this in February 1960. It was now clear that the English Stock was going to be extinguished or wound up, though at this stage no one knew quite how, but a new problem had begun to cause division and anxiety—the question of compensation for the stockholders. It must have been further highlighted by the decision made just after the sale to pay stockholders a dividend of 50 per cent,

12½ per cent for the current year to June 1960 and 37½ per cent as a bonus to make up for the lack of payments after the war. As had always been anticipated, the number of shares had increased since 1603, when there were 105. there were now 175: 25 Court shares, 50 Livery shares and 100 Yeomanry shares still worth £320, £160 and £80 respectively, amounting to a total of £24,000. The problem was finding the fairest way to compensate these stockholders.

To begin with, the constitutional committee wanted to repay them at par plus 100 per cent with no annuity. William Penman was starting to talk about the need for larger amounts of compensation while on the other hand a lot of people felt, generously, that the main aim of securing the Company's future was so important that compensation did not matter. Almost immediately, after the meeting of the Court in February 1960 the problem appeared to have been effectively solved within the constitutional committee by J.M. Rivington, who produced a scheme which after a few amendments was the one adopted in the Act of Parliament of 1961. It was proposed at a special Court meeting on 22 April 1960 and, after considerable debate, seconded by William Penman and agreed by a 15 to 1 majority.

As the family with probably the strongest links with the Stationers' Company of any, it was highly appropriate that John Mylne Rivington should have been the key figure at this difficult moment. No less than nine of his ancestors had been Masters of the Company and his great-grandfather, grandfather, father and cousin had successively held the office of Clerk to the Company from 1800 to 1957. J.M. Rivington himself had qualified as a barrister and then become a partner in the family publishing company. He too became Master in 1963-4 and his portrait hangs in the Stock Room.

Under his scheme the existing stockholders were repaid the value of their shares at par and then given annuities of £64, £32 or £16 for a Court, Livery or Yeomanry share. When one of these annuitants dies the share can pass only to someone who joined the Company before 1961, so that the number of annuitants is gradually decreasing. As previously, under the shares system an annuitant's widow can inherit his annuity; on her death it passes back again to the Company. Other schemes were discussed at the Court meeting of April 1960 but this was the one that met with general support, the only immediate change arising from a proposal by William Penman that the level of compensation should be increased from J.M. Rivington's original figure of 10 per cent to 20 per cent—the figures quoted above are at the 20 per cent level.

The special Court meeting of 22 April which had agreed this had followed another meeting of the Court on 5 April, at the end of which William Penman read out another long memorandum which he had drafted about the English Stock problem. In counsel's opinion, the previous December, the stockholders had been somewhat unfortunately described as being entitled to 'the lion's share of the income from the £630,000'; on the strength of this phrase but using it slightly out of context he included a table showing possible levels of compensation for the stockholders' loss of income based on their life expectancy. The figures are very high indeed. In Philip Unwin's words,

The £663,000 'windfall' from the property sale was the very heart and core of our heritage; such a stupendous piece of good fortune was unlikely ever to come our way again; and it was the majority view that the capital must be nurtured with the utmost care so as to provide income and growth for the future. This is not to say that, after our years in the wilderness, more than one of us did not look momentarily, with some longing, at the enticing terms suggested in the minority proposals, involving a substantial payment to stockholders, but to all but three of the stockholders there was never any real doubt as to the more prudent course for the future of the Company.[25]

William Penman set great store by this memorandum and this was the central cause of his dispute with the Company. After the meeting of 5 April it was circulated to all Court members as there was no time for it to be discussed. But the fact that it did not come up for discussion at the meeting of 22 April indicates that there was no real support for it. Penman seemed to be behaving as though he was involved in a purely commercial situation, failing to appreciate the very different way in which the Stationers' Company was regarded by its Liverymen.

On 26 July 1960 the letter to the Livery was sent out. This sets out in simple terms the background to the problem over the English Stock, together with the proposed solution of the Act of Parliament and the scheme of annuities, and invites the Livery to approve or disapprove. It had been under discussion since April and William Penman had been angling for a copy of his own memorandum about terms of compensation to be sent out with it to every member of the Livery. Because of the reception his memorandum received in the April Court there was never any question of this but Penman continued to press for its circulation, even insisting that the information in his memorandum was being deliberately suppressed. James Ousey was now Master. The exchanges between them became more and more difficult until finally his patience was exhausted. Sadly, Penman seems by this point to have become completely alienated from the rest of the Company.

On 28 September he resigned as Treasurer to the Company—he had been persuaded to withdraw his resignation from the Court as well. A month later without any authority at all he circulated a copy of his April memorandum to every member of the Livery together with a new covering letter which urged raising the level of compensation from 20 per cent to 50 per cent. Instead of being £16, £32 and £64 the annuities would be £40, £80 and £160 and the overall cost of the scheme would go up from £70,000 to £175,000; Penman said he thought the settlement as proposed was too generous to the Company. Within a few days the Master and Wardens responded with another letter to the Livery, firmly refuting Penman's memorandum and calmly pointing out that the 20 per cent level of compensation had in fact been suggested by him.

The whole situation might have been reminiscent of the comic relief in a Shakespearean tragedy had it not been potentially so serious. There was general regret

25 Unwin, pp.75-6.

38. *London Almanack* for 1893. Actual size 12½in. by 9½in.

for William Penman's resignation but universal condemnation for his unauthorised later action. He was called before the Court in November and referred to a committee of Past Masters on 7 December; James Ousey was too angry to attend. There was real anger at this hearing that Penman had been prepared to take the law into his own hands against the wishes of the majority but even now he would not give way, refusing to make any promises about not speaking outside the Court and refusing also to help with the process of obtaining the Act of Parliament. He continued his dispute to the bitter end, presenting a petition in the House of Lords against the Company's Bill—as he had every right to do—and thereby adding around £1,500 to the costs. All the papers relating to this affair, surviving in the Company's archive, are described here for the first time.

In spite of it all everybody's nerve held and the full process of consultation within the Company as required by Parliament was carried out scrupulously. When it came to the final ballots, both of the stockholders and the liverymen at the end of January 1961 only two people joined William Penman in voting against the Bill—his brother Victor and one other; he never did attract a following. His petition against the Bill meant a two-day hearing before a Select Committee of the House of Lords on 20-21 June 1961 where the Company was ably represented by J.M. Rivington. When it was announced at the Court meeting of 25 July that the Bill had received the Royal Assent and had become law on 19 July the praise and the plaudits were deservedly directed mainly to him.

The wording of the Act was largely that of Rivington's original scheme. It gives the Court the additional power to raise the level of the annuities if it feels this is required but they have always been left at the 20 per cent that was originally agreed. One much needed new feature which the Act created was a £25,000 fund for charitable payments, replacing the annual amount of £200 available under the 1681 by-laws, but its main purpose was of course the extinguishment of the English Stock. The effective date for this was set at 1 June 1961. Since annuities can only go to those who joined the Livery before that date they will eventually come to an end.

In 1990 there were 66 annuitants remaining, most of whom relinquished their dividend in favour of a Company charity of their choice. At the time of writing (1999) there are twenty-seven. In January 1962 the Stock Board was renamed the English Stock (Annuities) Board, as its only remaining duty was administering the annuities. In July 1984 this was taken over by the Finance Committee and the English Stock (Annuities) Board was abolished.

The English Stock's contribution to the Company was a very special one. Although it is now almost forty years since the Act of Parliament, the fact that the Stock Room stands next to the Hall and the Court Room means that it cannot be forgotten. Its determination that the 17th-century legacy of its almanacks should be carried on into the 20th century may well be seen as controversial but it was this determination that led first, to the rather tentative acquisition of property in Ludgate Hill and eventually, to the spectacular 1959 sale which, after two stormy years of negotiation leading up to the Act, should make a suitably triumphant ending to the story of the English Stock. Alas, it did not quite turn out as might have been expected from a windfall, which came at a time of growing national prosperity, of more than half a million pounds. During the 'never had it so good' 1960s the Company enjoyed a stability it had never known, before the oil crisis of November 1973 sent the Company fortunes plummeting once more. Disaster was averted in the 1990s, however, through careful management and a buoyant stock market, although the carefree optimism following the original sale is unlikely to be felt again.[26]

26 In the early 1980s, the Company was on the verge of bankruptcy but an astute treasurer, Peter King, new financial advisers, a policy of charging the Livery for everything, and of maximum letting of the Hall for commercial functions, saved the day.

CHAPTER SIX

Tradition and Innovation

The Company's Administration, Finance and Entertainment in a Changing World

PENELOPE HUNTING

Officers and Organisation

The structure of the Company has remained constant since 1560 when the Stationers were officially granted a livery of scarlet and brown-blue. Numbers have fluctuated but the hierarchy of Master, Wardens, the Court of Assistants, Liverymen and Freemen (the Yeomanry) remained steady. The Court of Assistants, or Ancients as the elders were called, has reigned supreme as the governing body despite periodic challenges (see p.43). While the structure of the Company remained the same, the duties of the officers changed over time. The Charter of Incorporation had endowed the Master and Wardens with extensive powers of search and inspection of printed matter, the regulation of printing and copyright and the right to discipline and fine offenders—duties which are no longer relevant. However, the Master still represents his Company in the City and provides leadership to the Court, in which he is assisted by the Upper and Under Wardens, who in the normal course of events will succeed him.

The Renter Wardens

The Renter Wardens, as their title suggests, were originally responsible for collecting rents from tenants of the Company's properties and quarterage from all members, whose names and addresses were entered in an account book which provided a valuable record until they were destroyed in the Blitz. The collection of quarterage—formerly paid quarterly but by the 19th century an annual subscription—from each member proved increasingly difficult and unrewarding. The Renter Wardens usually paid for the November dinner for the Livery out of the quarterage money, but as they had only collected £32 16s. in 1884, the Court repaid the cost of the previous November's dinner (£268 13s. 6d. including wine) and abolished quarterage. In 1887 the Renter Wardens were formally discharged of the duty of supplying the November dinner as they no longer kept accounts.[1] The number of Renter Wardens was increased from two to four from 1957.[2] They are chosen from senior Liverymen of 12 years' standing; they are no longer responsible for collecting money payable to the Company but are in attendance on Court days and at all social events.

---

1   Court Book c, 10 June 1884, 7 January 1887.
2   Court Book m, 10 April 1956.

40. *Left.*
Charles Rivington,
Clerk, 1829-69.

41. *Centre.*
Charles Robert
Rivington, Clerk,
1869-1916.

42. *Right.* Reginald
Thurston Rivington,
Clerk, 1916-57.

The Company has always had a small number of permanent officers and employed extra staff—cleaners, waiters (and nowadays waitresses) and, until 1849, watermen or 'whifflers' (see *Glossary*) for the barge as occasion demanded. The duties of the Clerk, Beadle, Hall keeper and Porter were defined at the beginning of the 19th century, coinciding with new appointments.

The Clerk

A by-law of 1694 required the Clerk to be knowledgeable in the laws of the realm, to register the Company's ordinances and assist the Master and Wardens in all the affairs of the Company. These broadly-based qualifications still applied in 1800 when three candidates, all lawyers, applied for the clerkship. In a ballot all the votes were for Henry Rivington, son of a bookseller, John Rivington II freed by patrimony in 1786.[3] In the years following Henry Rivington's appointment the Clerk's duties expanded to the point when he was acting as legal adviser, estate agent, archivist and information officer. In 1822 his salary was increased by £20 in acknowledgement of the extra work involved in researching the Company's legacies in order to satisfy the Charity Commissioners—the Commissioners' Report of 1837 revealed that an 'outdoor' Clerk was employed at Stationers' Hall as an assistant to Henry Rivington. Between 1800 and 1957 the clerkship was held in succession by four members of the Rivington family. The last three, Charles, Charles Robert, and Reginald Thurston Rivington, took a great interest in the history of the Company, which all their predecessors had ignored, and in the preservation of its records (see pp. 177, 181, 185, 186, 187-8, 192). Each of these three became Master of the Company. Charles Robert Rivington succeeded in disentangling the increasingly unsatis-

3   Court Book P, 26 March 1800.

factory organisation of the Copyright Registry, which was an anomaly in the way it had been set up by the Government, and had become more and more bureaucratic and beyond the power of Joseph Greenhill, the Registrar, to reform single-handed (see p.77).

With the end of the Rivington dynasty in 1957 Gordon St Patrick Wells, also a solicitor, was chosen from 22 applicants. His responsibilities were exhaustive—he was to attend every meeting of the Court, Stock Board and committees, collect rents and inspect properties, present cheques, keep accounts, arrange for the distribution of charities, deal with the register of books and fine art, report to the Charity Commissioners, deal with insurance, advise on legal matters, conduct the Company's correspondence, supervise staff and Hall lettings.[4] With such onerous tasks the Clerkship became full-time from 1959, and even then the Court was wary that the Clerk might find time to practise as a solicitor from the Hall.[5] Bundles of legal papers relating to his practice still come to light from time to time in cupboards and drawers at Stationers' Hall. After 17 years and having gained a reputation for being imperturbable, Wells acted briefly as Clerk Emeritus while he introduced his successor, Colonel R.A. 'Sascha' Rubens, to the Company in 1974. The Court realised that in modern times they could not expect to appoint a solicitor as a modestly paid full-time clerk and that the Company could be better served by a recently retired member of the armed forces whose salary would be supplemented by a service pension. The Court changed the by-laws accordingly. The new clerk, Sascha Rubens, a regular soldier with distinguished war service, an oenophile and bon viveur, was faced with a harder task than his predecessor because the Company's finances and activities were at a low ebb in the wake of the first

43. *Left.*
Gordon St Patrick Wells, Clerk, 1957-74, seen here sitting at the head of the table at the Renter Wardens' dinner, 1969.

44. *Centre.*
Colonel Alexander (Sascha) Rubens, Clerk, 1974-84, giving the toast to the Company at a Charter Dinner.

45. *Right.*
Captain Peter Hames, Clerk, 1984-97, giving the toast to the Company.

4   Court Book m, 12 February 1957.
5   Court Book m, 1 October 1959; Court Book n, 7 March 1961.

oil crisis of late 1973, in spite of the high hopes that the sale of the Ludgate Hill property in 1959 was going to revolutionise the Company's fortunes (see p.99).

Colonel Rubens' successor, Captain Peter Hames, Royal Navy, Clerk from 1984 to 1997, was given the brief of improving the level of Hall lettings to increase income. Hard work paid off, and more and more commercial bookings were made, steadily increasing income from hall hire year by year; but it meant more wear and tear which was offset by donations to a Hall Preservation Fund.

The first ordinances of the Stationers' Company had been approved by the Lord Chancellor and the Chief Justice in 1562, since when additions and revisions had been necessary in order to adapt to changing circumstances—the rules and ordinances were revised three times in the 17th century, and not again until 1877. They were revised in recent years—in 1979, 1992, 1995 and 1998. The revisions were carried out, under the supervision of the Court, by the Clerk, formerly a solicitor skilled in the use of legal language; those of the 1990s have an informality which contrasts with the legal niceties of earlier versions. In 1985-6 a list of the Company's objectives was drawn up for the first time in its history, which were subsequently itemised in a revised version of 'The Rules, Ordinances and Established Customs'.

The Beadle

The office of Beadle is the most ancient in the Company and City. A mid-19th-century advertisement for the office specified that the successful candidate must be married and middle-aged, and have knowledge of the trade of a publisher and bookseller. He was to reside at Stationers' Hall where his wife was to work as Hall keeper, cleaning the rooms and robes, making tea and coffee.[6] The 19th-century Court showed little respect for the office, and was greatly concerned that the Beadle should be kept in his place—outside the door during Court meetings, nor was he to presume to sit at table with the Master, Wardens and Court or to attend Livery dinners. He was put on a par with the porter, both of them being under the direction of the Treasurer of the English Stock. He had to carry out a number of trivial, menial tasks—tending the garden, cleaning the gateway, waiting on the Master and Wardens at their houses thrice weekly.[7] More consonant with the dignity of his ancient office was his duty of seeing that Liverymen were properly dressed on Lord Mayor's Day; robed and carrying the mace, he added dignity to processions. In addition he was the Company's record keeper—Thomas Hopkins, Beadle 1832-8, initiated the Beadle's Book, dated 1834; it is a unique source of cuttings, history and biographical information covering the years from 1786 to 1973. In the 19th century the Beadle was usually a Liveryman although he was required to disenfranchise himself if called upon to testify in Court regarding English Stock books. Like the Clerk, the Beadle was elected annually, a formality which gave the Court the option of dismissing a troublemaker. William Poulten, Beadle for 50 years (1890-1940), diversified. He acted as Secretary to the Publishers

6 Series 1, Box F, folder 7, vii.
7 Court Book Z, 2 February 1869.

SIR,

BY Virtue of a Precept from the Right Honourable the LORD MAYOR, you are defired by the MASTER and WARDENS of the Worfhipful Company of STATIONERS, to meet at *Stationers Hall*, on *Wednefday* the 9th Day of *November*, 1785, PRECISELY at Eleven of the Clock in the Forenoon, in your Livery Gown and Hood; from thence to proceed to *Guildhall*, to efcort the Right Hon. the LORD MAYOR to the *Three Cranes*, and then in your Barge with the LORD MAYOR to *Weftminfter*; and upon landing at *Blackfriars*, to walk before his Lord-fhip in the Proceffion to *Guildhall*, and afterwards return to your own Hall to Dinner.

N. B. The Mafter intends going from the Hall immediately after Eleven o'Clock.

*** *No Perfon will be admitted in the* Proceffion, *or on board the* Barge, *without his* Livery Gown: *And none but the* Livery *will be admit-tea to* Dine *at the* Hall *on that Day.*

MARSHALL SHEEPEY, Beadle.

Association and the Booksellers' Provident Institution (see p.5), and took on the duties of Registrar when the voluntary registry of books was set up in 1924. He was given permission to reside away from the Hall in 1905, and given an extra £50 p.a. in lieu of residence and fuel. His accommodation was given to a couple who were appointed as resident Hall keeper and Caretaker. In 1965 the Beadle, Douglas Rowland, was demoted to butler; he was succeeded by Stanley J. Osborne as both Beadle and the Clerk's Assistant.[8]

The Warehouse Keeper or Treasurer

The Warehouse Keeper or Treasurer of the English Stock was the guardian of the stock of books and paper in the Company's warehouse and was responsible for the associated financial transactions. It was a full-time salaried post, with living accommodation at

8   Court Book n, 6 April 1965.

Stationers' Hall for as long as the English Stock remained the life blood of the Company. From his office at the Hall he also directed the Beadle and Porter. Two Mr Greenhills, father and son, were Warehouse Keeper continuously from 1798 to 1883, when the Court decided to let the office lapse.[9] The Company's bankers, Messrs Gosling and Sharpe, took over the financial transactions while other business was allocated to the Clerk and to the Beadle under the direction of six professional Stock-keepers. It cannot have been a satisfactory arrangement for in 1885 Greenhill was re-appointed Treasurer.[10] When he finally retired, the office of Treasurer became an honorary position—Alderman G.R. Tyler was appointed in 1893, the year that he was also Lord Mayor and Master. From that time the Treasurer has always to be a senior member of the Court.[11] In 1907, Sir George Wyatt Truscott assumed responsibility for the Company's corporate accounts; the age-old form of the Wardens' Accounts, which had been the responsibility of the Under Warden as auditor and accountant, was modernised and became the province of the Treasurer. His duties widened with the interests of the Court. He also kept an eye on the Company's investments, and on income from Hall lettings, catering and the Registry until it was abolished in April 2000; an assistant was also appointed when necessary. For a period from 1932 until the ending of the English Stock in 1961 there were two Treasurers, one for the Company, another for the English Stock.

Registrar or Copyright Registering Officer

The copyright and legal deposit registry was a separate operation based at Stationers' Hall, the Registrar being remunerated by fees charged on a scale set down by law; but the Greenhills combined the two offices, operating the Registry from their office at Stationers' Hall. Following the Royal Commission on Copyright of 1878, the Clerk, C.R. Rivington, took over in 1883 and succeeded in running it fairly efficiently until statutory registration was abolished in 1912. In 1924 a voluntary registry was set up and run by a member of the office staff, generally the Beadle or Assistant Clerk (see p.111).

The Chaplain

The Company's first honorary chaplain was Rev. Henry Greenhill, son of the Treasurer Joseph Greenhill, appointed in 1892 and continuing until his death in 1907.[12] In 1849 a Liveryman, Rev. O.J. Owen, volunteered for the job but he was rebuffed because the Court had no intention of appointing a chaplain at that point. Latterly the Company's chaplain has been the incumbent of a City church.

---

9   Court Book c, 6 February 1883.
10 Court Book c, 2 March 1885. Joseph Greenhilll became Master in November 1890 on the death of J.E. Adlard.
11 Beadle's Book, p.91. Court Book d, 1 March 1893.
12 Court Book W, 9 January 1849; *ibid.*, d, 2 February 1892 and f, 7 May 1907.

Other Offices

Three generations of the Mylne family of surveyors looked after the Company's properties from 1776 to 1890 (see chapter 8). In addition, the 19th-century Company employed
a barge master and mate, a butler, a porter, a caretaker and a cook. The Company's
barge was given up in 1849-50; the Barge Master and his mate were made redundant in
1850. In the 1960s the Caretaker (now called Hall keeper) doubled as Company butler;
the Beadle latterly combined those duties with those of Registrar as well as being the
book keeper. Mounting office work has meant a large and more versatile staff—the
Clerk's Secretary also serves several committees and, now that Hall lettings have become
a major source of the Company's income, there is a full-time hall bookings manager and
assistant. Looking after potential clients has become an important part of the Hall
keeper's work; he also has an assistant. Extra staff are also taken on for special functions.
In addition Liverymen give a great deal of voluntary assistance. The working practices
of Stationers' Hall, in contrast to earlier times, have been revolutionised and it has
become a hive of industry.

Committees

The corporate business of the Company has remained under the government of the
Master, Wardens and Court of Assistants who relied increasingly on the specialised work
done by committees. The management of the English Stock was in effect in the hands of
a committee of the Master, Wardens, Treasurer and Stock-keepers, although there was no
such formal title; corporate activities were concentrated in the hands of the Master,
Wardens and Court which itself resembled a committee or forum. In the late 18th century
small *ad hoc* committees were formed to deal with particular subjects such as the barge and
fire engine (1766) or the repair of the Hall (1800).[13] The first to assist the work of the Court
substantially was the General Purposes Committee, appointed in 1846 with a wide-ranging
brief 'for the purpose of enquiring into, considering and reporting to this Court all such
matters as shall be from time to time referred to them'. It was to meet quarterly and it was
proposed that each man should receive a guinea for his attendance.[14] Henceforward any
subject could be put to the General Purposes Committee for consideration and the Court
came to rely heavily on its reports. To begin with the General Purposes Committee was
primarily concerned with domestic accounts, checking then presenting the bills of the
carpenter, bricklayer and Barge Master for payment, and reporting in 1848 that the Company was just £22 7s. 5d. in credit.[15] In 1959, the Master and Wardens' Committee took over
much of the work of the General Purposes Committee.

Investigations into the Company's finances were to pass to the Finance Committee, first
appointed in 1876 because a review of the situation was urgent. The appointment of the

13   Series 1, Box K, folder 2. Series 1, Box G, folder 3, iii, iv.
14   Court Book W, 7 July 1846, 3 October 1848.
15   Court Book W, 3 October 1848, 6 February 1849.

various committees reflected the current preoccupation of the Court: a School Committee commenced deliberations in 1852; a Wine Committee was first appointed in 1872, arousing itself whenever new stocks were required; a Copyright Committee was called in 1887 and one to consider the (declining) state of the English Stock in 1893. Less serious subjects were dealt with by the Festival Committee (1876) and the Master's Badge Committee (1878). In this century, the Court's concern over the imports of stationery from Germany in 1916 brought about a Stationery Committee to remonstrate with the Foreign Trade Department. Celebrations such as the 1951 Festival of Britain and the Company's Quatercentenary celebrations in 1957 were handled by committees. In the 1960s the General Purposes and House Committees combined to supervise building improvements at the Hall; an Investment Committee advised on the capital forthcoming from the sale of the Company's site on the corner of Ludgate Hill and Ave Maria Lane; a Welfare Committee was formed in 1970 to look after the needs of the Company's pensioners, and the Arts and Library Committee organised the new library from 1974 to 1990 when the library and archive came directly under the Library Trustees (see p.198). The Committee of the Future took on a formidable task in producing a wide-ranging report which covered all aspects of the Company (1985). Remarkably, the Court accepted 40 out of its 46 recommendations. The Court prepared for the future by streamlining its business, reducing the number of courts to eight in 1989, in order to encourage younger and busier members to stand for election, encouraging Liverymen to take an active part in Company affairs and strengthening ties with the trade associations. Ten years later the New Millennium Committee, which made its first report in May 1996, took another look at the Company's objectives and its role in the City. The Trades of the Guild Committee was formed in 1974 to further links between the Company, captains of industry and trade organisations, a goal that continues to be pursued by the Trade and Industry Forum of Liverymen appointed to liaise with trade associations for mutual benefit (see p.19). To ensure that the Company kept pace with advances in technology, manufacturing and the specialisation of the industries, trades and skills with which it is associated, the definition of the trades of the guild was widened and updated in 1992. The trades and occupations which qualify a candidate for admission to the Company by servitude or redemption now include a wide range from electronic image assembling to librarianship.

For many years of the 20th century the Livery Committee was one of the most effective committees. Its founding Chairman, R.A. Austen-Leigh, gave a first-hand account of its dynamic early years, aptly titled 'Seven Years of Peaceful Agitation'.[16] He described how members of the Livery, who re-assembled after the First World War when times were hard and Company activities few and far between, expressed their views—'some of them of a highly revolutionary not to say bolshevik character'. These 'bolshevik' views were filtered through a committee and presented in rational terms to the Court. The proposals, which now seem tame enough, included annual election of Liverymen to the Court, an advisory

16   Originally the title of a talk given at a Livery Lunch, 1927, published as a booklet in 1928, ZCKA Box II.

committee to promote the interests of the Livery, rooms at the Hall for the use of the Livery in the advancement of their trades, the reintroduction of Livery dinners, and permission to see the accounts. A joint negotiating committee under Edward Unwin was formed. Most of the concessions it wrung from the Court were trivial—Livery dances (from 1925), a ladies' banquet (1928)—but there was one major concession, that of two Livery representatives on the Court from 1926 (see p.250).[17]

The Livery Committee did not continue its impetus for reform beyond the mid-1960s. Perhaps its last substantial achievement was the inauguration in 1970 of *The Stationer and Newspaper Maker* which currently comes out three times a year. Although much of its coverage is parochial, it provides a useful record of current Company events, profiles of living or recently deceased members and occasional historical articles.

Finances

The first report of the Finance Committee, set up by the Court in 1876, defined the sources of the Company's income:[18] dividends, rent from leasehold warehouses in the garden and the freehold house no. 3 Clements Court, one sixth of the rents and profits from the Wood Street estate, fines and fees, quarterage. The Stationers had entered the 19th century in a prosperous financial state, as the Clerk reported in 1800—its income had recently increased to £1,700 owing to the increase in the number of Freemen and Liverymen admitted. It continued to rise with the increase in cloathings to an all-time high of 517 in 1810, accompanied by a rise in the amount paid for admission to the Livery to £50 in 1809, followed in 1817 by an increase in fines and fees paid by newly elected Assistants—£20 to the Company, £3 into the Poor Box and £200 to avoid the offices of Warden and Master.

In 1820 Court and committee fees were doubled from 10s. 6d. to 21s., and a report of 1869 revealed that the Stationers' Company was the 15th richest out of 58 livery companies in terms of total gross income.[19] The wealth of the City livery companies was under public scrutiny at the time: there was widespread suspicion that funds intended for charitable purposes were being diverted to subsidise extravagant Livery dinners, and in some Companies these suspicions were justified. The authorities reproached the Stationers for neglecting to distribute the loan charities and for failing to keep separate accounts; a new scheme was devised in 1858 which applied the loan charities to the Company's school (see p.135). The Court may have been guilty of negligence in this area but there was no suggestion of extravagance—caution rather than prodigality pervaded Stationers' Hall. Dinners held at the Hall were substantial but there was no increase in their number—on the contrary, in the 1880s Court dinners were reduced from six a year to four. Nor was there

17 Court Book h, 13 April 1920, 26 July 1921. R.A. Austen-Leigh, 'Seven Years of Peaceful Agitation' (1928), ZCKA Box II. See also Livery Committee Minute Book 1920-31.
18 Court Book b, 4 April 1876.
19 Total gross income p.a. was given as £1,626, only slightly less than the Fishmongers' Company with £1,698. *City Press* November 1869, Beadle's Book, p.28.

any extravagant spending on the Hall—repairs were completed in 1801 for a modest £1,309 and in 1825 alterations to the Court Room cost £1,600. By 1850 the Company's barge and fire engine had been disposed of as unnecessary. The foundation and maintenance of the Stationers' Company's School in 1861, which might have been a financial drain on the Company, was supported by loan charities, the Wood Street estate and personal donations, with only occasional contributions and prizes from corporate funds. There was some investment in property on Ludgate Hill in the early 19th century, but it was not until the 20th century that the Company extended its property-holding to the south with purchases on Ludgate Hill, forming the substantial site which was largely destroyed by enemy action in 1940, and sold in 1959.

The second half of the 19th century, however, was not a prosperous era for the Company—hence the appointment of the Finance Committee (1876), the appearance of the first printed balance sheet (1885) and the disappearance of venison from the menu. Underlying reasons for financial stringency were public criticism and the decline of the English Stock—in 1850 the profit from publications stood at £4,000, in 1880 just £2,000 'and is gradually declining'. Slices of capital did come the Company's way in the 1870s with the sale of the Dark House at Billingsgate (£3,400 in 1874) and £40,000 from the sale of the Pellipar estate in Ireland to the Skinners' Company (1875). The £40,000 was paid by instalments and the sum was partially invested in railway companies and partially spent on building expenses in the 1880s. The rebuilding of houses at Amen Corner and Ave Maria Lane cost £40,000; the new Stock Room and improvements at Stationers' Hall cost some £9,380—the latter was paid for by the sale of Madras Railway stock and Metropolitan Board of Works stock originally purchased with the proceeds from the Irish estate.[20]

The report of the Finance Committee predicted some improvement in the Company's finances once leases were renewed (shortly) and it recommended adjustments in fines and fees.[21] Thus in 1880 fees rose to new heights—admission to the Freedom by service or patrimony £5, by redemption £30, admission to the Livery £70, to the Court £80 and the fine in lieu of serving as Under and Upper Warden and Master £200.[22] The increases did not have the desired effect and were reversed in 1896 as the number of Liverymen fell.

Another longstanding, regular source of income was quarterage which could involve the Renter Wardens having to track down members in their homes. The difficulty of collection (or possibly the disinclination of those responsible), combined with the reduced number of the Company, yielded only £32 16s. in quarterage in 1884, so the subscription was abolished—to be reintroduced in 1990.

The early years of the 20th century brought financial crisis. The Wardens' bank account was overdrawn and there was no money to pay pensions or Court fees. A

20 Report of Master, Wardens and Stock-keepers 26 January 1887, Court Book c, following 1 February 1887.
21 Report of 27 March 1876, Committee Minute Book 1876-1928, pp.100-2.
22 Court Book b, 4 May 1880. Printed in full in front of Renter Wardens' Accounts 1888.

temporary solution was provided by an advance of £125 from the Stock-keepers while the General Purposes Committee was called upon to investigate.[23] As a result of that committee's recommendations economies were imposed—the Hendon dinner and the payment of all charitable subscriptions and donations were suspended. Court fees were cut by half, the surplus cost of Bibles and Prayer Books presented to apprentices was transferred from the corporate account to Robert Low's charity. Finally, it was mooted that the income of the Company might be augmented by capitalising on one of the Company's chief assets—Stationers' Hall itself. This idea was pursued by a special committeee and escalated into a full-blown plan to make the Hall 'a desirable home or centre of co-operation for the various societies connected with the trades from which the Livery was drawn'. This would necessitate the extension of the Hall and plans were submitted by H.W. Wills, F.R.I.B.A. in 1918, but to no avail.[24] The idea, however, was soon to be taken up by the Livery Committee.

The circumstances which led to the General Strike of 1926 (when some 150-200 men from the City's police reserve slept in the hall and Stock Room for five nights)[25] were not conducive to financial prosperity. The 1930s brought some financial reforms in the submission of the accounts of the Master and Wardens, the English Stock and charities to the auditors, Messrs. Jackson and Pixley.[26] Rents were raised and the Company's pensions reduced; more drastic measures were adopted in 1938 with the suspension of Livery Dinners and committee fees; Court fees were halved and luncheons simplified.[27]

The bombing of the Wood Street estate and fire damage at and around the Hall in 1940 brought a loss of rents and left a desolate site at the corner of Ludgate Hill with Ave Maria Lane. During the war English Stock dividends were suspended, resuming in 1949 at just 2½ per cent. In these post-war years the Company was forced to live off its meagre capital—there was no revenue from tenants or Hall lettings, and war damage compensation was not enough to cover the total cost of restoring the Hall and installing new kitchens, offices and cloakrooms. Meanwhile the potentially valuable site facing St Paul's Cathedral awaited planning permission before any decision could be taken about redevelopment. There was much debate on the course the Company should take before the Court decided to offer the site for sale with planning permission. The prospect of undertaking the redevelopment was too daunting, the possibility of immediate capital tempting. Finally the freehold site was sold to the Colonial Mutual Life Assurance Society in 1959 for what was then the astounding sum of £663,000, the highest rate per acre yet paid for land in the City (see p.99).

For the first time in its history the Company found itself possessed of a large capital sum. The stockbrokers, Messrs Fielding Newson-Smith and Capel-Cure, Linton, Clarke and Co, advised investing £50,000 in equities, and the Court accordingly instructed the

24 Court Book g, 8 January 1918, *ibid.*, h, pp.33-6 for report of 8 October 1918, with 5 November 1918.
25 Court Book i, 1 June 1926.
26 Court Book j, 31 July 1934.
27 Court Book k, 5 April 1938.

Treasurer to select whatever he thought fit.[28] Plans to invest the largest sum in property foundered through the Finance Committee's lack of direction; an Investment Sub-Committee appointed by the Court met once only, in May 1959, and it did not minute its proceedings. It was not until April 1963 that the General Purposes Committee proposed that a professional adviser should be appointed to assist the Investment Committee.[29] Matters were further complicated by the contentious issue of the winding up of the English Stock by Act of Parliament of July 1961 (see pp.101-2) which allocated £25,000 from the English Stock for charitable uses and settled annuities upon shareholders (see pp.102, 105). The Investment Committee continued to strive to oversee the management of the Company's newly acquired resources but by the time of the Master's Report for 1971-2 its work was beginning to be undermined by the problem of inflation and a review of the Company's income and expenditure since 1966 showed that investment income had done no more than keep pace with 'the inescapable rise in our expenditure'.[30] In consequence a number of economy measures were introduced including a reduction of Court and committee fees and savings in domestic catering. The Livery, which for a few years during the 1960s was able to give free dinners, was once again asked to subscribe to their cost; and following an appeal by the Master and Wardens 77 English Stock annuitants surrendered their payments 'with a view to improving the Company's income at a time of financial stringency'.[31] By 1981 the worst was over and the Court noted with approval an increase of £700 in the Company's gross annual income. The trend continued with the introduction of higher fines and fees and the raising of the hire charge for the use of the Hall (1982).[32] Efforts to increase Hall lettings intensified and within four years of the appointment of a new Clerk in 1984 Hall hire income had quadrupled.

Hall hire became big business but increased use meant more wear and tear which had to be dealt with by a schedule of regular renovation during the summer recess. In addition, in 1988, wet rot was discovered in the roof of the Card Room which cost some £75,000 to eradicate, and new sources of income were looked for. A Hall Preservation Fund had been set up in 1984, to which Liverymen made generous donations. A Report on the Future Finances of the Company (1990) drew attention to the need to augment the annual income of the Company by £27,000, and this was achieved by the reintroduction of quarterage of £65 per annum in 1990 (Liverymen over 65 paid half the sum), to be increased annually by the cost of inflation.[33] The recession of the early 1990s, although less severe than that of 1973-4, hit the Company's two main sources of income, Hall lettings and investments. Stricter budget control was exercised and the Treasurer re-organised the presentation of the accounts to make them more comprehensible to the layman.

28   Court Book n, 7 March 1961.
29   *Ibid.*, 7 May 1963.
30   Livery List 1972-3.
31   *The Stationer and Newspaper Maker*, 14, summer 1976.
32   Court Book p, 3 February 1981, 27 July 1982.
33   'The Story of the reintroduction of Quarterage 1990'.

47. The Renter
Wardens' provision
of a 'sufficient
dinner' for the
Master, Wardens
and Court, 1969. A
'one-off' revival.

Ceremony and Entertainment

The chief ceremony of the Company's year is the election of the Master and Wardens
in early July. It retains its traditional form, with the new Master making a solemn
declaration that he will 'truly order and govern all the Fellowship of the Mistery and
Company' before being robed, and invested with the Master's badge. The election was
formerly celebrated at the Election Feast held on the Sunday after St Peter's Day (29
June), the day after the ceremony. This dinner and the one in honour of the new Lord
Mayor were the chief feasts of the Company's calendar in the 1570s when it was also the
custom for the Court to dine together after the quarter day Court meetings. As time
went on additional dinners, entertainments, ceremonies and church services became
part of the Company's tradition; dates were sometimes altered, in times of hardship
dinners were suspended and venison came and went from the menu. Nevertheless, the
Company's two main feasts are now the Charter Dinner in May and the Civic Dinner
in November; Court dinners are still held regularly and two special events, 'Cakes and
Ale' on Ash Wednesday and the Richard Johnson service in June have been kept up for
the last two hundred years.

Livery Dinners were and are renowned, and invitations have always been sought after. James Boswell describes in his journal how he and Sir Joshua Reynolds persuaded the bookseller Charles Dilly and the Clerk to invite them to one of the Company's Venison Feasts at Stationers' Hall on 12 August 1790. The menu included 15 haunches of venison, and as many pasties with 'other good substantial dishes' enjoyed by 225 Liverymen and their guests. After the feast came port, sherry and Mountain (a type of Malaga wine), tea, coffee and a game of whist—'I, being full of wine ... then supt and drank more but was very much intoxicated and could not recollect much of what passed'.[34] Perhaps there were too many guests like Boswell and Reynolds attending the Company's Livery Dinners, so the Renter Wardens were instructed that the November dinner was to be frugal and they were not to invite their personal friends.

The Venison Feasts originated in the will of John Sweeting (1659) specifying that his estate should provide a memorial to himself, a pair of gloves for the Master, payment for a sermon in August, two dinners for 'Bachelors that are Booksellers free of the Company of Stationers, Shopkeepers of Themselves in the City of London', also a dinner for the Master, Wardens, Assistants, Clerk and Livery on the day the sermon was preached. The dinner was usually referred to as the August dinner or, after it became customary to dine on venison (from c.1676), the Venison Feast or Dinner. Legacies left to the Company by William Lambe and Evan Tyler were put towards this dinner, which after 1875 was sometimes held in July.

In the 19th century the Lord Mayor's Dinner in November was a hearty affair for the entire Livery, accompanied by musical entertainment—beginning with a sung Latin grace, followed by the national anthem, as many as a further thirteen vocal performances; it included the courteous ceremony of the Loving Cup, when the two-handled goblet is passed from guest to guest, the previous drinker standing with his back to the drinker, on guard to defend him from being stabbed. The November dinner, at which the Lord Mayor, the Sheriffs and officers of the Corporation of London are in attendance, has been known as the Civic Dinner since 1963—it is the more formal of the Company's two Livery Dinners and full evening dress is worn. The Charter Dinner in May commemorates the granting of the Royal Charter of May 1557 and is the occasion when guests from the trades associated with the guild are entertained at the Hall. Since 1991 there has also been a dinner following the February Court, when the Master, Wardens and Assistants entertain the Masters and Clerks of other City companies with the object of strengthening ties between them. A summer Livery wine party now marks the election of the new Master and Wardens, with a similar party at Christmas for the Livery and guests, who include the office staff. At a June luncheon there is a presentation of prizes and awards to those who have received grants under the Educational Charity. In 1970 a Freemen's dinner was inaugurated, now held annually and there has been a Freemen's Concert since 1993.

---

34 Transcript of James Boswell's Journal, 12 August 1790. Series 1, Box L, folder 6, vi.

In addition to the two Livery Dinners and the Court dinners, for the greater part of the 19th century the Court also enjoyed Cater's dinner which was held on 1 December after the distribution of Theophilus Cater's charity; small legacies from Daniel Midwinter (1750), Richard Brooke (1722) and William Gill (1798) also contributed to the cost of Cater's dinner. Similarly, Alderman Wright's will directed that £26 3s. should be spent on a dinner for the Master, Wardens and Assistants on the day that Wright's charity was distributed.

In the first half of the 19th century it was customary for the new Master and Wardens to issue invitations to their Inauguration dinner and occasionally a group of newly-elected Assistants would give a dinner. In December 1877, the Master and Wardens' dinner was combined with Cater's dinner and this became regular following a review of the Company's entertainments in 1881. A Ladies' Banquet was first held in 1893 and there was a flurry of social activities for the Livery in the 1920s as a result of pressure from the Livery Committee.

If the menus are any indication, Victorian appetites were gargantuan and dinners long. The meal invariably began with turtle soup; salmon and stewed eels were favoured and specialities included 'chines' of mutton, braised hare and marrow pudding. Obviously, venison was the *pièce de résistance* of the Venison Dinner, preceded by three kinds of soup, five fish dishes and nine choices of poultry. As well as venison the menu included duck-lings, turkey poults (pullets) and gosling, followed by ten different puddings from blanc-mange to plum, with desserts of hothouse grapes and pineapples.[35] J.R. Riddell, who master-minded many initiatives in the 1920s, urged improvements in the catering. (Company cooks were successively Robert Devers, J. & T. Staples, Robert Palmer, J.T. Swayne, Messrs Thorogood & Co., Mrs Milligan, the wife of the butler and Hallkeeper.) The Company has always used outside caterers for large-scale dinners and in 1984, as part of the drive to maximise the use of the Hall, new caterers were engaged in addition to the Company's own steward or Catering Manager for smaller and domestic functions.

'Cakes and Ale' on Ash Wednesday is the most intriguing of the Company's traditions, and one of the most enduring. John Norton specified that cakes, wine and ale be provided for members of the Company who attended the Ash Wednesday service, as prescribed in his will of 1612—hardly an epicurean feast yet sufficient incentive. In the 19th century 'Cakes and Ale' took the form of buns made to a traditional recipe, now lost, and ale distributed in the Stock Room at the Hall by the caretaker and his wife. If Liverymen came in person they were entitled to eat 'what buns they like', to take six more away with them 'and drink what ale they think fit'. Some Liverymen sent servants to collect their quota of buns in which case the servant was given a bun for himself and, if adult, a glass of ale. A 'bun list' of 1837 records that the Master received four dozen and the Wardens three dozen buns each, the total for the Livery being 454 buns[36]—the propriety of such consumption on the first day of Lent is questionable. Once the buns

---

35   Menu, 15 August 1861. Series 1, Box L, folder 2, ii c. See also folders 1, 4, 5.
36   Ash Wednesday arrangements 1837, 1839. Series 1, Box L, folder 2, i.

48. Order of
procession of the
state barges for
Lord Mayor's Day,
1843, when the
Stationers' barge
led.

INCORPORATED 1827.

THE

ORDER OF PROCESSION

FOR

THE BARGES,

AS REGULATED BY THE

Right Honourable the LORD MAYOR and Court of ALDERMEN of the CITY OF LONDON, to be observed on *Thursday* the 9th Day of NOVEMBER, 1843.

To Anchor on Lambeth Side.		To Anchor on Westminster Side.	
1	STATIONERS.	7	MERCHANT TAILORS.
2	APOTHECARIES.	8	SKINNERS.
3	TALLOW CHANDLERS.	9	GOLDSMITHS.
4	CLOTH WORKERS.	10	FISHMONGERS.
5	VINTNERS.	11	DRAPERS.
6	IRONMONGERS.	12	GROCERS.

THE CITY BARGE TO CLOSE THE PROCESSION.

IT IS ORDERED,

THAT the said Barges be rowed from *Blackfriars Bridge* to Westminster in Procession, as above directed, and to return in the same manner, each Barge to hold its proper rank and to keep an equal distance from each other, so that the whole Procession be formed in a regular Line.

IT IS FURTHER ORDERED,

THAT the *Court of the Watermen's Company* do on that Day attend on the River to see the same duly performed, and that a Copy of this Order be delivered to the Master of each Company concerned, who is desired to conform to the same.

Clerk.

Watermen and Lightermen's Hall,

November, 18

STATIONERS' HALL,

JULY 5th, 1836.

SIR,

THE Master and Wardens request the pleasure of your Company, with Two Ladies, on board the Barge, on Thursday the 28th of July, to proceed to Richmond to Dinner, at Three o'Clock precisely; and they beg you will inform the Treasurer, before the 26th, whether or not you intend to be of the Party.

The Barge will be at the Stairs, on the North-west Side of Westminster Bridge, and will move at *Ten o'Clock in the Morning precisely*, and will return to Westminster Bridge in the Evening;—leaving Richmond at *Seven for half-past Seven o'Clock precisely.*

THOMAS HOPKINS, Beadle.

and ale had been distributed, Liverymen processed, gowned and robed, to St Faith's chapel under St Paul's for the Ash Wednesday service. Afterwards, the Court took coffee or chocolate, with dinner later—the dinner was discontinued in 1849. For some sixty years, until the closure of the Company's school, the service was enlivened by the choir of the Stationers' School, replaced since 1986 by the Company's choir.

The ceremonies and entertainments involving the Company's barge ranged from the most stately to the purely pleasurable. The Stationers' first barge was built in 1680, its sixth and last was made by Searle in 1826 and sold in 1850.[37] A state barge was a luxury and many livery companies chose to hire one on the few occasions in the year when a barge was needed.

37   M. Osborne, *The State Barges of the Stationers' Company 1680-1850* (1972).

The highlight of the civic year, when the new Lord Mayor proceeded to Westminster to take the oath, had been marked by a river procession from the 15th century. If a livery company boasted an Alderman, Sheriff or even the Lord Mayor, participation in the barge procession was *de rigueur*. The Barge Master would be ordered to start preparations in October, his Mate, 18 oarsmen, whifflers and musicians would be alerted, the barge banners, hangings, cushions and livery for the crew spruced or re-newed for the occasion. With more than a fair share of Lord Mayors in the first half of the 19th century (six), the expense of maintaining the Stationers' barge seemed to be justified—Sir John Key, successively Sheriff, Alderman, Lord Mayor, and Master of the Stationers' Company in 1830, enjoyed the use of the Company's barge on several occasions.

Those attending the Lord Mayor in the Company's barge on Lord Mayor's Day made a detour to Lambeth Palace to deliver the traditional gift of almanacks to the Archbishop of Canterbury. The barge would be moored while its Liverymen passengers were served with refreshments and the new almanack presented. In 1845 there were 32 aboard the Stationers' barge, each Liveryman was given a pint of wine, new bread and old cheese, while the watermen and attendants were content with ale.[38]

Liverymen of the Company joined the solemn funeral procession which escorted the remains of Admiral Nelson from Greenwich to St Paul's in January 1806, they watched the opening of the new London Bridge in 1831 and attended the King to Greenwich in 1835. On Lord Mayor's Day 1843 the Stationers' barge led the procession of barges to Westminster, this Company being the most junior of the 12 represented.[39]

In June or July the Company barge was used for the summer outing to Richmond, an excursion enjoyed by members of the Court and the Stock Board, the Clerk, Treasurer, Surveyor and their ladies who embarked at Westminster for Richmond where coaches transported the party to the Star and Garter hotel on Richmond Hill for dinner at 3 p.m. After the sale of the barge the Stationers hired a vessel for the Richmond outing or ventured elsewhere by carriage—in 1875 the recently re-opened Alexandra Palace was fixed upon for the ladies' summer entertainment. In 1994, there was a revival of the river excursion to Richmond—it was not possible to recapture the dignity of the Company's state barge, but on a hot July day a launch was hired by the Master, Richard Hasleden and the Immediate Past Master, Peter Rippon, who invited the Court and guests to go by river to lunch at the Star and Garter, now a home for disabled servicemen.

The upkeep of the barge, barge-house, the salaries of the Barge Master and Mate, the expense of hiring oarsmen, musicians and whifflers was a luxury few companies could afford by 1850, and the City's state barge was used for the last time in 1856. The Stationers had decided to dispose of their barge soon after Lord Mayor's Day 1849, it being 'inexpedient to retain the use of the Company's Barge ... a great expence without an

38 *Illustrated London News*, 15 November 1845, p.22.
39 Order of Procession for the Barges, 9 November 1843.

50. Programme for the Livery ball, October 1957, in celebration of the quatercentenary of the granting of the first Charter, 1557.

adequate object'.[40] The barge was sold in April 1850 to Mr Hall for £150 and the former Barge Master, Richard Morton, and his mate, George Morton, were given £4 and £2 respectively—the equivalent of a year's salary. The barge house at Lambeth, on a lease from the Archbishop of Canterbury, was offered to Messrs George Searle and Sons for a rent of £10 per annum.[41] The Stationers' barge became the Exeter College boathouse at Oxford, passed to University College in 1873 but was broken up or otherwise disposed of by 1883 when University College commissioned a new one.[42]

In the 1870s, a Committee of Liverymen organised balls at the Hall, and in June 1893 a ladies' banquet was held, with suitably dainty menu cards.[43] Fewer than a third of those present were women, nevertheless the success of the evening justified the repetition of

40   Court Book X, 4 December 1949.
41   *Ibid.*, 26 March, 9 April, 4 June 1850.

51. Presentation by the Master, Ray Tindle, to the Earl of Stockton (Harold Macmillan, Prime Minister 1957-1963) in the presence of the Prince of Wales, 1985.

the ladies' dinner either at the Hall, the Hotel Metropole or Hotel Cecil until 1905. The Livery Committee revived the practice in 1928 when, at a cost of 10 shillings a head, 146 were present, presided over by R.A. Austen-Leigh.

The six regular dinners exclusively for members of the Court seem to have grown wearisome by 1875 when it was decided that the May Court dinner should be replaced by a banquet to which 25 distinguished guests were invited; and in 1881 the Court decided that the number of its annual dinners was to be reduced from six to four and more guests invited; the inauguration dinner was amalgamated with Cater's, and Liverymen were allowed to introduce a guest at the Lord Mayor's Dinner.[44] This was not an economy measure, as the Accounts for 1886-7 show; expenditure on dinners, luncheons and entertainments was the largest item—£1,000, with another £300 spent on wine.[45] The purchase of wine was by this date the responsibility of the Wine Committee, who were under instruction not to purchase any more wine in one year than had been drunk the previous year. Regulation and control had been imposed in 1872, not before time,

42   'The Oxford College Barges', notes by Norman Dix, May 1995.
43   Menus for Ladies' Banquets 1893-1905. Series 1, Box L, folder 3.
44   Court Book c, 2 August, 4 October 1881.
45   Court Book c, 30 March 1887.

as until then the junior members of the Stock Board had taken it upon themselves to sample and select wines for the Company without regard to supplier or price.[46]

Dinners were suspended on the outbreak of war in 1939 and, in any case, the damage inflicted upon Stationers' Hall in 1940 left little scope for entertainments; the first since the end of the war being a small dinner in 1951. It was not until the new kitchens and the restoration of the Hall were complete in 1957 that full-scale dinners became feasible, coinciding with the quatercentenary celebrations marking the grant of the Company's Royal Charter of May 1557. The Quatercentenary Dinner was attended by the Prime Minister, Rt. Hon. Harold Macmillan (who proposed the toast to the Company), by Sir Denis Truscott, the Lord Mayor and Lord Astor of Hever; boys from the Company's school and trumpeters of the Royal Marines took part in a masque.

The Company had adopted 45 Commando the Royal Marines in 1949, since when ties have been cemented at social events, by the presentation of the Queen's and Regimental Colours which hang in the Hall, and by the orchestra of the Royal Marines' School of Music which plays regularly at Stationers' Hall.

Musical entertainment has long been enjoyed at the Company's dinners and during outings on the barge. Concerts were held at Stationers' Hall in the late 17th century when the Society of Gentlemen, Lovers of Musick performed there in honour of St Cecilia (a Roman martyr of the third century later famous as the patron saint of music and musicians). The St Cecilia's day recital at the Hall became renowned with the performance of Purcell's second ode written for the occasion in 1692—'Hail! Bright Cecilia'. Concerts and celebrations surrounding St Cecilia's day (22 November) were popular for some twenty years afterwards. The Musicians' Company revived the tradition of the St Cecilia festival with a service at St Paul's Cathedral in 1905[47] and, following the 'Homage to Purcell' recital at Stationers' Hall in 1968, the Master, Charles Rivington, wistfully drew attention to the late 17th-century St Cecilia's day concerts which had made the Hall one of the musical centres of London.[48] On 22 November 1992 the tradition was revived with the performance of the ode composed by Purcell 300 years previously, by the choir and orchestra of 'Fiori Musicali'. Corporate sponsorship enabled the St Ceciliatide International Festival of Music to be repeated at Stationers' Hall for a week in November 1995, with, of course, dinner afterwards, and it is now a regular event in the Company's year.

---

46 Court Book a, 6 August 1872.
47 The Musicians' Company was granted the use of Stationers' Hall for meetings and dinners from 1905. Court Book f, 6 June 1905.
48 Past Master's Report, Livery List 1969-70.

TO THE MEMORY OF
OVERSEAS IN THE
PATIENCE AND

OLD BOYS OF THE
WORLD WAR 1939
FRIENDSHIP AND

THOSE WHO DIED
1945 THEY GAVE
NOW REST FROM

AT HOME AND
ALL WITH COURAGE
THEIR LABOUR

CHAPTER SEVEN

The Charities, the School and Technical Training

PENELOPE HUNTING

The Provision of Pensions for the Poor

The Stationers' Company has long been responsible for awarding pensions to poor freemen and widows. The provision of regular payments to the poor and needy has undergone considerable change, particularly in the decades since the end of the Second World War. The introduction of state pensions on the one hand and the enormous decrease in the value of money on the other has made the bequests of earlier centuries inadequate for their original purpose and these have been adapted and re-organised to work efficiently in a modern context.

The Company's corporate obligation was vested in the English Stock whose letters patent stipulated that £200 per annum of the profits were to be used in pensions which were doled out at quarterly Pensions Courts in March, June, September and December. These were abolished in 1973 when the Court ruled that pensioners were no longer required to attend at the hall.[1] In earlier times men felt a pious duty to leave money to support the poor and old. Bequests made between 1567 and 1797 are listed in the *Abstract of charitable donations in the disposal of the Court of Assistants ...* (1926). Of these, one woman (Mrs Beata Wilkins, died 1773, widow of the printer, William Wilkins) and nine men, several of them non-Stationers, left money in trust to the Company to be distributed to the poor, sometimes with the terms spelt out minutely. William Lambe, a Clothworker, left money in 1567 for a penny a week and a pennyworth of bread to be doled out to six poor Stationers or their widows. In 1795 Richard Johnson, a sad bachelor and paper merchant, died before he could achieve his wish of making a fortune by the age of forty. He left his property to the Company to be divided half-yearly, among 'five very poor widows, who should have seen better days, above the age of sixty, whose husbands were liverymen and in a good way of business, and either stationers, printers, booksellers or binders'.[2]

Nineteenth-century Stationers seem to have been very much concerned with the plight of their elderly poor but, judging from the phrasing of their bequests, they seem to have considered it more of a civic than a pious duty to look after those unable to earn a living. The Stationers had no almshouse and were therefore unable to rehouse

52. The Stationers' Company's School memorial window to boys killed in the World Wars, which was moved to Hornsey Parish Church in 1983.

---

1 Court Book o, 3 July 1973.
2 *Charitable Donations and Benefactions in the disposal of the Court of Assistants of the Worshipful Company of Stationers* (1926).

53. Luke Hansard aged 77, sketched by Samuel Lane and inscribed by Hansard for his sons, 29 October 1828.

the 14 old and needy men and women required by the terms of bequest; the charitable donors concentrated instead on the provision of annuities and pensions, some specifying that the money be used for men or women of their own branch of the trades of the Guild. John Nichols (1745-1826) and his near contemporary, Luke Hansard (1752-1828) printer to the House of Commons, foreshadowed the employers' pension schemes of later times by making over sums of money for pensions for their own employees to be administered by the Company. Luke Hansard gave the Company £1,000 in Consols in 1818, to be used for annuities of £10 a year to 'my old and early fellow-workman, James Larman, now in his 68th year and free of this Company ... to be continued to his wife for her life', and to his brother, 'William Larman, Pressman ... now in his 64th year, and free of this Company'. The residue would go for grants of £5 each to four elderly Freemen. Luke Hansard's second benefaction of £1,500 was to be used to pension two of his warehousemen at six guineas a year and to provide a copy of the prayer book and psalms neatly bound to be given to every apprentice bound at Stationers' Hall. He calculated the interest would allow for 200 copies a year at 2s. 7d. a copy.[3] It now pays for one every now and again.

In 1820, the pensions from the Company's corporate funds were between 10s.6d. and £2 a quarter. In May 1883, with the impending threat of a Royal Commission report on the City companies, the Court voted to increase this to £8 for four pensioners and £4 for the rest. 'The money derived', according to the Commission's published report of 1884, 'from an appropriation of the profits of the monopoly of almanacs', which between 1681 and 1884 had risen from £200 to £344 per annum.[4]

The corporate pensions were reasonably straightforward to administer, even if the money grew less and less adequate in real terms, but there was a bewildering number of small bequests which became increasingly outmoded and anomalous: 12 pensioners still received 2d. loaves from William Lambe's charity; 18 poor got £1 from Thomas Guy's charity, and there were many other small sums to be awarded regularly.[5] Particularly problematic was Mrs Elizabeth Baldwin's gift of five greatcoats for five poor Liverymen to be given in the first week of December. By 1919, the money only stretched to one coat costing £4. William Bowyer junior's endowment of 1777 included an annuity for a journeyman compositor who must be 'a man of good life and conversation, a regular worshipper, able to read and construe Latin ... and at least read Greek fluently with accents', brought up piously and virtuously 'at Merchant Taylors or some other public school'. Such a man was increasingly difficult to find.[6]

The re-organisation of parochial charities in 1893 relieved the Company of the duty of attending a service in memory of Theophilus Cater, who had left money in 1718 to poor parishioners of St Martin within Ludgate and Christchurch, Newgate Street, and of making payments to the minister, clerk, sexton and reader of St Martin's Church .[7] Two years later the Church Commissioners excused the Company from the duty of distributing payments to poor parishioners, but the Court continued to distribute £1 to each of 14 poor Freemen in December.

The laborious business of awarding pensions to recipients personally and in accordance with the wishes of the donor was simplified in 1917.[8] Even so, amateur methods of distribution were still in operation after the Second World War and the Company continued to dole out 50 small pensions. In the hard winter of 1962-3 the pensioners were given money to pay for half a ton of coal or the equivalent.[9]

3   This indicates the level of printer entry into the trade. See also Chapter Two.
4   *House of Commons, Reports from Commissioners, Inspectors and others, London City Livery Companies* (1884), vol. 5, p.278.
5   Stationers' Company Pensions List 1918-29.
6   *Charitable Donations and Benefactions in the disposal of the Court of Assistants of the Worshipful Company of Stationers* (1926).
7   Court Book d, 7 November 1893.
8   Minutes of the Pensions Committee 6 February 1917, p.177, Committee Minute Book 1876-1928.
9   Livery List 1963-4.

The Stationers' and Newspaper Makers' Company Act of 1961 which extinguished the English Stock gave the long-awaited opportunity to rationalise the Company's pensions. A new fund, Charity '61, was set up with £25,000 from the Stock which was able to give grants to a wide variety of national, trade and other charities ranging from the Book Trade Benevolent Fund to the British Honduras Hurricane Fund. In 1967 the Charity Commissioners approved a new scheme for merging all the multifarious small trusts and this meant that the amounts paid in pensions could be increased. Pensioners ceased to collect their due at quarterly pension courts, the cost of journeying to the Hall sometimes being more than the amount given in pension. In place of this, Liverymen began to make regular visits to retired or sick members of the Company living alone in their own homes. The new scheme perpetuates the benefactors' wishes through a welfare fund which gives financial assistance to elderly freemen, widows and other poor folk who have been engaged in the trades associated with the Company. The responsibility for the disbursement of the Company's Charities Fund rests with the Charitable Trusts Committee, subject to the approval of the Court; various trade benevolent associations, the Church, the Royal Marines, civic and special appeals, national charities and one chosen by the current Master are the beneficiaries.

The Loan Charities

Educating the young and helping those setting out in life was one of the Company's age-old objectives and a number of wealthy Stationers made bequests to the Company, in accordance with a time-honoured custom of the City, to be used in loans to young men wishing to set up in trade on their own account. But times change and the loan charities fell into desuetude, to be transformed in the 19th and 20th centuries to fit the changing needs of later generations of young people.

The earliest of these was that of William Norton (1527-93), one of the original signatories of the Charter of 1557, printer of the so-called Bishop's Bible and three times Master of the Company. He left property in the City in trust to Christ's Hospital which was to provide £6 13s. 4d. per annum for the Stationers' Company; £6 to be used in a loan to a young freeman, and the remaining 13s. 4d. to be shared between the Master, Wardens, Clerk and Beadle. His nephew, apprentice and successor, John Norton (d. 1612) was King's Printer in Greek, Latin and Hebrew, an Alderman of London and, like his uncle before him, three times Master of the Company; he was buried in St Faith's under St Paul's Cathedral. He was a wealthy man whose major legacy to the Company was £1,000 to be invested in land and the rents and income to be applied in loans to young Stationers. To this the Company added £150 from William Norton's bequest to the parish of St Faith and poor Stationers, and in 1604, a further £50 from the bequest of Henry Billage, Citizen and Dyer, making a total of £1,200 which was used to purchase property in Wood Street in 1619.

Another loan charity was that of George Bishop (1569-1611), Liveryman and Alderman, who left the Company property in Shropshire. The income from this was to provide

54. Flyleaf of the autograph manuscript of Richard Johnson's *Paper Maker and Stationer's Assistant*, 1793, setting out the terms of his bequest to the Company.

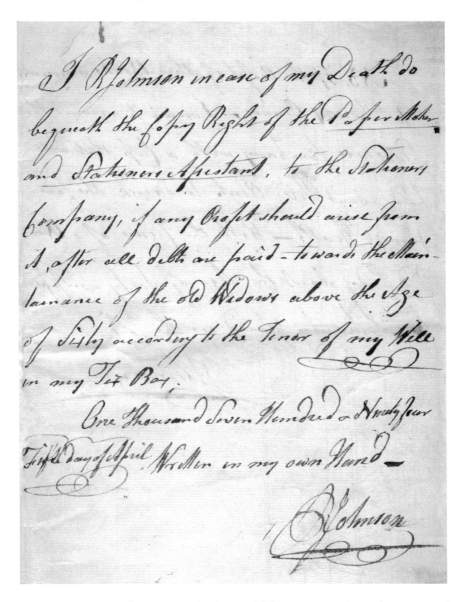

£6 per annum for loans to young freemen, which would become void 'in the event of negligence on the part of the Company to carry it out', £6 to Christ's Hospital and £10 for a preacher at St Paul's Cross. By the will of Christopher Meredith (*d.*1653) rents from property in St Paul's churchyard were to be laid out in loans to poor freemen. Evan Tyler (*d.*1682), printer and bookseller in Edinburgh and London, Master of the Company in 1671, specified in his will that £500 should provide loans over a four-year term to 10 young Stationers; £120 was to provide an annual collation for the Master and Wardens.

Early bequests often included provision for corporate dinners and for sermons to be preached on particular occasions. John Norton, among other bequests, left provision for a sermon on Ash Wednesday, 2d. a week and a loaf of bread to 12 poor people and from the residue, cakes, wine and ale for the Stationers 'either before or after the service' (see p.119). Richard Johnson wished the Master and Wardens to go to Hendon on the anniversary of his father's death to inspect his father's tomb, in which he himself was buried, and to hear a sermon preached on the text of 'Vita humana bulla est', 'human life's a bubble' and afterwards to dine.[10] The Hendon dinner was discontinued in 1917 and the grave is now inspected by Robert Baynes, the last headmaster of the school and a Liveryman. For a number of years the service and sermon was held in St Martin's within Ludgate; it now takes place in St Bride's Church; in place of a dinner for Master and Wardens, the service is now followed by a Livery luncheon.

Administering the charitable trusts required abilities which the Company did not necessarily have. It needed skill to invest the capital to best advantage or to purchase and manage property to ensure that there was sufficient income to fulfil the donors' wishes. The value of money and property fluctuated, records got lost or were destroyed, the trustees varied in competence and conscientiousness and did not always keep separate financial accounts. The loan charities posed special problems. It was not easy to identify those young men at the start of their careers who would benefit from a loan, and because there was no penalty for failure to repay, recovering the money was particularly difficult. Over the years the system gradually fell into disuse with the result that the income was gradually subsumed into the Company's general fund. The Charity Commissioners reported in 1830 that 'no sums of money had been for many years applied in loans according to the direction of the several wills'.[11]

'Nothing is now applied in loans' from William Norton's charity, the report stated. Payment from John Norton's and Henry Billage's loan charities had ceased and the accounts had been confused with the Company's corporate account. Income from Christopher Meredith's charity had been absorbed into the general funds and no loans were forthcoming from Tyler's charity of 1682, of which £500 lay undisposed.

The Origins of the Stationers' Company's School

Apart from the loan charities, the Commissioners were tolerably satisfied that the Company was fulfilling its trustee duties. The Attorney-General nevertheless filed a suit for breach of trust against the Stationers in the Court of Chancery, in that 'for many years the Company has applied no sums in loans according to the directions of the donors' but had retained the same for its own use. Secondly, the system of carrying over the funds, including rents which had increased dramatically over the centuries, into the general account of the Company was unacceptable. The Clerk, C.R. Rivington, rose to the defence. He pointed out that the Company expended in voluntary charity an amount far in excess of the amount due in loans. He estimated that the annual sum received from the loan charities was £264 1s. 11d. whereas the Company gave £342 10s. annually in voluntary charity, mostly pensions, not loans. He also maintained that the

---

10   See Robin Myers, 'Vita humana bulla est; Richard Johnson (1757-93)', *The Stationer and Newspaper Maker*, 28 and 29, summer and autumn, 1982.

11   House of Commons, *Reports from Commissioners, Inspectors and others, London City Livery Companies* (1884), vol. 5, pp.278-85.

55. *The Book of Bequests*; transcript of Evan Tyler's will, 1682, leaving £500 for loans to young Stationers.

present Court of Assistants was unaware of the existence of the loan charities and in any case would prefer to continue awarding pensions to the poor rather than revert to the 'obsolete system of loans'. The Clerk clearly resented the amount of time he had been obliged to devote to the investigation of wills and bequests in the archives, but he was willing to consider reforms and to keep separate accounts for each charity.[12] The case was heard before the Master of the Rolls on 26 May 1830. The Court of Assistants was absolved, but in future the charitable funds were to be kept separately and a new scheme for the regulation and management of the loan charities was to be devised, which eventually led to the foundation of the Stationers' Company's School in 1858, the Company's major educational endeavour of the 19th century. Whereupon the Company heaved a sigh of relief and went back to sleep for another 21 years.

It was not until 1851 that positive steps were taken and a new scheme for the loan charities devised. The suggestion was that the Company should boost its reputation for philanthropy by using the arrears of income from the loan charities to build and endow almshouses for the Company's aged poor as other livery companies had done.[13] The

12　Minutes of 23 March 1830, Proceedings of the Charity Commissioners 1829-30, *Report of the Charity Commissioners* (1830), vol. xxii, pp.76-89.

13　Court Book X, 4 March 1851.

Attorney-General did not approve; his solicitor wrote to the Clerk in January 1852 suggesting an alternative idea—'the establishment of a school in connection with the Company'. The Court responded with alacrity and it was agreed that the property and income of the loan charities, originally intended for young people, should be applied to educational purposes.[14] The committee appointed to undertake the task was a weighty one, composed of Alderman Sir John Key, Alderman Sir William Magnay, Alderman Francis Graham Moon, the Master, Wardens and six members of the Court.[15] It reviewed the accounts and found that £5,316 was available from the loan charities to build a school for the sons of Freemen and Liverymen.[16] After this promising start there was a delay of three years before further steps were taken. William Mylne, the Company's surveyor, was then instructed to make inquiries regarding a site and building expenses. Research was put in hand to ascertain where Freemen resided with a view to building the proposed school within easy reach of their homes. The Company then advertised in the London press for a freehold site within a mile and a half of Ludgate Street. Among those considered were a disused burial ground for Irish vagrants in Golden Lane, three houses in Great Ormond Street and the Welsh Charity Schools in Gray's Inn Road, which were being vacated.[17] By the end of 1857 an empty printing office in Bolt Court off Fleet Street had been fixed on as a suitable location. It was at the very heart of the printing and publishing district of London and there was every reason to believe that the school would attract the sons of those working in the printing and allied trades; it was also conveniently close to Stationers' Hall where the school governors met.

Bolt Court was at the north end of a narrow alley, opposite the Bolt and Tun inn from which it took its name. Its most famous resident was Dr Johnson (1709-84) who lived at number 8 from 1776 until his death. Fire destroyed the house in 1819; it was rebuilt as a printing office and owned by Thomas Bensley and his sons. Bensley (d. 1833) was an exponent of 'fine' printing and Master of the Company in 1825. Negotiations for the printing office and adjoining house were completed early in 1858 and £5,750 was offered.[18] Funds entrusted to the Company were used for the purchase and the Company also acquired neighbouring premises in Hole in the Wall Court and at 17 Johnson's Court.[19]

Mr James Arding, who described himself as a surveyor and builder of Dorset Street, produced plans and estimates for the new schoolroom and classrooms and for the conversion of an area for a playground on the north side. Two ground plans for the

14   Court Book X, 13 January 1852.
15   *Ibid.*, 3 February 1852.
16   *Ibid.*, 2 March 1852; Court Book Y, 6 March 1855. For a general history of the school see Robert Baynes, *A History of the Stationers' Company's School 1858-1983* (1987).
17   Copy of C. Rivington's affidavit to Court of Chancery, 9 February 1856, Brown box School, unclassified.
18   Court Book Y, 23 December 1857 and 12 January 1858.
19   C. Rivington, Notice to liverymen 5 March 1861. For Johnson's house see H.B. Wheatley, *London Past and Present* (1891) vol. i, pp.216-7. G.W. Thornbury and Edward Walford, *Old and New London* (1883-5), vol. i, pt i, pp.110, 114. James Boswell, *The Life of Samuel Johnson*, ed. John Canning (1991), pp.169, 303, 352.

school survive, dated March 1859, and the following year Arding repaired the house alongside for the headmaster.²⁰

Arding's outside estimate of £2,000 indicates that the Stationers' School was as simple in style as it was in plan, and a brief description in *Building News* confirms this. A large central window on the north side of the school was gabled, the internal walls were lined with matchboarding to five feet and a queen-post roof added some dignity to the large schoolroom. *Building News* saw the school as an expression of the vigour of the Stationers' Company compared with other livery companies which it declared were 'already practically defunct'. The report concluded that there was little doubt that the school would soon be rated with the Merchant Taylors, the City of London and St Paul's schools.²¹

It took three years to build the school at Bolt Court (1858-61) at a cost of some £8,000, which the Clerk informed the Livery was paid entirely out of the loan charities, while the extension of the site to the west was paid for by the donations from members of the Court and Livery—among them, John Murray II, Andrew Spottiswoode, three Rivingtons and the Master, Henry Foss.²²

With the school buildings nearing completion it was time to appoint a headmaster. The Company's advertisement offering a salary of £180 per annum attracted the astonishing number of 91 applicants, whittled down to four on a shortlist from which A.K. Isbister emerged as the clear favourite.²³ He had previously been headmaster of an Islington school and more recently head of the English department at Jews' College in Finsbury Square, but his early career had been less conventional and more colourful. Alexander Kennedy Isbister was born on a trading settlement of the Hudson's Bay Company in Rupert's Land, Saskatchewan, Canada. His grandfather had worked for the Hudson's Bay Company and had married an Indian woman named Agathas whose Indian features were strikingly marked in her grandson. At the age of 16 Alexander followed his father and grandfather by joining the same company, and pursued a harsh, adventurous life as a fur trader and explorer. In an age when his mixed blood prevented promotion in the Hudson's Bay Company, the young man abandoned the wilds of Canada for Aberdeen and Edinburgh universities. He evidently possessed an innate ability to teach, write and reason, for by 1872 he was the editor of the *Educational Times*, and Dean of the College of Preceptors; he had been admitted to the Bar and obtained a law degree as well as acting as agent for the Red River Settlement and carrying out his duties as headmaster of the Stationers' Company's School; by 1883 he had written 23 school textbooks. ²⁴

20 Plans V53 and 54, Box V. V54 is dated 30 March 1859 and signed by James Arding and James Arding junior. Stationers' School Minute Book 1858-95 for details relating to the building of the school November 1858-June 1859. Court Book Y, 2 October 1860.
21 *Building News*, 19 April 1861, p.335.
22 C. Rivington, Notice to liverymen 5 March 1861.
23 Stationers' School Minute Book 1858-95, 29 January, 5 February 1861.
24 I am grateful to Robert Baynes for reading a draft of this section, for letting me see the proof of his booklet *Alexander Kennedy Isbister* published by the Old Stationers' Association (1995), and for a copy of Professor Barry Cooper's article 'Alexander Kennedy Isbister. A Respectable Victorian' in *Canadian Ethnic Studies* vol. xvii, p.2, 1985.

The Court Minutes do not reveal the reasons for the choice of this exceptional man for the headship but his commanding presence and wide experience must have created a strong impression. A former pupil remembered him as 'A great man, over six feet high, his gown and mortar-board and person reeking of tobacco; his pipe had a hookah, and a large one at that, and with en suite tubing as large as could be seen outside illustrations from Arabian Nights Entertainments'.[25]

Another old boy described Isbister when he was nearing retirement. 'His entrance to the School was impressive to small boys as he moved slowly in carpet slippers with cap and gown hanging loosely much below his shoulders.'[26]

Isbister knew what was expected of him, for the principles on which the Stationers' Company's School was founded were formally approved by the Court of Chancery and printed (1858). Carefully worded clauses specified the fees, the curriculum and the respective responsibilities of the headmaster and the governors. In planning the school the Clerk had estimated that about 385 Liverymen and 800 Freemen of the Company were living in or near London in 1856. As it was calculated that about three-quarters of the Freedom consisted of journeymen or assistants engaged in the printing, stationery, bookselling and bookbinding trades, it was decided that what was required was a lower-class day school at a fee of 6s. a quarter to provide 'a liberal and useful education to the sons of liverymen and freemen', so long as they were 'not afflicted with any contagious disease or convicted of any crime'.[27] The first pupils to enrol were indeed the sons of Freemen and Liverymen but, by the first day of term, 8 April 1861, 55 boys aged seven to twelve attended; they included the sons of wine merchants, surgeons, a leather factor, and an assistant at the British Museum.[28] By 1862 there were 66 pupils; 40 were the sons of Stationers of the 'middle ranks ... scarcely any from the poorer members of the Company'. The other 26 were described as sons of 'Aliens' or non-Stationers.

The school originally offered instruction in the Christian religion, reading, writing, arithmetic, land surveying, book-keeping, geography, drawing and designing, general English literature and composition, sacred and profane history. Isbister, supported by the governors, applied for changes in the original curriculum to cater for the cleverer boys and establish the school officially as a middle-class school.[29] The Master of the Rolls, in his wisdom, preferred the status quo. In spite of this ruling, Isbister added physical science to the curriculum and by 1873 Greek, Latin and French, with instruction in vocal music and drilling after school hours. Thus, although the school did not fulfil its intended function as a lower-class school in some respects, it soon acquired the standards of a middle-class one. William Gilbert, an independent commentator generally hostile to livery companies, wrote in *The City; an Enquiry* (1877), 'as excellent an education can be obtained in the

---

25   *The Stationer,* July 1935, description by F.P. Knights, an old boy of the school.
26   *The Stationer,* July 1935, an old boy, H.O.W. Moorgate's recollection of the aged Isbister.
27   *The Scheme for the Regulation and administration of the Charities founded by William Norton, George Bishop, Christopher Meredith and John Norton under the management of the Stationers' Company* (1858).
28   Stationers' School register of scholars 1861-1913.
29   Stationers' School Minute Book, 3 June 1862.

Stationers' Company's School as in any school in the country, not excluding Eton, Harrow, Westminster, Charterhouse, Winchester or King's College, London'.

The Company was immensely proud of its school in those early days and members were generous in their provision of scholarships and prizes. In 1868 Edmund Hodgson, head of the firm of book auctioneers and twice Master of the Stationers' Company (in 1866-7 and 1867-8), gave the first scholarship of £20 per annum. Thomas Browne, a bookseller of Paternoster Row, a partner in Longmans and Upper Warden in 1857-8, left the school £5,000 for scholarships and a bronze medal and a purse containing £5 to be awarded to the pupil coming first in the midsummer examinations. Henry Foss, a bookseller and twice Master (1860-1 and 1862-3), gave a prize for the complete works of Shakespeare to be awarded annually, and there were prizes from Charles Grimwade, wholesale stationer and Renter Warden (1859-60), and from Joshua Butterworth, law bookseller in Fleet Street, Master in 1894 (see p.162); Henry Cecil Sotheran (Master in 1895) left the school £300, Herbert Fitch (Master 1922), made a bequest and the widow of Sir Thomas Vezey Strong, Master (1903-4), Lord Mayor (1910-11), endowed a scholarship in his name in 1924. In 1967 these were all collected into a single Prize and Scholarship Fund.

There was an annual prizegiving at Stationers' Hall when the Master and Wardens made the presentations. In 1873, a grateful winner of the Edmund Hodgson scholarship wrote to the Clerk to express his gratitude for the education he had received under the painstaking guidance of Mr Isbister and his staff which had enabled him to be articled to a solicitor. 'We all have reason to be proud of our School,' he wrote, 'which although it has been only a short time established already takes a high place among the public schools of London.'[30]

In 1880 Isbister reported to the governors that the method of teaching at the school was 'that of our most successful public schools, modified ... with greater attention to those studies which have a direct application to the practical business of life'. He advised masters to teach their pupils to think and avoid making them learn by rote.

The school examinations were conducted by an external examiner. His report was invariably favourable and strictures related to buildings and equipment, not to the standard achieved by the boys. The reservation expressed in 1889 was that the boys worked so well and happily that they deserved more commodious surroundings; and in 1891 the examiner reported that the chemistry papers had been only moderately well answered which was not to be wondered at considering the lack of scientific apparatus. A proper science laboratory was required to keep abreast of the times, a comment that was to be made several times.[31]

Within five years of its opening, the school was in need of additional accommodation. The Company's surveyor, R.W. Mylne, managed to juggle rooms around so as to extend a classroom.[32] But by 1869 there were 180 pupils in buildings designed to accommodate

30   Court Book a, 4 March 1873.
31   Examiners' reports 1889, 1891, Brown box School, unclassified.
32   Stationers' School Minute Book 14 December 1866.

70, and there was little that could be done to make space at Bolt Court where the school was hemmed in by printing offices and warehouses. Nor could the Company have afforded to pay the increasingly high price of property in the area. Eventually, in 1877, the Committee recognised that the school would have to move and estate agents were asked to report on the sale value of the buildings at Bolt Court.[33] It was to be another 14 years before agreement was reached that the school should move to Ferme Park, Hornsey. In the meanwhile the school struggled through its last years at Bolt Court.

Isbister retired in 1880 and, in spite of the admission of choristers from the Temple and Lincoln's Inn, the numbers fell. In the February before the school moved out of Bolt Court there were just 83 pupils. The main reason was that by the 1880s the City was no longer a residential district and parents objected to their children having to go by train to Fleet Street every day. Isbister's successor, Henry Chettle, complained of the heavy expense of repairing the building and looked forward to new premises. He had received many applications from residents of north London who had heard about the school's relocation at Hornsey and hoped that the school would establish itself as a local centre of education 'and not improbably the local centre for a large part of north London'.[34]

Several alternatives had been considered at West End Lane, Turnham Green and at the rear of the Public Record Office, before the Charity Commissioners approved the Company's purchase in 1892 of land at Ferme Park, Hornsey at a cost of £3,375. A second plot was bought for £2,800 in 1895, paid for by contributions from liverymen.[35] The first building to be erected on the site was a temporary structure built by J. Britton to a design by William Whiddington (1893) and known affectionately as the Tin Temple. It was in use until 1939. Three other architects were invited to submit plans for the permanent building. The commission went to G.G. Stanham, the others having backed out. His instruction was to design a school to accommodate 250 day boys within a budget of £10,000. In the event the cost was a little over £15,510. Stanham's plans were submitted to the Charity Commissioners, who at first witheld their approval, and Stanham was obliged to accept numerous modifications from the Commissioners' architect, E.W. Christian, as well as a reduction of £1,000 in the cost of construction.[36] The style of the building was described as 14th-century Gothic with a large central hall as the main feature. It was completed by 30 October 1894 and formally opened by the Lord Mayor.[37]

The old school at Bolt Court immediately sold to the City of London Parochial Trustees for £8,250. It has been an educational establishment ever since. The London County Council bought it for the newly-founded School of Photo-Engraving and

33 Stationers' School Minute Book 9 January 1877.
34 Court Book d, 13 January 1891, 7 February 1893.
35 Legal papers 186, 287. Stationers' School Minute Book 8 January, 29 January 1895.
36 School Committee, Minute Books, 19 January, 2 March 1892, 15 Febuary 1893. Court Book d, 12 January 1892. School Ledger f.253.
37 *The Builder* 17 November 1894, p.359.

Lithography, known as the Bolt Court School, later to amalgamate with the St Bride School of Printing, to become the London School of Printing (see p.10). The Bolt Court School was rebuilt in 1911 and is now occupied by a branch of the City Literary Institute.

The move out of the City to Hornsey brought a change in the nature of the school which, as the headmaster had anticipated, became a local community school. In Bolt Court, between 1861 and 1864, the school had had 61 sons of Freemen and Liverymen as well as the 'Sons of Aliens'. In contrast, out of 189 admissions to the Hornsey school between January 1910 and June 1913 there was only one Stationer's son.[38] The school had changed its role; it no longer fulfilled its original objective of educating the sons of freemen and liverymen but had succeeded in becoming a local suburban school. Greatly increased facilities were needed to bring the school up to the standard it aimed at, but at the turn of the century the Company could not have provided sufficient capital for significant expansion. Although a chemical laboratory, which had been recommended in 1891, was built in 1901, the facilities still fell short of the requirements of a high-grade secondary school. Then Middlesex County Council and Hornsey Council came to the rescue by agreeing to pay for six new classrooms and a workshop which were opened in 1912. Strangely enough, the improvements failed to raise standards and the number of pupils dropped to about half. The appointment of a new headmaster, John Huck, in 1913, was expected to introduce reforms but these were inevitably shelved during the First World War and it was not until after the armistice that the school at Hornsey began to expand and flourish. A new organ was installed in memory of the Old Boys killed in the War and this encouraged musical activities. The school choir was asked to sing at the Stationers' Company's Richard Johnson service when it was held in Hendon and at the Ash Wednesday service in St Faith's, the latter continuing until the closure of the school in 1983 (see p.144). In the last years, the boys came to Stationers' Hall before the service and were regaled with sausage and mash in the Stock Room under the aegis of the Beadle, while their elders joined the Livery for the latter-day equivalent of Norton's 'cakes and ale' in the Hall. In 1938 Liverymen, Old Boys and parents subscribed to the purchase of a playing field at Winchmore Hill and by December 1939 two extensions to the school were completed, and the 'temporary' Tin Temple which had been in use for 46 years was at last demolished.

The early inter-war years produced a number of boys who went on to distinguished careers. Several also played an active part in the Stationers' Company. Since the closure of the school, a continuing link has been forged by the admission of Old Stationers to the Freedom whether or not they worked in the Trades of the Guild. Some who joined the Livery before the school closed were, most notably, Kenneth Day, Archibald (Archie) Donaldson OBE, editor of the *Dental Journal*, founder of the Dental Association

38 Stationers' School Register of Scholars 1861-1913.

Museum and worker for Quaker causes, who helped with cataloguing the Company's library, and Past Master George Riddell, OBE (d. 1998).

The First World War had caused stagnation; the Second caused some upheaval. Two hundred and seventy-two boys with 26 staff were evacuated to Wisbech in September 1939 and billeted on local families while attending classes at Wisbech Grammar School, Queen's School and in assorted church halls. There were many, mostly predictable, problems, as a visiting alderman reported. Growing boys are huge eaters and there were numerous complaints that the billeting allowance was 'not sufficient to feed the boy'. Although rationing had not yet been introduced, one boy was expelled from five or six billets because he ate too much.[39] In 1940 the mayor and corporation of Wisbech were awarded the Company's Silver Medal.

During the Blitz of 1940 the Wood Street estate in the City, which the Company had purchased in 1619 from the bequests of John and William Norton, George Bishop, Christopher Meredith and Henry Billage, was destroyed (see p.117). Rather than undertake the responsibility of redeveloping it after the war, the Company decided to sell it for what then seemed the enormous price of £25,000 and in 1946 the Clerk reported that £11,731 had been credited to the School Governors' fund as the school's proportion of the proceeds; a further £14,456 was due in war damage compensation.[40]

The school at Hornsey suffered only minor war damage of shattered panes of glass, broken roof tiles and the loss of a cycle shed. More than 400 boys re-assembled at the school after the war but the preparatory school for the seven- to twelve-year-olds, separately housed at Oakfield Road from 1932, never re-opened, having been eliminated by the 1944 Education Act.[41] Old Boys were killed during the hostilities and in 1950 their memory was honoured by a stained glass window in the school assembly hall.

The school entered the post-war years as a successful non-fee-paying north London Grammar School with voluntary aided status, which brought an increase in local authority funding yet allowed the Stationers' Company to retain a two-thirds majority on the Board of Governors. There followed some of the school's best years; the arrangement worked and the school functioned well. The headmaster responsible for setting the school on its feet after the disruption of the war was S.C. Nunn, who is remembered as a quiet, kindly man and a shrewd judge of character. Competition was encouraged by the house system and discipline was enforced by prefects as well as staff. All sixth formers had prefectoral powers and could give detentions for offences which ranged from assault and battery to eating two puddings at dinner.[42]

The 1960s were tumultuous years in many spheres, not least in the re-organisation of local government and education. The London Government Act of 1963 replaced Middlesex County Council with nine boroughs, and the Stationers' School, which had

39   Extract from report of 16 September 1939 S8/29, Brown box School, unclassified.
40   Court Book k, p.575, 5 December 1944, 12 December 1947.
41   Robert Baynes, *A History of the Stationers' Company's School 1858-1983* (1987), pp.55, 59-60, and private information from Mr Baynes.
42   School Prefects' Detention Book 1945-46, Brown box School, unclassified.

previously been in the Borough of Hornsey, found that its local education authority was now the much larger Borough of Haringey. The school inspectors repeatedly stressed the need to modernise the school and its equipment, and the Company was app-roached for financial assistance in building extensions. The Court, without much discussion of the matter, regretted that the Company could not contribute on the scale required and in 1964 took the only way it saw of financing needed improvements by applying for voluntary controlled status for the school. The Ministry of Education took over such capital costs as new buildings and running costs including staff salaries, but the Company lost its two-thirds majority on the Board of Governors and now had only six governors out of eighteen. For a few years it continued to take an interest in the well-being of the school, contributing towards the cost of equipment for a language laboratory and computer room, then quite an innovation. One Old Boy recalls the early years of the new technology in the school which he believes launched him on a successful career in computing.

The London Borough of Haringey, meanwhile, drew up a schools development plan and when this was approved in 1967 the Stationers' Company's School was converted from a selected entry grammar school into one of the 14 comprehensives in the borough. The entire character and organisation of the school changed when 214 chil-dren and staff from the William Forster secondary modern school joined forces with Stationers', swelling the numbers for 1967-68 to 785. By 1973 they had risen to over 1,200.[43] Moreover, these were children of mixed ability from a multi-ethnic community—some entered the school unable to read or write English. The headmaster, Robert Baynes, calculated that about a quarter of his pupils were of Cypriot origin, a quarter Caribbean, a quarter Anglo-Saxon/Celtic and the remaining quarter came from all corners of the globe with a preponderance of Asians. He rose to the challenge and when the school was inspected in July 1968 tribute was paid to its smooth running, to the integration of pupils of different abilities, the competence of the teachers and the leadership of the headmaster, but, as always throughout the school's 107-year history, now more than ever, 'the need for additional accommodation cannot be overemphasised'.[44]

With a decline in the number of pupils over the next decade, space was at less of a premium but other problems came to the fore with the publication of a Green Paper on the re-organisation of Haringey secondary schools in 1977. It concluded that the borough could not maintain 14 comprehensive schools and Stationers', with its out-dated buildings and as a single sex school at a time when these were going out of fashion with educational theorists, was immediately under threat. Parents took fright and the intake of pupils fell. Governors, parents, teachers, pupils and Old Boys mounted a vigorous campaign to save the school from closure. Over 25,000 people signed a petition, the local M.P., Hugh Rossi, and the playwright Arnold Wesker lent their

---

43 Past Masters' annual report, Livery List, 1972-73.
44 Review of Secondary Education Type Schools 1968, Stationers' School Comprehensive Reorganisation
    correspondence c.1960-79.

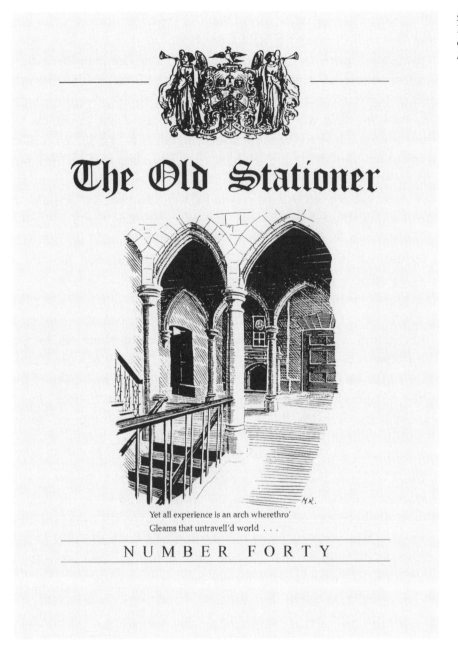

56. The school at Hornsey; cover design of *The Old Stationer*.

support and a deputation put its case to Dr Rhodes Boyson. Sir Keith Joseph, Secretary of State for Education and Science, was adamant and gave his approval to Haringey's decision which was, in fact, implementing a government policy directive to local education authorities.

The Stationers' School closed in July 1983 and the final edition of the school magazine *The Stationer* was published that month. The war memorial window was moved to Hornsey parish church; the organ went to a girls' school on the Isle of Wight; the pupils and some of the staff were transferred to the Langham School. The cups and trophies were taken to Stationers' Hall and some have since been given as educational awards under the Company's Educational Trust. When Reed's School had its silver trophies stolen, the Company was able to replace the most valuable with one from the former Stationers' Company's School. The centenary window was reinstalled in the Stock Room at Stationers' Hall, the portraits of the headmasters rehung on the stairs leading up to the library and the school records were put in safekeeping at the Hall where Mr Baynes and an Old Stationer honorary archivist have charge of them. The buildings were eventually bulldozed by Haringey Council.

A dwindling core of Old Stationers continues to lunch together, play football and reminisce. Their magazine, the *Old Stationer*, still circulates to members of the Old Stationers' Association and in 1996 they held a centenary dinner of the association at Stationers' Hall, attended by the Master and Wardens and the clerk.

What steps did the Company take to stave off the school's closure? Over the years the school came to be more and more integrated in the local community and to grow away from its City roots. Particularly after the revolutionary changes of 1964, the Court seemed to lose interest in what had once been its pride and joy, the flagship of its charities. Now that the dust has settled and the full facts are known, it is clear that, even if the Company had been quicker off the mark, the school was doomed because central government and local authority were both set on its closure. The headmaster understood what they were up against, but there was disappointment and resentment among staff and boys that the Company did not take active steps to save the school.

The Educational Charity

The fact is that the Company was *not* quick off the mark because the consultative document which the borough sent for consideration in 1980 was not drawn to the attention of the Master and Wardens' Committee for some weeks after it had been received. At which point it appointed a committee under the chairmanship of Sir Derek Greenaway who, with David Wyndham-Smith, was empowered to take legal advice and negotiate with Haringey Council and the Charity Commissioners. It was clear that the school's fate was sealed and that the committee must concentrate on salvaging what could be salvaged. The objectives now were 'I. To realise the maximum value of the property' and '2. To get approval from the Charity Commisioners to use the money outside Haringey with as much freedom as possible.'[45] The problem was that the existing trust deed stipulated that the trust money had to be spent on the Haringey school. The Council fought hard to gain control of the property. Among a number of proposals which were utterly unacceptable to the Court were the suggestions that the Company donate the building to Haringey for its own use, that the site be turned into a public park to be called Stationers' Park, or that the land be sold and the proceeds used to finance one of the remaining comprehensive schools in the borough. There followed four and a half years of hard bargaining and much legal consultation. Counsel's advice was that the Company should obtain a new trust deed which should refer back to the

45 'The Educational Charity. Brief Background Facts' [1986]. Stationers' archive, the educational charity.

original terms of the loan bequests which stipulated financial assistance to young Stationers. The Charity Commission agreed to this in principle although it restricted the educational uses to which the money could be put but this was the best result that could be obtained. The final result, after a battle royal with Haringey, was that the borough bought the property from the Company for £1 million, and the Charity Commissioners approved a new trust deed for the money to be invested in an educational charity for young people under the age of twenty-five (though this age limit might be waived in exceptional circumstances), normally working in the printing, stationery, publishing or associated trades. When negotiations were finally concluded and the new charity established, Sir Derek Greenaway and David Wyndham-Smith gave way to younger men and Alan Brooker succeeded to the chair.

The new trust took over the administration of existing educational funds, such as the Francis Mathew Memorial travelling scholarship (Francis Mathew was manager of *The Times* from 1946 to 1965), and the Prize and Scholarship Fund originally intended for pupils of the Stationers' Company's School. Awards are given to students in the trades of the guild. Those who qualify may be doing journalism courses at the City University, craft bookbinding or paper conservation at Camberwell College of Arts and Crafts or studying media and communications, for the City and Guilds examinations. In its first decade the new educational charity gave preference to applications by former pupils of the Stationers' Company's School, but by 1995 the youngest boy in the school had turned 25 and no longer came within the terms of the trust.

The Duchess of York presented the first six major scholarships of up to £5,000 at the *Excellence '87* exhibition.[46] Since those early days the charity has broadened its terms of reference. It provides an annual bursary for Reed's School, at one time gave a number of grants to students of the London College of Printing, as it then was, and has equipped school printing departments to encourage schoolboys and girls to take an interest in printing. It has funded printing equipment at Reed's School, Cobham; King Edward's, Witley; Wisbech Grammar School; King's School, Canterbury; and Chigwell, Durham and Bootham Schools. Since 1999 it has added an Islington school. The Company's Schools Liaison Committee keeps in touch with them and an annual schools day is held at Stationers' Hall. The trust also hosts an annual awards luncheon at the hall in June each year for the trust's prize winners.

The Stationers' Company and Technical Education

In 1873 the Stationers' Company was drawn into the movement for technical education through the influence of Sir Sydney Waterlow, Master and Lord Mayor (1872-3). Whole-hearted involvement with the improvement of technical education in the printing trades came in the 1920s, largely owing to Liveryman J.R. Riddell.

---

46 *Excellence '87* brochure, Stationers' Company library, ZCKA Box 6. The event was organised at Stationers' Hall by the Master, Allen Thompson and his wife, liveryman Josephine Thompson.

The St Bride Foundation Institute founded as an evening institute in 1894 was one of the success stories of the movement for technical education. Day classes started in 1912. The first Principal J.R. Riddell (Principal 1912-39) persuaded the Company to give prizes to students of the St Bride Printing School; he urged the Company to forge closer links with the printing trades and was the driving force behind the formation of the Stationers' Company and London County Council Printing Industry Technical Board. Situated in St Bride Lane and with a printing school, library and recreational facilities, the St Bride Foundation Institute was backed from the outset by the London County Council Technical Board, the Linotype Company, the Master Printers' Association and the Printers' Managers and Overseers' Association. Cholmeley Austen Leigh of Spottiswoode and Co. and a liveryman of the Stationers' Company, was an early supporter; several members of the Company were on the Board of Governors and in the first decades of this century Edward Unwin senior, W. Howard Hazell, Lord Riddell and of course J.R. Riddell (all of them liverymen of the Company) actively promoted the work of the St Bride Printing School, which in 1922 moved into larger premises south of the river and became the London School of Printing. With the establishment of the Stationers' Company and Printing Industry Technical Board in 1920 students from the Printing School came to Stationers' Hall to take examinations, to receive certificates and awards and to listen to lectures.

During the 1890s, however, the Stationers were deaf to appeals for financial support from both the London County Council Technical Education Board and from the City and Guilds Institute. The London County Council persevered, approaching the Stationers again in 1910 in the hope that the Company might provide a scholarship for research work in book binding. This elicited the customary reply of insufficient funds, although the General Purposes Committee thought that the Company could support an annual prize of five guineas and a silver medal to be offered in the examinations at the City and Guilds Institute in South Kensington.[47] The idea caught on and in 1912 the Company gave three prizes to student-apprentices living within a 20-mile radius of Stationers' Hall who obtained the highest marks in the Honours examinations in Typography, Bookbinding and Lithography.[48] The prizes were awarded annually until the Stationers' Company Printing and Industry Technical Board was founded and the prizes transferred to that Board's examinees.

The Court was to discover that the giving of prizes did not bring power. It was thought that in view of the Company's generosity and the fact that 'there are few industries which send a greater number of students to be examined by the Institute' a representative Stationer should have a place on the Council of the City and Guilds but the application was tactfully refused.[49] While the Court recovered its equilibrium, a letter arrived from

47 Court Book g, 1 November, 6 December 1910.
48 Livery List 1911, 1912.
49 Court Book g, 6 March 1917.

J.R. Riddell of the St Bride Printing School inviting a representative of his Company to attend a meeting 'to further the cause of technical education in the printing business' (1917).[50] The invitation was accepted and the Company was soon committed to the cause.

The Stationers' Company and Printing Industry Technical Board

Edward Unwin, already familiar with Riddell and the St Bride Foundation through his chairmanship of the Printing School Committee, attended the meeting and reported to the Company favourably, whereupon the Court agreed unanimously on 'the urgent necessity of improved technical education'. The meeting concluded in haste: 'warning was given of the attempted approach of hostile aircraft and in obedience to official instructions members of the Court took cover in the basement'.[51]

With the return to normality after the First World War, an annual meeting to further technical education was held at Stationers' Hall, the Company donated medals and prizes to students at the St Bride Printing School and took positive steps to improve technical education through the Stationers' Company and Printing Industry Technical Board which organised craft lectures and examinations at Stationers' Hall.[52]

The first chairman was Edward Unwin, Master 1920-1, and J.R. Riddell soon became its honorary secretary, who was responsible with the Stationers' Company for drawing up a scheme for examinations (Unwin and G.B. Eyre represented the Company on the examinations committee) and appointing examiners. The trade associations were asked to contribute not less than five guineas a year; candidates paid a fee of 1s. 6d. 372 students entered for the first examinations in 1921, and by 1936 there were 1,252; the first examinations were in composing, cylinder machine operating, lithography and book-binding, later extending to cover 21 subjects.[53]

The board also founded a series of craft lectures at Stationers' Hall, held in the winter months, which superseded the trade lectures at St Bride's (1917-22) after the St Bride Printing School had moved to larger premises in Stamford Street.[54] There the Company usually made an annual donation of £25 to its funds. The inaugural lecture was given by the Rt. Hon. Lord Riddell, whose printing interests spanned *Country Life* and the *News of the World*. His subject, chosen to appeal to the aspiring young men in his audience, was The Printing Business as a Career.[55] The lectures were followed by discussion. The lectures were later published in six handsome volumes which included an account of the proceedings and a brief biography of the Master of the Company.[56] They continued

---

50 Court Book g, 2 October 1917.
51 Court Book h, April 1920.
52 For later developments see Chapter One.
53 Minutes of the Stationers' Company and Printing Industry Technical Board 1920-52, St Bride Printing Library. Minutes of Meetings of SCPITB 1921-45. Court Book h, 2 November and 7 December 1920.
54 It changed its name to the London School of Printing.
55 Lord Riddell was no relation to J.R. or G.L. Riddell.
56 The volumes were presented to the Company by J.R. Riddell and his son Dr George Riddell and are now in the Company's library.

until the winter of 1939-40 when they were cancelled 'due to national emergency', as were the examinations of the Standing Committee of the Printing Industry Technical Board— in any case the increasing number of candidates (1,590 in 1939) made it unlikely that the examinees could continue to be accommodated at Stationers' Hall, even though the examinations were spread over several evenings.

When the situation was reviewed after the Second World War the board's trustees concluded that technical examinations in the printing and associated trades would be better conducted by the City and Guilds Institute which had national status and was by that time working effectively as an examining body. A note of 1945 indicated that the continuance of the Printing Industry Technical Board, was 'no longer justified' and in 1952 it was finally acknowledged that lectures and instruction in the printing trades were being adequately provided elsewhere. Edward Unwin junior, who had succeeded his father on the board, supplied a fitting epitaph to the valuable work of the Stationers' Company and Printing Industry Technical Board, the Beadle was given two guineas for his trouble and remaining funds were allocated to the St Bride Foundation.[57]

In 1957 the Company started a new series of annual Livery Lectures, given by men of wide practical experience in subjects that are relevant to the printing and associated industries.

Charities and education stand together in the Company's list of objectives. The Company's pensioners and those who have fallen on hard times continue to be beneficiaries but larger sums are given to the sponsorship of book trade charities such as the Book Trade Benevolent Society, the Printers' Charitable Corporation and the Bookbinders' Charitable Society. In addition the Company makes donations to a wide variety of good causes, chiefly those with City connections such as the Corporation of London Widows' and Orphans' Fund, the Guildhall School of Music, and the National Library for the Blind. Since the closure of the Company's school and the setting up of the Educational Charity in the mid-1980s, the largest donations have been made in grants to young people in the book and allied trades and the setting up of printing departments in a number of schools.

57 30 April 1952, Minutes of Stationers' Company and Printing Industry Technical Board.

CHAPTER EIGHT

The Stationers' Hall

ANN SAUNDERS

This volume on the Stationers' Company and its Hall begins properly in 1800 but, if we are to understand the history of the building, we must start the story some twenty-five years earlier. On 7 May 1776, John Rivington being Master, the Court of Assistants:

> Resolved that this matter be referred back to the Stock keepers to consult the Surveyor as to the manner in which he would propose to cover the vacant Ground before the Hall and case the outsides of the Buildings from which the Old Houses have been pulled down for the present; and to procure a Plan to be hereafter executed.[1]

Two months later, on 2 July 'Mr Mylne the Surveyor attending', a plan was laid before the Court.

This was the first time that Robert Mylne is mentioned in the Court Books; three generations of the family were to serve the Company as Surveyors. It is with him that this chapter must begin since it was he who gave the Hall its present appearance.

Robert Mylne (1733-1811) was descended from a long line of Scottish master masons. Three of his ancestors had served the entire Stuart dynasty as Master Masons to the Scottish Crown; his father, Thomas, was surveyor to the City of Edinburgh. In 1754, at the age of 21, having served a thorough apprenticeship as a carpenter, Robert set out for Rome, travelling in less affluent conditions, but at the same time as Robert Adam. In 1758, he won the Silver Medal for architecture at St Luke's Academy, an honour never before achieved by a Briton, and made several useful friendships, including the artist and engraver Giovanni Battista Piranesi. He returned home in the following year, reaching London in July, when designs were being sought for a new bridge over the Thames at Blackfriars. Mylne entered the competition, was short-listed and in February 1760 was declared the winner. That one so young and so untried should succeed was considered a marvel, by Mylne himself as well as by such critics as Dr Johnson; nevertheless his design, spanning the river in nine elegant, elliptical arches, was carried to completion and was opened in November 1769, the doctor and the architect having, by that time, become friends. Piranesi published a superb engraving of the bridge while under construction.

The young engineer's name must have been well known in responsible City circles, not only for his work on the bridge but also as Surveyor to St Paul's Cathedral and to

---

1 Court Book M, 7 May 1776.

the New River Company. An entry in Mylne's diary for 8 January 1782, however, hints that it may have been no chance that the Stationers' Company's choice fell on him during John Rivington's Mastership: 'Paid bills of £524 16s. 3d. work done for Mr Rivington which, as an old friend, I surveyed for nothing'.[2]

The handling of so much work without reward by way of friendship suggests a long and close relationship but there is no indication of how or when it began. In a later generation, this friendship was to be cemented by marriage.

The buildings to be put in Mylne's care lay on the north side of Ludgate Hill and extended over the best part of an acre. The Stationers had purchased for £3,500 the Hall and site in 1611 from the Earl of Abergavenny and his sons; in the 14th century, the property had belonged to the Countess of Pembroke, founder of Pembroke College, Cambridge.[3] Everything was swept away in the Great Fire of 1666, but the Stationers rebuilt their Hall with the aid of Peter Mills, the City Surveyor. On 13 August 1669, he made his entry in the *Survey of Building Sites*: 'five foundacions set out the day abovesaid scituate in Avemaria Lane belonging to the said Company containing upon the front North and South 96 foot from the middle of each party wall; and in depth East and West 40 foot'.[4]

A battered and rather puzzling ground plan among the Stationers' archives may have some relationship to the entry.[5] It is on stout unwatermarked paper, measuring 13 by 28 inches; the endorsement reads 'The Company of ye stationers fayer plots' and the same 17th-century hand has identified the rooms along the north side:

> The warehouse and court room
> Wardens Roome
> Skreene [beyond which the Hall extends without further identification]
> Loby and stayr / lobby for atendauncs
> Ye Courthouse / kichin
> Ye Wardens room

The range of buildings on the west (left-hand) side, which today forms the administration block, is unlabelled; to the east (right-hand) are faint outlines for the small houses that had been, and would be again, on Ave Maria Lane; to the south, Cock Alley is marked and a scale in feet is given. The outline of the Hall, however, is far more like an actual survey of a building in existence, delineated in pen and wash, the windows corresponding to those of the present Hall, but on the south-east corner the outline of an unrealised structure has been added in what looks like a later hand. It is labelled

---

2   The MS diaries are in the possession of the Royal Institute of British Architects. The text was published in 1955 by Sir Albert Richardson.

3   For a fuller discussion of the medieval site, see Ann Saunders, 'The Stationers' Hall', in *The Stationers' Company and the Booktrade 1550-1990*, ed. Robin Myers and Michael Harris (1997).

4   Printed by the London Topographical Society, 1962, No. 97, f.52v.

5   Stationers' Archives, Box G (2) 21. Professor Michael Cooper of City University gave careful study to this plan, for which I am most grateful.

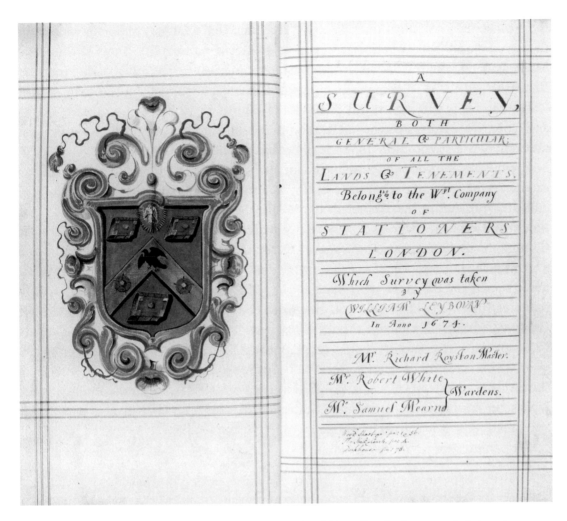

Parlor, but does not equate with any known building. In the bottom left-hand corner of the sheet, what appears to be the same hand has added a sketch of a doorway with a round window above it, and the outline of a moulding, possibly for a cornice.

The precise dating of this sheet remains a puzzle but it does establish that the Court Room has occupied its present position ever since the post-fire rebuilding. In the absence of archaeological evidence, we cannot be certain that the builder used the foundations of Abergavenny House for the new Hall, but it seems more likely than not. The proportions of the easternmost lobby, kitchen and Wardens' room correspond closely with those of the present-day Stock Room and Crush Landing. The rebuilding, begun briskly in 1669, thereafter went slowly and was not completed until 1673.[6]

Life was getting back to normal. In 1674, the Company commissioned William Leybourn to make a survey of all their land and tenements which he did in great detail

6 Robert Wapshott or Wapshol was paid £905 for brickwork, drains, slating and plastering; Henry Foord (or Ford) had £732 for the carpentry work and Mr Pollard received £33 for the painting. On 6 November 1674 Stephen Colledge was engaged to panel the Hall with wainscotting for £300; this unfortunate man was later to be the last to be executed for expressing treasonable opinions in print.

in a handsomely bound volume,[7] showing the Hall itself with tiny buildings to the east in the Inner and Outer Courts, as well as properties in Cock Alley, Amen Corner, Ave Maria Lane, Great Wood Street, Milk Street, Friar Alley and the Dark House in Billingsgate. These had come as bequests or had been acquired as investments by the English Stock, which indeed still owned the Hall itself.

Leybourn's survey provides much fascinating detail about these small properties, but unfortunately gives no more than the outline of the Hall. A document of 1 March 1757, however, does allow us a glimpse of the interior of the Court Room. This is a contract drawn up between the Company and William Robinson of Friday Street[8] for the enlargement and redecoration of the Court Room and lobby. Attached to the agreement are scaled ground plans, a wash drawing of the south front, a section through the building showing the space allotted to warehousing and carefully executed designs for the decoration of the room which pay particular attention to the handsome fireplace and the design of the ceiling.

On 21 June 1771, the English Stock finally conveyed the Hall and garden to the Company, though it retained the other properties. Two years later, in 1773, a careful inventory was drawn up in a large volume, giving details of every tenement and warehouse, with the ownership and terms of occupancy of each.[9] The total income from all the property amounted to £686 7s. 0d. of which £519 3s. 0d. went to the English Stock. It was perhaps because of this new beginning that such an able man as Mylne was appointed as Surveyor to the Company.

The Minutes for 2 July 1776 read:

> Mr Mylne the Surveyor attending laid before this Court ... a Plan for rebuilding on the Companys Ground in Ave Maria Lane, Amen Corner and Stationers Court to be hereinafter executed; and proposing that the vacant Ground should be inclosed with an open Palisadoe and that the outsides of the Old Buildings should be cased for the present in rough cast.

Resolved:

> That the vacant ground shall be forthwith inclosed and the outside of the Buildings cased as proposed by Mr. Mylne.

The 'palisadoe' may well have been erected—the eastern approach from Ave Maria Lane has always been the unprotected approach to the site—but no major action was taken with regard to the Hall. The Court Minutes, re-inforced by Mylne's diaries, show him frequently in attendance as required, dealing with a multiplicity of small problems

---

7   Stationers' Archives, *Survey of all the lands and tenements belonging to the Worshipful Company of Stationers, London, which Survey was taken by William Leybourn in anno 1674.*

8   Howard Colvin, *A Biographical Dictionary of British Architects*, 3rd ed. (1995), p.831, describes him as 'of Bow Lane'. In 1733, Robinson published a 32-page volume entitled *Proportional Architecture*. He was among those who tendered for work on the new Mansion House. I am most grateful to Dr Sally Jeffery, architectural historian to the Corporation of London, and to Simon Bradley of the *Buildings of England*, for helpful discussions over this contract.

9   A partial transcription is given in Blagden, pp.223-4.

and enquiries—the renewal of leases,[10] an argument, happily resolved without litigation, over the erection of a wall at the west end of the garden by Mr Rowley,[11] repairs to the Treasurer's apartments,[12] the whitewashing of the Hall, lobby and Stock Keeper's rooms[13] in the summer of 1788.

Then, in the summer of 1789, major work required on the old Hall became urgent. Mylne reported to the Master, Thomas Field:[14]

July 25th 1789

Sir

According to your request, I reviewed and examined the Walls of Stationers Hall, and find, that altho' they are in general very thick and strong, there is a defect in one part of them.—

In the East side, or front Wall, towards the Court there is a bulge or swelling outwards, in the Brickwork, of the upper part of the 2nd pier from the great Door of entrance into the Hall, where the Rainwater pipe is fixed to the Wall on the outside.—

The Wall is very fair and aparently sound, in the inside; where the plaister work and every thing else stands remarkably well.—

I am induced to suspect, that the wall at this place in question, is split in the middle of its thicknefs, longways; and that the outer face of it, is swelled outwards, by some cause, which does not appear and which may be owing to the arches of the Circular upper Row of windows, or to some timber in the middle of the thickness of the said Wall being rotten.—The inner part of the thicknefs of the wall stands well, as I said before; and supports its share of the weight of the Roof with sufficient stability.—But the outside should have something done to it; and I aprehend, if care is taken, the whole may be set to rights from the outside, without breaking thro' into the inside or even dirtying the new Whitewashing and Varnishing done to the Hall last Season.—

Some years agoe, I had occasion to examine the whole of the Roof, and recomended to the Company to take off, the present heavy tyling, and cover it with a light slating on boarding.—Something like that or Copper Covering should be put on it, that the Roof may rest with a lefs weight on the side walls, which stand very well in almost all their parts, but would be in a much better state and likely to stand longer, if such an alteration or improvement was made to this Building.—

A few weeks later on 1 September Mylne reported yet again, emphasising the need for a new roof.[15] He was asked for an estimate, appeared before the Court of 6 October to answer questions, and was asked to deliver his advice in writing. This he did in a letter of 19 October:[16]

10 Court Book O, 3 April 1792.
11 Court Book O, 16 November 1789, 24 November 1790, 12 January 1791, 4 February 1779.
12 Court Book N, 2 August 1785.
13 Court Book O, 1 July 1788.
14 Stationers' Archives, Box G, 14, i.
15 Court Book O, 1 September 1787, 6 October, 3 November 1789; 13 April, 1 June 1790.
16 Stationers' Archives, Box G, 14, iii.

1st The great utility and propriety of taking off, the present tyle covering, repairing the timbers, and putting on a new good slate covering at £175, as estimated;—In order to lighten the great weight thereof, which is charged, first, on the strength of the roof itself, and ultimately on the side walls.—

2nd That the present Tyle Covering requires to be new rip't and relaid, at all events, at this time; from the laths and other circumstances being bad; which, with other expenses contingent thereon, would in itself amount to £50 or more.—

3rd That the Side and one End Walls are defective, about ten feet down from the Gutters, and all round by a small thicknefs of their outer surface of the brickwork, from 4 to 9 Ins in thicknefs, being detached, seperated [sic], and having no bond with the inner thicknefs of 3 feet of sound brickwork, which is sufficiently strong to maintain the building and support the Roof, (when lightened as above mentioned,) for 100 years to come, proper care being taken of it.

4th That if the Building and its Roof is left in its present situation, and each part of it was to be repaired, as it becomes defective, in the same manner, as that lately done, on the front or East side;—There will not be an expectancy of its duration, but that it most probably will be required to be rebuilt, in a third part of that time.—

and lastly

That the best thing which could be done by the Company, would be to case the two sides and south end, with a thin sheeting of stone, from the Ground to the top of the Parapet; Which casing would protect all its defective parts from the weather; and would give an opurtunity [sic] of removing the thin substance of brickwork above mentioned round the upper part of it; which is an injury to its strength, and will always be a subject of repair.—

Faced with considerable expense, the Court required time to consider and it was ten years before a special committee was set up and the work put in hand. Almost inevitably, further defects were revealed once the task had begun and the committee were forced to authorise additional expenditure. On 3 March 1800 they reported what they had done, 'flattering themselves when finished the repairs will give satisfaction not only to the Members of the Court but to the Company at large'.[17]

A second report followed a few weeks later but at last the work was complete.

A comparison of engravings from *The London Almanack* for 1782 and 1802 gives us some idea of the changes wrought on the Hall. The earlier illustration shows it with the original pairs of windows each with a semi-circular clerestory window above. The entrance in the south-east corner is approached by steps, though a tree partially obscures the doorhood, but we can see clearly that the undercroft of the Hall is now a semi-basement for warehousing. A better representation of the pre-Mylne Hall is provided by a 1781 drawing by Carter; the building can be seen clearly, set apart from the outside world by handsome railings and a decorative gateway. These presumably

17 Muniment Room, Series I G, 3, iii, iv.

provided the recommended 'Palisadoe' though no bill for them can be found among the archives.

The 1802 Almanack gives us a first sight of the re-fronted Hall in all its up-to-date elegance. The brickwork had disappeared behind a stone facing, the sheltering doorhood had been replaced by a flatter treatment of the entrance, and the upper row of oval windows had vanished behind square Coade stone panels adorned with putti representing the Four Seasons. A large patera and an oblong plaque with griffins completed the new decorations. The need to repair the Hall had provided an opportunity to give it a modernising face-lift, bringing its appearance into harmony with the changes which were transforming the late 18th-century City. Behind the new façade, Stephen Colledge's wainscotting still snugly lined the Hall.

Naturally enough, the Stationers were proud of their Hall and wished to adorn it. On 13 April 1778 the Court heard that a painting intended as a present for them from Alderman Josiah Boydell was now finished. The Court resolved 'That Mr. West the painter thereof be requested to acknowledge by an Inscription on such painting (in such

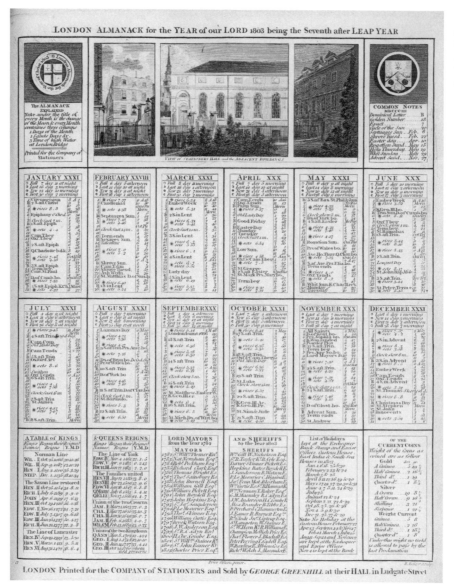

60. *Raven's Almanack* for 1803, showing the refaced east front of the Hall. Actual size 9in. by 7in.

Manner as he shall think proper) that the same is the Gift of Mr. Boydell to this Company of Stationers.'[18]

This was the enormous canvas (90 by 110 inches) which now fills the west end of the Court Room. It represents an otherwise unrecorded scene from English history; King Alfred, in hiding from the Danish invaders, divides his family's last loaf with a beggar or pilgrim; the family, standing behind him, do not look best pleased. The artist and his family served as models for the characters.

Alderman Boydell's generosity called forth similar beneficence from other members of the Company. In 1801, Alderman Thomas Cadell presented a large round-headed,

18   Court Book N, 13 April 1779. I am most grateful to Dr Elizabeth Einberg of the Tate Gallery for helpful discussion of the painting. See also Helmut von Erffa and Allen Storey, *The Paintings of Benjamin West* (1986), pp.187-8.

painted glass window which was inserted into the north wall of the Hall.[19] It was the work of the master craftsman, Francis Eginton (1737-1805). Glass from the post-fire windows, with the arms of the City and the Company, was respectfully retained and inserted; additional panels were provided by the artist. John Nichols (Master 1804), printer and historian of the book trade, considered it 'most brilliant ornament and admirably executed', and published an engraving of it in the *Gentleman's Magazine* in 1814.[20] The whole operation cost £418 17s. 4d.; the bill was met by Cadell's executors in June 1803, the Company contributing £90 towards the repair of brickwork and plaster.

During the 35 years that he served the Company as Surveyor, Robert Mylne waited upon the Stationers at the Hall, or inspected Company property, or represented their interests at City Corporation committees on more than a hundred occasions. The laconic entries in his diaries[21] give no information about his personal relationship with the Company, although he mentions dining at Stationers' Hall on 1 December 1810. Less than six months later, on 5 May 1811, he was dead. By his own wishes, he was buried in St Paul's Cathedral near to Sir Christopher Wren; his son was elected to succeed him as Company Surveyor on 24 June 1811.

William Chadwell Mylne (1781-1863) served the Company for 52 years, until his death. Apart from giving devoted attention to the Company's increasingly time-worn properties in Wood Street and Billingsgate, his main service was a general overhaul of the premises in 1825-6 and, more particularly, a re-ordering of the Court Room with the construction of an additional western extension, today called the Card Room. Expert advice was sought from Robert Smirke, later to be Sir Robert, the architect of the British Museum,[22] who expressed approval of the Surveyor's plans; a detailed specification was drawn up;[23] estimates for the work were sought and the lowest, from Mr Mansfield for £1,047, was accepted; requests to use the Hall were to be refused while building work was in progress. William Robinson's graceful ceiling remained undisturbed in the Court Room as did the fireplace. A supporting row of columns was set across the newly created opening between the two rooms; they were to be of scagliola work, painted to look like marble; the firm employed was to be either Brown of Carmarthen Street or Sealy of Pedlars Acre, Covent Garden. The new room was an irregular octagon; lacking windows, it was lit from above by a rectangular lantern. The whole undertaking, with the refurbishment of the Hall and kitchens, cost £1,652.

Meantime, another £1,038 5s. 8d. had had to be laid out on repairs to the Court Room, and further, smaller sums were spent at intervals during the stewardship of the second Mylne.

William Chadwell died on Christmas Day 1863. His son, Robert William, reported the death to the Court on 12 January 1864 and offered himself in his father's place; he was

19   Court Book N, 18 December 1800, 4 May, 25 May 1802, 1 November 1803. Box G, 10, 2.
20   *Gentleman's Magazine*, 1814, vol. 84, pt 2, p.417.
21   A.E. Richardson, *Robert Mylne, Architect and Engineer* (1955).
22   Court Book S, 17 June, 2 August, 4 October 1825.
23   Box G, 3, viii.

61. *Left.* The painted north window donated by Thomas Cadell, 1801.

62. *Right.* Window, installed 1894, replacing Cadell's window and showing William Caxton offering the first fruits of his press to Edward IV.

elected to it on 1 March and remained in the post till his own death in 1890. The minute reporting his decease spoke of his 'long and honourable connection with this Company' and conveyed sympathy to the family but only the most formal correspondence survives[24] and there are many fewer references to him in the Court Books than to his father and grandfather. In February 1867 he had to deal with the Universal Private Telegraph Company; one of their workmen 'who neither asked nor obtained permission to enter upon the premises', had come in and passed a wire over the roof of the Hall.

> The Telegraph Company appears to be established for communications between various Banking and other large Establishments in the Metropolis, and the wire passing over [the roof] is fixed between the premises of Messrs. Longman and Co., Paternoster Row, and Messrs. Strahan of Ludgate Hill.[25]

The Company recovered from this outrageous display of modernity and was sufficiently mollified to permit a second wire to be put in place the following year.

24   Box G, p.14, xi–xiv.
25   Court Book Z, 5 February 1867.

In August 1875 plans were made to create a new way through so that the Court Room might be approached without going through the Hall.[26] This would have involved inserting a gallery and in the end nothing came of it.

As the years pass, there are even fewer references to the third Mylne than might be expected, and a feeling grows that perhaps relationships were not entirely satisfactory between the Company and its Surveyor. In November 1879, the entry in the Court Book runs:

> That it be referred to the Clerk acting under the instructions of the Master and Wardens to take such steps as they may deem necessary for ascertaining the precise position of Mr. Mylne in his relation to the Company as their Surveyor appointed by the Resolution of the Court dated 1 March 1864.[27]

Four years later, there were distinct hints of trouble:

> 6 November 1883[28]
>
> The Court was informed that Mr. Mylne had submitted to the Stock Board an account of Messrs Bailey & Son amounting to £164.10/-s for supplying Hot water pipes in the new Warehouse now vacant situate in Ave Maria Lane which was not provided for in the Contract with Messrs Patman and Fotheringham and for which expenditure the Board had not given any precise authority and a Report from Mr. Mylne dated the 31st day of October last thereon having been read,

It was resolved unanimously that

> Henceforth no expenditure of any kind not already sanctioned to be incurred or directed or authorised by the Surveyor on behalf of the Company without the previous authority of the Stock Board or a Committee at the Court of the Company signified to the Surveyor by a memorandum in writing signed by the Master and countersigned by the Clerk and delivered to the Surveyor before the expenditure is incurred.

And that a copy of the preceding resolution be forwarded to Mr Mylne.

Towards the end of 1886, the Court was presented with a letter from Mylne claiming £112 'to be paid for plans partially adopted'. He wrote:

> I cannot proceed further until an assurance be given that my commission of the moiety of five per cent on the contract sum will be paid in full by or before the first week in October.

It was by then 2 November and the Court observed grimly that

> No progress appeared to have been made with the buildings up to Michaelmas Day although the contract was signed on the 27th day of August last.[29]

---

26 Court Book b, 3 August 1875.
27 Court Book b, 4 November 1879.
28 Court Book c, 6 November 1883.
29 Court Book c, 2 November 1886.

The Court decided to defer the matter till a future, unspecified, meeting. Just over a year later, on 10 January 1888, Mylne wrote to the Court again. His letter was read out but there is no hint of the contents and the letter does not survive. The Clerk was instructed to reply but, once again, no record remains of anything that may have passed; two and a half years later, the Surveyor was dead.

It is probably significant that Mylne's name is never minuted in relation to the greatest change to take place in the Hall during the 1880s. In 1885 the Master, Edmund Waller, presented the Company with two new stained glass windows for the west wall. They depicted St Cecilia and William Tyndale—the saint to represent the Company's musical affinities, Tyndale because of his translation of the Bible into English. They were the work of Mayer's, the Munich firm of stained glass manufacturers who maintained a London office until 1914. Their workmanship was superb but by the 1880s their designs in the heavy style of the Gothic Revival, made popular by Pugin, were going out of fashion in favour of the Art Nouveau; but the older style was to the taste of the wealthy City men for whom Mayer represented the best that money could buy.

Joshua Butterworth, who came of a family of 18th-century Fleet Street law booksellers, was bound to the trade and admitted to the Livery when he was 21; he was Renter Warden at 30 but was not called into Court until he was 72 and at 77 became Master. He had other, non-trade, antiquarian interests—both he and his father were admitted fellow of the Society of Antiquaries of London within a few months of each other. Those who signed Joshua Butterworth's election certificate in January 1848, described him as 'a gentleman conversant with the history and literature of this country ... likely to become a useful and valuable member thereof'. On his admission, he presented—in those days you just picked up such things and gave them away or kept them and gloated over them—a portion of the Roman pavement found in Gresham Street. He was an active fellow and three years later he had the Society's collections of ballads, proclamations and broadsides rearranged and bound. A number of items relate to the Stationers' Company and the collection is still one of the prize possessions of the Antiquaries' library. In 1888 he presented the Company with the Shakespeare window as a companion piece to those of Tyndale and St Cecilia which his friend Edmund Waller, a successful fancy stationer in Fleet Street, donated as his gift as Master in 1885. None of the worthies in the west windows—Caxton, Cranmer, St Cecilia, Shakespeare or Tyndale—was a member of the Stationers' Company.

In June 1893, while Upper Warden, Butterworth wrote to the Court pointing out that 'It is frequently remarked that the present north window should be replaced by one more in accord with the West windows'.[30] He planned the north window as his gift as Master in 1894, and begged for 'permission to remove' the Cadell window at his own expense 'and replace it with a stained glass window to be executed by the artists who provided the West windows ... The design I have chosen,' he wrote, 'is one connected with the Company's

30 Court Book d, 6 June 1893.

trade and includes the Company's arms and insignia with the device of several eminent printers who were members of the Company in the sixteenth century.'

A huge new window was accordingly inserted, filled with a wholly fictitious scene of Caxton displaying his press to Edward IV and his Queen, Elizabeth Woodville.[31] The anonymous artists appear, from the Germanic style of their work, to have been working in-house for Mayer and Butterworth may have directed them for the main subject to Daniel Maclise's vast 1856 painting of the same subject at Knebworth. The Maclise is a much more exact representation of a printing house interior, but no more historically correct. The surround of the picture contains the devices of eminent early printers, all except one being members of the Company; Wynkyn de Worde, Caxton's successor, was not a Stationer. Above him is the device of Reyner Wolf, who though a foreigner was four times Master of the Company, dying, like Butterworth, in office in 1573. Below that is Richard Tottel, first law publisher of Fleet Street, to whom in some sense Butterworth's were successors. On one side is John Day, first printer of Anglo-Saxon and of music and the first English printer to use italics. He used several devices and this one, punning on his name, shows an angel arousing another with the motto 'Arise for it is day': the art of printing dispelling the night of ignorance. This was the kind of thing which particularly appealed to Victorian romantic patriots. Bottom right is Hugh Singleton, an original member of the Stationers' Company. Top centre are the Company's arms with the dates— 1403, that of the first coming together of the manuscript text-writers and illuminators, and 1557, the year of the Company's incorporation. For good measure the artist added (bottom centre) the last of the Company's six ceremonial barges which was sold in 1850. Cadell's painted glass vanished and while we must for ever regret the loss, there is no doubt it would not have accorded with the style of the west windows.

In the 1980s and 1990s several events were commemorated in stained glass, albeit cost necessitated a smaller scale of operations—a stained glass window in the Stock Room marked the closure of the Company's school in 1983; in 1984 the granting of the Honorary Freedom and Livery to the Prince of Wales, and in 1987 the quincentenary of paper making in England, were celebrated by windows on the east side of the Hall.

Returning to Mylne, the building works to which the 1886 Minute refers must have been the reconstruction of the eastern wing of the Company's premises.[32] Since the fire, this had been a three-storey warehouse; at its heart was the Stock Room where that side of the Stationers' business was transacted; the end of the range had provided accommodation for the Treasurer. There is scarcely any mention of this part of the building in either the Court Books or the miscellaneous papers; if they were still largely of post-fire construction, then indeed it was time that they should receive attention. The east wing was rebuilt in Portland stone. The panelling in the Stock Room, which may well be attributed to Henry Foord, was retained and adapted. A friendly little half-hexagonal

---

31 Much of the description of the north window is based on the text of a talk given at the Caxton window centenary celebration by Robin Myers, 4 May 1994.

32 Court Book c, 2 November 1886.

bay-window was added on the southern side with an hexagonal lantern above it; this must surely have been to Robert William Mylne's design and is today the one characteristic feature of Stationers' Hall visible and familiar to the public as they hurry along Ave Maria Lane or glance up Stationers' Court, which was once Cock Alley.

Before the end of the 19th century, the Company had managed to rid itself of several encumbering responsibilities. In 1874, the City acquired the Dark House for the development of Billingsgate Market, and in the following year the Company sold its interest in the Pellipar Estate in Ireland to the Skinners' Company for £40,000. The Wood Street property remained with the Company.

Judging from the Court Minutes, life continued tranquilly enough during the early years of the 20th century. The new Surveyor was Henry Dawson who, in 1905, succeeded in getting the rateable value of the Hall and offices reduced from £2,900 to £2,300. New heating apparatus was installed for £240 and consideration was given to the advisability of installing a lift for use during Livery dinners—would a device able to raise two hundredweight be sufficient? In the end nothing was done.[33] An antiquarian book exhibition was held in the Hall in 1904, French booksellers were entertained in 1908, and in 1911 the Royal Colonial Institute hired the Hall to welcome the President of Tasmania. In the same year, it was discovered that there were rats in the kitchens, and precautions had to be taken. Messrs Simpkin Marshall, who had been tenants since 1858, rented the basement under the Hall; their occupancy involved a good deal of alteration work, for which the Stationers' Company refused to pay half, though it did spend £225 5s. od. on modern kitchen equipment, and also contributed £1 7s. 6d. towards the cost of false teeth for a poor Freeman.

In October 1915, the Court 'resolved that the premium paid for insurance against aircraft risks upon buildings in their occupations the property of this Company amounting to £31 19s. be shared in equal moieties between Landlords and tenants'.[34] In 1919, it was proposed that an association should be formed to build over the Garden,[35] thus providing offices which could be let for £1,000 a year, but nothing came of the suggestion though the Company was looking earnestly at how its income could be increased by more widespread letting of the Hall—the newly equipped kitchens were felt to be a great asset. Routine repairs were carried out conscientiously but, when major alterations were mooted, the General Purposes Committee reported sharply that 'No progress can be made until some of the wealthier members of the Company come forward with substantial contributions'.[36] The matter was not raised again.

With the outbreak of the Second World War, the 2nd Battalion of the London Rifle Brigade was temporarily billeted in the Hall. This was coped with smoothly enough, but real danger to the old building came a year later. On 15 October 1940, an incendiary

33 Court Book b, 1 March 1881.
34 Court Book g, 5 October 1915.
35 Court Book h, 14 January 1919.
36 Court Book j, 30 July 1935.

bomb destroyed the roof of the Hall and Court Room, bringing down the elegant ceilings; the flames consumed the Court gowns, some of the portraits[37] and shields of the Masters' arms, and 'nearly all the filed copies of the works registered at the Hall'. The Archbishop of Canterbury and other well-wishers expressed their regrets, a resolution was passed 'that all items of historical or intrinsic interest' should 'be removed to a place of comparative safety', and that a temporary protective roof should be put over the building.[38] Mr Rivington, the Clerk, managed to find space for the valuables in the strong rooms at Cunard House, Leadenhall Street. Captain Douglas Harold Cox, one of the Stock Keepers, offered his father's cap and gown; Edward Hanslope Cox had been Master in 1916, and the clothing was accepted gratefully for the use of the present Master. Astonishingly, the stained-glass windows in the Hall remained relatively intact.

Worse was to come. The appalling raid of 29-30 December quite literally devastated the whole area round the Hall. On 14 January 1941, the Court was informed that 13-17 Ave Maria Lane, Amen Corner, 4 Stationers' Hall Court, 20 and 22 Ludgate Hill, 11, 12 and 13 Wood Street, as well as the Company's premises in Clements Court and Feathers Court, had all been destroyed by enemy action. The tenants occupying these buildings had, understandably, disclaimed their leases, thereby removing a good part of the Company's income. Further damage had been done to the Hall, and some of the windows of the Stock Room. All around the Hall, the destruction seemed complete.

Long afterwards, Ian Norrie assessed the devastation—and the reaction to it:

> The climax came on the night of 29-30 December when Paternoster Row and the surrounding streets were nearly all demolished. Longmans could supply between five and six thousand titles on 28 December but only twelve on the following Monday. Whitaker's were burned out, with all their records, but even so *The Bookseller* appeared on 21 January 1941, as usual, in Geoffrey Faber's phrase, 'without a hair out of place'. Simpkin's premises and total stocks were destroyed, a disaster from which the trade never completely recovered.

The City bookseller, Hubert Wilson, writing under the pseudonym Petrel, described the desolation in a memorable article in *The Bookseller*:

> It is the eve of the new year—and the hub of the English book trade lies in smoking ruins. Such a scene of destruction I have never seen or imagined ... With many others Simpkin's, Whitaker's, Longman's, Nelson's, Hutchinson's and, further afield, Collins and Eyre and Spottiswoode, are gutted shells. In their basements on Monday afternoon, glowed and shuddered the remnants of a million books. Gusts of hot air and acrid smoke blew across the streets, and around the outskirts of the devastation played the jets from the firemen's hoses.
>
> This would have been bad enough by itself. But these famous houses, and the streets in which they stood, marked only the boundaries of a scene of destruction so complete, so utterly irretrievable that it held me spellbound. Nowhere were pavements or road surfaces to

37 Including that of Elizabeth Leake, Samuel Richardson's second wife.
38 Court Book k, 5 November 1952.

63. The dome of
St Paul's among
the surrounding
bomb-flattened
area, 1940.

64. A painting of the bomb damage around the Hall.

be seen. From Warwick Square on the west to Ivy Lane in the east, from the Row nearly to Newgate Street, there lies now an undulating sea of broken yellow bricks. As I picked my way gingerly across from brick to brick, hot gouts of sulphurous fumes from buried fires seeped up between my feet; desultory flames played in the remains of a rafter here or a floor joint there, and on either side the smoking causeway fell sharply away into cavernous glowing holes, once basements full of stock, now the crematories of the City's book world. I looked around me in what was Paternoster Square and recognised nothing but a pillar box, the top beneath my feet; there was nothing left to recognise. Here and there half a wall stood in dangerous solitude, two or three stories high, giving form and significance to the desolation, and that was all. I was quite alone (for I had found my way in through a passage unsuspected by the police) and no living thing was to be seen.[39]

Back at Stationers' Hall, Messrs Dawson reported on 1 April 1941 that the erection of an independent steel roof would cost £1,500, but that the money should be recoverable from the War Damage Commission.[40]

The evacuation and storage of the fixtures and fittings such as the screen, the Royal arms and the chiffoniers in the Hall, the mantelpiece and mirror in the Court Room, the carving in the Stock Room, and the eight large tables and benches and the inlaid card tables, was undertaken with the advice and assistance of Sir Eric Maclagan, Director of the Victoria and Albert Museum, Mr Ralph Edwards, Keeper of Woodwork, and Mr

39   Ian Norrie, *Mumby's Publishing and Bookselling in the Twentieth Century* (1982), pp.87-8.
40   Court Book k, 1 April, 6 May 1941.

Jack and Mr Bennit of the Ministry of Works; the treasures were evacuated to Friar Park, Henley on Thames, the home of Lady David. In spite of everything, Court and Committee Meetings continued to be held at Stationers' Hall, those attending being cheered and sustained with hot coffee brewed by Mr Pitch the Beadle.

Work on a new, more permanent roof had begun by 1948 by Messrs Henry Dawson and Son with much of the detailed repairs under the supervision of Geoffrey H. Gurney, FRIBA, FRICS, who became Architect and Surveyor to the Company. It was possible to open the Hall to the public in August 1951, during the Festival of Britain, with a display of the Company's archives and treasures. In the following February,[41] the Court was informed that the restoration work was complete, though not all the costs were recoverable from the War Damage Commission, the Company needing to find £1,830 16s. 10d. On 4 May 1957, the Livery were at last able to dine together in their own Hall.

The unexpected and extraordinary windfall from the sale of the Ludgate Hill/Ave Maria Lane corner site (see p.99) made possible a further and most welcome rationalisation and refurbishment of the building. The low, westernmost range of warehousing against the remains of the City Wall, most recently used by Messrs Butterworth, was converted into proper, centrally-heated accommodation for the Clerk and for the Company staff. A passage and staircase were inserted to give an internal connection with the Court Room; this gave access to roof space in the western wing where it became possible to create a room for the Master's personal use. The kitchens were re-equipped to the highest standards. A new entrance, and an ingenious landing, onto which large assemblies may spill, was inserted into the staircase leading up to the Stock Room in the eastern wing. All this was the responsibility of Geoffrey Gurney.

So, how can we best sum up this miscellany of the centuries which make up the involved—and evolved—structure which is Stationers' Hall? Perhaps the best plan is to take a walk around the courtyard, through the building and into the garden. We should start in Ave Maria Lane, where some sort of gateway must have barred the entrance to the Countess of Pembroke's inn.[42] Today, the entrance runs under the now empty Colonial Mutual Life Assurance Building. The elder Mylne's elegant iron railings, which once protected Stationers' Court from the outside world, have gone presumably for wartime salvage; today's asphalt provides parking space for a few cars and for the delivery vans which service functions held within the building, but across the courtyard we can see the refined, Neo-classical façade of the eastern side of the Hall, re-fronted in stone by Robert Mylne in 1799-1800. Every detail lends serenity—the doorway at the southern end, reached by semi-circular steps and flanked by handsome iron lamp-standards, the four slender, round-headed windows, the frieze of Coade stone putti above the cornice—even the pattern of the tie-beams which hold the stone facing securely to Robert Wapshot's 17th-century brickwork.

41 Court Book l, 5 February 1952.
42 See Ann Saunders, 'The Stationers' Hall', *op. cit.*

65. Hanslip
Fletcher's drawing
of the Court
Room and Card
Room in the 1920s.

Adjacent, to our right, on the north side of the courtyard, is the eastern wing, remodelled in the 1880s by Robert William Mylne, Robert's grandson, the third Mylne to be Surveyor to the Company. Faced in Portland stone, the Flemish Renaissance façade, with bands of carving with the date 1887 and a tapering hexagonal lantern, has an endearing incongruity when contrasted with the earlier work. The lie of the land and the need to gain space necessitate an entrance at semi-basement level—a part of the post-war remodelling, which now provides cloakroom facilities. Stairs lead up to the Crush Landing, where hang portraits of those Masters who have also served in the office of Lord Mayor; Sir Sydney Hedley Waterlow, who filled both offices in 1872, is on the stair. Around the landing are Alderman John Crowder (Master and Lord Mayor 1829) by Sir William Beechey, Sir George Blades, later Lord Ebbisham (Master and Lord Mayor 1926), by Lindsay Williams, Sir John Boydell (Master 1783; Lord Mayor 1790) by John Graham with St Paul's in the background, Sir William Waterlow (Master and Lord Mayor 1929) by George Harcourt and Sir Clive Martin (Lord Mayor 1999) by David Cobley. On the landing and stairs are two fine 17th-century chest-buffets, a handsome mid-Victorian longcase clock, and a model of the Stationers' Barge of 1820, presented by Victor Harrison, Master 1947-8. On the way up to the Stock Room hangs a painting, on loan from the family, of Sir John Key (Master 1830; Lord Mayor 1831-2) by a follower of Sir Thomas Lawrence, and on the landing are portraits of William Bowyer, senior, a benefactor to the Company, and Robert Nelson, the historian of Islington, donated by John Nichols.

The Stock Room is a dignified introduction to the delights that are still to come. Rectangular, save for a broad bay window, some of the panelling dates back to the 17th century; the garlands above the chimney piece may be the work of Henry Ford. Around the cornice are 59 heraldic shields with the arms of the families associated with the Company; 30 of them have survived from the 18th century, the remainder have been restored. When new, they were carried in procession when Sir Stephen Theodore Janssen became Lord Mayor in 1754; he was the first Stationer to achieve the City's highest office (without having had to translate to one of the Great Twelve companies), having been Master of the Company from 1749-51. There is a handsome plasterwork ceiling, and in the bay window is a coat of arms taken from the library window of the Stationers' Company's School when it closed in 1983; the two windows on the north side have decorative Victorian glass, one of them with a small portrait of the Queen herself. On the panelling are inscribed lists of those Stationers who have served as Lord Mayor, of the Honorary Freemen and Liverymen, the Clerks to the Company (four Rivingtons among them), the Chairmen of the Livery Committee, founded in 1920, and, in the Hall, the Silver Medallists but not, unfortunately, the Beadles.

The eight portraits here form an interesting collection. Over the fireplace is a small portrait of Mary Tudor, probably copied by Eschenburg after Anthony Mor;[43] it is fitting that she should have pride of place since she presented the Company with its first Charter. On the east wall hang William Strahan (Master 1774) by Sir William Beechey after Sir Joshua Reynolds, William Waller (Master 1885) by Henry Code, Andrew Strahan by William Owen, and John Nichols F.S.A. (Master 1804) by John Wood, with a benign, round, bespectacled face and a substantial book on the table. The gathering on the west wall, nearest to the Hall, is equally distinguished—John Mylne Rivington (Master 1963-4) by Cosmo Clark; Harold Macmillan, Earl of Stockton, Honorary Freeman and Liveryman, aged 90, by Gandee Vaikunthavasan, and Sir Derek Greenaway (Master 1974) by Michael Noakes.

Four steps down from the Stock Room and we are in the Great Hall, a truly amazing survival after all the vicissitudes of the centuries. Stephen Colledge's panelling still sits serenely around the walls; the superb segmental-headed, Corinthian-columned screen, probably the work of Henry Ford, spans the southern end; display cabinets have been let into it to hold the Company's plate. More plate is on view at the northern end, in two skilfully adapted chiffoniers. Eight modern painted acrylic banners, with the arms of Stationer Lord Mayors, hang from the walls, and all around the panelling stand 65 heraldic shields, mostly of the 18th century. There are no paintings here but a pennant, belonging to the Scriveners' Company, is set high on the western wall.

The ceiling, skilfully re-created after wartime destruction, is to the eldest Mylne's design—a long rectangle enclosing five circles of varying size, a painting of St John, copied from the war-torn original, in the centre. The stained-glass windows in the north and west walls have miraculously survived the bombing of the last war.

Eight Charles II oak refectory tables still stand in the Hall; the benches to them at present rest in the gallery above the screen. They have been hard used over the centuries and had need of restoration, though they will give centuries more service yet. From the

43 Donated by Past Masters Wilfrid Hodgson and Charles Rivington.

start, the Hall had been intended to provide the Company with an income by being let out for suitable civic and other functions, though we may note that on 7 February 1774 its use was denied to the Adam brothers for the drawing of their lottery which was to finance the Adelphi development.[44] The Hall still fulfils this usage most handsomely and is in demand throughout the year to provide the setting for all sorts of gatherings; a whole section of the office staff is now needed to deal with the lettings.

A short flight of steps leads up from the Hall to a landing where hang portraits of Charles Robert Rivington (Clerk 1869-1916; Master 1921) by Sir Charles Holmes, and Ralph David Blumenfeld (Deputy Master 1934) by Neville Lewis. From here, a staircase runs to the Muniment Room and Library (see pp.198-9).

We are now entering the western arm of the building, where the most severe bomb damage was done, and where much post-war rebuilding in red brick was needed. Messrs Henry Dawson were responsible for the work with Geoffrey Gurney as the Architect and Surveyor. The re-constructed ante-room is now an elongated octagon with a plain ceiling—previously, it had been oval. At the four corners are shell-headed niches which hold a Regency mahogany bracket clock of c.1820, a small pottery figure of Herbert Fitch (Master 1922-3), a bronze head of Edward VIII by Francis Doyle Jones—the Prince was Master of the Company in 1934-5 when he was still Prince of Wales—and a neat little figure of Shakespeare. Around the walls hang portraits of the astronomer and almanack maker Tycho Wing by Van der Bank, of Matthew Prior and of Sir Richard Steele (both after Kneller) and James Round (Master 1740 and 1741). Two exquisite card tables, inlaid with mother-of-pearl, stand against the wall.

From here, we enter the Court Room, the first apartment to be reconstructed after the Great Fire; the beauty of the room is such as to put it on a level of importance with the Hall itself, and the skill employed in the post-war rebuilding and restoration cannot be praised too highly.

It is a large rectangular room, with four windows in the south wall which look onto the inner courtyard, now a garden. On the opposite wall is a fireplace with a deal surround, its swags and garlands carved in astonishingly high relief. This presumably dates from the 17th-century re-construction since William Robinson was instructed, in 1757, to re-use 'the old woodwork from the chimney',[45] but the contract between him and the Company gives no clue to the hand responsible for the overmantel nor to its date.

The deep coving and the main compartments of the ceiling follow Robinson's drawing, and the alternating medallions and flowers of the cornice match the Company's written instructions to him. The decorations within the compartments and within

44 Court Book M, 7 February 1774.

45 Stationers' Archives, Deed 482. The drawing attached to the contract shows the carved surround clearly and recognisably with a square frame above it, perhaps for a mirror, and a triangular pediment to complete the whole. What we have is an astonishingly delicate rococo chinoiserie fantasy—a riot in wood and gilded plaster of scrolls and swirls and fruit and foliage with an eagle in the centre and two triumphant mytho-logical ho-ho birds—symbols of good fortune—perched on the top corners. The contract makes no mention of it; there is no reference in the Court Books.

66 & 67. The Court Room in the 1930s showing the plasterwork ceiling.

the coving are later, dating presumably from William Chadwell Mylne's alterations and refurbishment of 1825-6. The plasterwork books which hover so realistically in their red and green bindings seem to have more in spirit with the early 19th than the mid-18th century. The red and green volumes on the south and west sides are closed; on the other sides, the leather-covered books are open; to the east we can see the opening words of St Mark's Gospel and on the north we have St John's, 'In the Beginning was the Word'.

The second Mylne's great achievement was to open up and enlarge the Court Room to the west, into what had been lumber space, but which is now known as the Card Room. Proximity of other buildings meant that there was no window space in the walls, but Mylne solved the problems of lighting and ventilation with an ingenious overhead lantern. Two Corinthian pillars, painted to look like black marble, appear to support the back wall; another pair once formed a screen between the two sections of the suite, but they were not replaced in the post-war restoration.

On the south wall, flanked by two windows on each side, is the Company's Charter, granted by Charles II on 22 May 1684, with a splendid portrait of the monarch on the top membrane.[46] The portraits in the Court Room are of Thomas Cadell (Master 1798) by Sir William Beechey, Sir Thomas Wright (Master 1777-8; Lord Mayor 1785) by an unknown artist, Samuel Richardson (Master 1754) by Joseph Highmore, and Luke

46 For the troubles of the Livery Companies during Charles II's reign when King and Corporation were in conflict over the matter of the succession, see J. Levin, *The Charter Controversy in the City of London 1660-1688 and its consequences* (1969). For the Stationers' problems, see Blagden, pp.153-77.

Hansard, printer to the House of Commons, by Samuel Lane. The Master's lofty chair, with the Company's arms, stands in the corner by the window.

68. The Company's garden in 2000.

On the west wall of the Card Room hangs West's painting of King Alfred and the Beggar; nearby are portraits, including Charles Whittingham, founder of the Chiswick Press, by Thomas Williams.

A jib-door in the south-western corner leads onto a landing, from which the Master's Room may be entered, and a staircase twists downwards to the westernmost range of buildings, once storage space for Messrs Butterworth, but now housing the Company's offices. In the corridor hang two fine pen drawings of the Hall, dated 1925 and 1931, by Hanslip Fletcher, and in the Clerk's office is another interior, this time an oil painting by A.R. Thomson, R.A. This unassuming single-storey structure with a deeply pitched, tiled roof, is an astonishing survival. It must date from the 17th century; though it does not appear on Ogilby and Morgan's Map of 1676-9, wooden window frames and oak doors, so heavy that they require a hard push from the shoulder to open them, assert that it cannot be much later.

The door leads out to the inner courtyard, a pleasant shady garden with an enormous plane tree in the centre planted about 1800; it grows on the spot where, it is said, undesirable books were burnt in the 17th century. From the far side, a covered passageway leads into the outer court and back to Ave Maria Lane and Ludgate Hill, where began our exploration of this complex and beloved building, an amazing survival in 20th-century London.

CHAPTER NINE

From Past to Present

The Archive, the Library and the Company's Heritage

ROBIN MYERS

PART I: THE ARCHIVE AS A RECORD OF COMPANY HISTORY

'The chief glory of the Company in the eyes of the world is our records,' wrote Sidney Hodgson to the Master in 1959 or 1960. 'Not only do they register the original publications of Shakespeare and Milton, but the wonderfully complete series of registers and court books constitutes a volume of bibliographical evidence which no other institution can ever match.'[1]

Whereas on the Continent the archives of government censors provide much information about the history of the book trade, in England there was no similar formal apparatus and the records of the Stationers' Company are the fullest source. The bombing of Paternoster Row and St Paul's Churchyard, where so many publishers had their offices up to the Blitz in 1940, makes the survival of the Stationers' archive all the more important.

The Records themselves[2]

The Stationers' records are remarkably complete and well preserved.[3] The muniment room houses the entry books and copyright registers (1556-1842) whose official purpose up to 1695 was to facilitate control of the press, although, from an early stage, they were used by the members of the Company to establish ownership and to protect copyright; membership records from 1555; Court Orders from 1602, draft Court Minutes or 'waste books' (1661-1957); the records of the English Stock; charitable bequests, lists of pensioners (1608-1929), surveys, reports, property deeds, financial records (1605-1909); royal charters, patents, and 90 boxes of miscellanea. Ninety-three volumes of copyright registers (1842-1911) and 567 packets of entry forms, were transferred to the Public Record Office in July 1912, after the Company's administration of copyright and legal deposit ended. With hindsight we can see it would have been better to retain the registers to 1862, when the registrar reorganised the entry books to accommodate the pamphlet and non-book materials coming in, in the wake of the Fine Art Copyright Act. The legal deposit registers (1842-1924) remained at the Hall.

69. A corner of the Company's library showing the run of almanacks, and the Charles Rivington bequest of early Rivington imprints.

---

1 Memorandum (1959 or 1960), Sidney Hodgson papers, Muniment Room.
2 See Appendix 4 and Myers, pp.21-308.
3 See Myers appendixes A and B, pp.335-40, and D, pp.343-50.

70. A leaf from Thomas Werreat's writing and arithmetic exercise book, 1685.

Later Acquisitions

An accretion of miscellanea has enriched and augmented the archive. How the charming exercise book of Thomas Werreat (1685) was acquired is unknown;[4] the papers of George Hawkins, Treasurer of the English Stock (1766-80) who died at the Hall, were among his effects, as were those of Richard Johnson (1757-93).

In recent years, others, descendants of families with Stationers' Company connections, have donated collections of papers—the Kellie bookbinding archive (1767-1962), auction house and personal papers belonging to the Hodgson family, and miscellaneous Rivington family papers (1787-1932);[5] a collection of Bentley family papers (1785-1877) was deposited in 1985; 140 Tottel family documents (1448-1719) were acquired at auction in

---

4   See 'Work in progress; and could be all according to Cocker', Myers, *Stationer and Newspaper Maker*, 20, autumn, 1979.
5   Mrs Alyson Henderson (née Kellie) donated the Kellie archive in 1985, Wilfrid Hodgson, the Hodgson archive in 1995, and Charles and Christopher Rivington, the Rivington papers at various times.

1981;[6] in 1986, a collection of family papers (1740s to 1840s), of the 18th-century king's printers, the Basketts, was bought at auction and donated to the archive.[7]

Finding Aids: Catalogues and Indexes

It was the custom for the retiring Clerk to transfer the records to his successor during his first Court. In March 1681, John Lilly handed the records to John Garret, listing what was transferred in the Court Orders.[8]

'In 1925, through the good offices of Mr. R.A.Austen-Leigh, permission was received from the Worshipful Company of Stationers ... to print ... [a] synopsis of the extant records to the close of the 18th century.'[9]

Abstracts of the Court books were compiled for office use by John Noorthouck in 1778, John Battiscombe in 1843, and C.R. Rivington in 1869. There are office indexes from 1919.[10] H.R. Plomer's catalogue is necessarily inadequate because he could include only such records as the Clerk chose to or was able to find for him. It was superseded by Myers, *Stationers' Company Archive* in 1990, but in the late 1960s, the Beadle's younger son, Michael Osborne, then teaching history at the Company's School, made a shelf list of the contents of the muniment room. He was also the author of *The State Barges of the Stationers' Company 1680-1850* (1972).

Storage: From 'Stone Repository' to Muniment Room

In February 1830, a few months after Charles Rivington (1806-76) succeeded his uncle as Clerk,[11] the Court ordered him to investigate 'the mode in which the Company's Books and Documents are preserved and how they are secured against accident and fire'.[12]

His report gives a clear account of the way the records were kept:[13]

> The Company was formerly not insensible of the security of their Records and Documents, and some years ago a Stone repository was built for their preservation and that of the Plate in the Cellar under the Office in the North East corner of the Hall. But from the extreme dampness of situation, it is understood that it was impossible to use it for any other purpose than for the Plate ... for had the Books and Writings been suffered to remain in it, they would probably have been rendered illegible.

At the time of reporting, the Court Books, apprentice and other membership records, the entry books, ledgers of Wardens' Accounts and 'other miscellaneous books' were

---

6 Calendared by Anna Greening 1989-90, and fully described in, 'A 16th-century stationer and his business connections ...', *The Book Trade and its Customers* ..., pp.1-8 (see Appendix II).
7 By Peter and Olga Rippon and others; C.A. Rivington calendared them in 1987; Mrs Virginia Baskett Leach of Virginia, U.S.A. donated her research papers into the Baskett genealogy.
8 See *Myers*, Appendix B, pp.339-40.
9 A.W. Pollard, Hon. Secretary of the Bibliographical Society, preface to H.R. Plomer, 'A Catalogue of Records at Stationers' Hall', 1926 (see Appendix 2).
10 Copies in the muniment room; Alison Shell and Alison Emblow, *An Index to Court Books E F & G, 1679 to 1717*, to be published by the Bibliographical Society. J.D. Lee indexed the Orders from 1983.
11 Charles Rivington resigned (1869) on being called into Court.
12 Court Book T, 2 February 1830.   13 Court Book T, 2 March 1830.

kept in 'two wooden presses, standing at the Head of the Staircase leading from the Hall to the entrance from Ludgate Street'. The case of drawers whose contents had been listed in 1772 still stood in the Court Room. The Treasurer, George Greenhill, kept the English Stock records in 'a thin iron chest' which, in the Clerk's opinion, 'would not afford much security in case of fire'. Obsolete documents, dismissed in 1772 as 'odd papers in 2 or 3 Old Cases', were relegated to a wainscot chest in a room behind the Court room and in due course lost sight of.

The Court continued to concern itself with the problem of storage for a few years and in 1833 appointed a committee to consider erecting a 'Repository for the preservation of the Company's documents'. Another five years passed—there was another enquiry into the 'state of the safe closet'—six years later, in July 1839, a new committee was urged to make haste in deciding on plans for a building in the centre of the garden. No more was heard of the matter and the records continued to be kept in the old haphazard way.

Between the wars the principal records were kept in a large safe at the head of the stairs leading to the Stock Room, with the apprenticeship records piled on top in dusty confusion while the rest lay forgotten in cupboards and chests about the Hall. When Plomer catalogued the records in 1926 he found the Renter Wardens' quarterage books (1646-1800) 'done up in brown paper parcels and placed in the loft'.[14] They were the sole archival casualty of the War—the Public Record Office took the major records into safe custody from 1940.[15]

The Blitz revealed how vulnerable the records were and how carelessly they had been looked after in the years since Charles Rivington's report of 1842. The wainscot chest was found after the air raid in a closet next to the wine bin at the south end of the Hall where the Musicians' Company, not having their own hall, kept their regalia. On being opened it was found to contain ledger books and documents, some of major archival importance.[16]

Sidney Hodgson and his bibliographical friends were most excited by the discovery and Mr Hodgson read a paper to the Bibliographical Society describing the material.[17] Frank (later Sir Frank) Francis of the British Museum and Honorary Secretary of the Bibliographical Society wrote to the Master seeking permission to: 'make a full list of these documents, indexing the names where desirable and calendaring all the separate documents ... My Council has no doubt that you would be conferring a great benefit on the world of scholarship if you would give favourable consideration to the proposal.'[18]

---

14   Plomer, 'Catalogue'.

15   Court Book k, 4 May 1940. As soon as Graham Pollard warned Hodgson that they were at risk, he rushed to the Hall after one of the worst raids on the City, 15 October 1941, when a bomb fell between the Hall and the Court Room but was too late to save the quarterage books. See Hodgson, 'Papers and documents recently found at Stationers' Hall,' 1944 (see Appendix 2).

16   These were sheets of draft court minutes, 1682-92 (disturbed, crucial years in the Company's history), the only surviving journal of the English Stock (1650-98), the earliest extant volumes of dividend payments (1644-1753), 200 packets of wardens' and treasurers' vouchers (1680-1800), unique printed folio livery lists (1733-1832) and six sets of a four-volume printed index of the copyright registry (1842-1907) all described in Hodgson, *Papers* and listed in *Myers*, Appendix E, pp.351-5.

17   Hodgson, 'Papers and Documents' 23-36 (see Appendix 2).

18   Undated draft letter, Bibliographical Society archives.

Nothing more was heard of the matter, as so often in the history of the Company, and the long lost documents disappeared for another 44 years only to reappear in July 1988 when Sir Frank's daughter came across three tin trunks labelled 'Sidney Hodgson' in clearing up her father's papers. The lost documents had been lent to Francis for his consideration in 1944, and when he retired the trunks, long forgotten, went from the British Museum to his new home. The contents are now safely stowed at Stationers' Hall.

Sidney Hodgson was eager to use the closet as a muniment room.[19] Ellic Howe donated the royalties from his history of the London Society of Compositors to provide a safe door and a Regency card table and two chairs were moved in. It was formally opened as a muniment room by Sir Hilary Jenkinson, Keeper of the Public Records, at a luncheon in 1949. In this chilly cave, Sidney Hodgson, newly created honorary archivist, spent many happy hours sorting and annotating the post-blitz discoveries (in biro) in his distinctive hand, comments ranging from the informative to the crisp 'keep this—very important'.

The new room was not large enough for all the records and as a search room, cramped, without natural light, with such thick walls that it was almost as cold in summer as in winter and with the door open, draughty: but working with the safe door closed (which dropped on its hinges as time passed and took strength to open or close) had its dangers. Professor D.F. McKenzie was once forgotten and locked in, to be released by the Beadle doing his rounds at the end of the day. Visiting scholars often preferred to spread out their work on the Hall refectory tables.

In 1980 damp rot from the adjacent wine bin threatened the archive; a team of Court Assistants transferred it to a much larger upstairs room out of the way of Hall traffic, a single flight of stairs from the library. It was well suited for a permanent repository, its only drawback being that it was directly beneath the tank room, a grave hazard until the Company's Surveyor devised a method of diverting any overflow. For 18 months the records were left in piles on makeshift rickety shelving or heaped on the floor until, in 1983, the Court and the Treasurer finally gave way to pressure from the Archivist and wall-to-wall shelving, elementary but effective humidity control and a plan chest were installed. The Company's plate was moved into the closet from the silver vaults below the Hall, and the new arrangement given Ellic Howe's blessing: 'Your new disposition for the Muniments appear to be completely sensible and I would be the last to object that the brass plate at the entrance to my burial vault will lead to silver rather than muniments.'[20]

---

19 The major records in folio and a vast accumulation of miscellaneous documents were shelved in the cupboards, the quarto waste minutes and apprentice memorandum books were put in the wainscot chest. The Musicians' records and regalia were put in the basement safe room which housed the Company's plate, and the gowns in a room above the Court Room from which they were ousted again in 1980.

20 Ellic Howe to Robin Myers 1982; the safe door bore a plaque commemorating his donation.

71. A selection of the Company's historic records.

Care and Conservation of the Records

The Court Books were originally wrappered or bound in limp vellum, rebound in reverse calf in the 18th century and rebacked at intervals thereafter.[21] Sidney Hodgson saved Liber A and other badly water-damaged volumes from irreparable decay by having them laminated at the Public Record Office bindery in 1950.[22]

Mr Hodgson was a power in the land but Robin Myers had no budget, even for an emergency, and had to make do with unskilled volunteers until such time as a conservation programme could be organised with the bookbinding and conservation

---

21 There is no record of this, but it is inferred from the style of binding.
22 Lamination was a fashionable thing in the 1950s but it was later found that the leaves tended to stick together and had to be pulled apart which, if not done with care, caused damage. For Liber A see *Glossary* p.250.

department of Camberwell College of Art whose lecturers were liverymen.[23] It was a *quid pro quo*—the archivist giving occasional lectures, showing the records to conservation students and advising on diploma projects based on the Stationers' records in return for supplying documents for student repair under supervision.[24] In 1993 Allen Thompson, as chairman of the library trust, who had the archives very much at heart, arranged for a regular budget to be administered by the library trust, with payment for conservation and annual refurbishing of the Muniment Room.

The Keepers of the Records

The Clerk had always been responsible for keeping the records, although the Treasurer had the entry books, copyright registers and English Stock records in his care until the Registry was re-organised on George Greenhill's retirement in 1883 (see pp.73-9). In due course archival visitors and routine enquiries were delegated to the Beadle.

Sidney Hodgson made the records his special mission, and after he was called into Court in 1941 had the power to promote them. He sought the advice of the foremost archivists, bibliographers, and conservation experts. He worked according to the lights of the day and although some of his cavalier custodial practices—writing in biro on original documents, taking material away to his office, storing documents in old pieces of cardboard—would shock today's Society of Archivists, it was his dedication over some 35 years which laid the foundation of the special repository on which his successors could build. This was recognised in December 1969, when, 'pursuant to the orders of 4th November, 1969 the Master, Charles Rivington, announced his intention to present the Company's silver medal to Mr. Hodgson', then in his 94th year. The citation specified 'his great work in keeping and preserving the unique and important archives of the Company.'[25]

'Words fail me,' Sidney Hodgson wrote to the Master, 'when I endeavour to convey to you the intense pleasure it gave me when you presented me with the silver medal ... which for years I had coveted but which I never anticipated could ever have happened.'[26]

Charles Rivington's enthusiasm for the Company's history matched Mr Hodgson's own, and with his encouragement an exhibition of the Company's archival treasures was mounted for the inauguration of National Library Week in March 1969 accompanied by a printed catalogue.[27]

James Moran, who followed Mr Hodgson briefly as Archivist, was chiefly interested in setting up the new library (see below). When he died suddenly in 1978 Robin Myers was invited to succeed him and has tried to build on Mr Hodgson's foundations, turning the archive into a research centre and making it more widely known.

23 Ray Wright, Douglas East, David Collins and Bill Topping.
24 The programme continues, despite education funding cuts, the death of Ray Wright and retirement of the others.
25 Court Book O, 4 December 1969.
26 Sidney Hodgson to Charles Rivington, Master, Hodgson papers, Muniment Room.
27 See Appendix 2.

From 'Writings & Papers' to Archives: the Beginning

The first document to evoke something of a book trade archive, evolving out of a collection of office records and legal documents, is a 17th-century abstract of the Court Books, a chunky quarto bound in reverse calf which was begun by John Lilly, the Clerk (1673-81), continued by order of the Court to 1701 and thereafter piecemeal to 1776. A small quarto catalogue of 1772 in marbled wrappers and labelled 'an Account of Writings and Papers Contained in a Case of Drawers in the Court Room of the Hall', was compiled when the English Stock which had hitherto owned the Hall conveyed it to the Company. The case, or chest of drawers had three locks, the keys being kept, one by the Master, the second by the Treasurer and the third by the Clerk, an ancient form of protection ensuring that no-one had sole access to the contents.[28]

Access and Use of the Archive (1770s to 1840s)

In the slow 18th-century dawn of scholarly interest in the Company's records, the battle cry of 'public access' was far off and the Company continued to regard its Hall as its castle, and its documents as legal records and working office papers. So it looked with the deepest suspicion on those who might wish to look round, such as Joseph Ames (1689-1759) who wanted to see the portraits of early printers at Stationers' Hall for inclusion in his *A Catalogue of English Heads: or, an account of about two thousand prints*, 1748. In a much quoted letter he complained that, 'some of those persons treat folks as if they came as spies into their affairs'.[29] When he came to collect material for the *Typographical Antiquities*, 1749, he was obliged to look in the Rolls Chapel and elsewhere for copies of the Company's charters and patents which he transcribed for the information they contained on the workings of the early book trade.[30]

Ames's motives, like those of his fellow antiquaries and bibliophiles, were innocuous enough. All of them were concerned with the dating of early books, and hoped to verify imprint dates from the Stationers' entry books and to establish the working years of printers in the imprints from the apprentice records. In addition the 18th century's romantic passion for Shakespeare led to an obsession with his chronology. The entry books would establish the order of his plays once and for all, so they thought, as well as revealing the existence of hitherto unknown early plays and of ballads, which also absorbed them greatly.[31]

William Herbert (1718-96), revising the *Typographical Antiquities* in the 1780s, fared better than Ames had done. As a print and map seller, a Citizen and Draper, a friend of Lockyer Davis, 'the learned bookseller' who was Master of the Company in 1779, he had

---

28 Sidney Hodgson engaged Major A.C.S. Hall to sort the Company's legal documents in 1950, box and list them (see Appendix 1).

29 Joseph Ames to Maurice Johnson, quoted by T.F. Dibdin, preface to the *Typographical Antiquities*, 3rd ed. (1810).

30 Ames's *Typographical Antiquities* (1749), and William Herbert's three-volume revision (1785-90) can be found in the Bibliographical Society's library.

31 See Appendix 4.

72. A page from *Register A*, the Company's oldest volume, showing items of receipts, 17 July 1557.

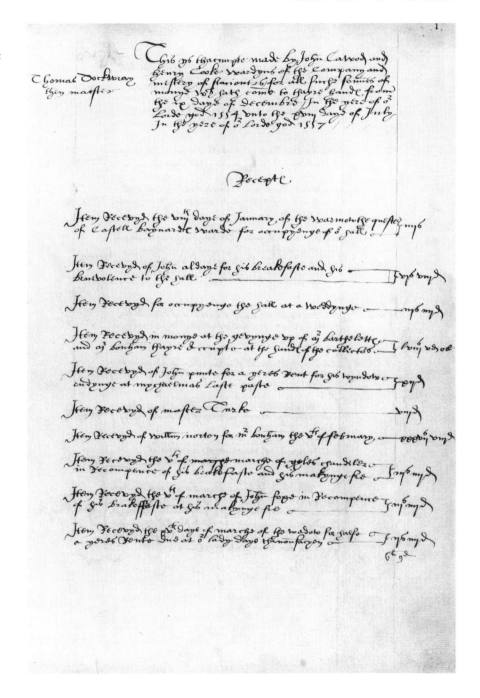

excellent credentials. His ties with the Company included binding his orphaned nephew, Isaac Herbert, to Samuel Hayes, bookseller and Stationer in 1787. He dined in the hall on a number of occasions, noted down the list of benefactors on the wall (long since disappeared) and was allowed to borrow Register A and Liber B (see *Glossary*, p.250) the company's earliest records, one at a time and copy them out in the comfort of his private library at Cheshunt. His transcripts in quarto notebooks bound in blue boards re-using waste charts and later bound into vellum covers, with his very rare heraldic

73. A page from William Herbert's transcript, *c.*1786, of the Apprentice Register for July to December 1576.

bookplate, are now an archival resource in their own right.[32] In April 1997, the Company acquired at auction a further Herbert notebook containing his annotated transcription of the Apprentices, Freemen and Livery (1576-1605) contained in Liber B.[33]

Among the first visitors to the records was the Shakespeare editor, George Steevens, whom Herbert described as his 'respectable friend' (mistakenly as it turned out). He was

32 George Chalmers bought them at the sale of Herbert's books in 1798 and applied to use the entry books a fortnight later. He put his spade shield bookplates in them. See Robin Myers, 'Stationers' company bibliographers ... Ames to Arber' in *Pioneers in Bibliography* (1988), pp.40-2.

33 It formerly belonged to Sir Thomas Phillipps (1795-1872), its blue boards protected by Phillipps' characteristic 'Middle Hill boards'.

introduced by Thomas Longman II (1730-97), a man of consequence in the Company, though not called into Court. Steevens, let loose on the entry books, marked in red ink all the entries he was transcribing for his Shakespeare chronology with his initials, an asterisk and the date of his visit (for example G*S 1774).[34]

When Edmund Malone, the greatest of the early Shakespeare scholars, who had been twice permitted to borrow Liber B, 'on his giving a Receipt for the same, with a Promise to return it,'[35] asked again in 1800, 'It was ordered that the Books be left with the Treasurer for Mr. Malone's inspection, but that they are not to be taken from the hall.'[36] We deduce that a new century brought tighter control and the new clerk, Henry Rivington (appointed in March 1800), was going to run the office very differently from his easy-going predecessor, Joseph Baldwin (Clerk 1776-1800).

Supervision of visitors was left to the warehouse keepers, George and Joseph Greenhill, with some disastrous results.[37] John Payne Collier (1789-1883) wormed his way into their favour and found opportunities to insert fictional ballad titles in the margins or between lines in Liber B.[38] He published his forgeries in *Extracts from the registers of the Stationers' Company ... 1557 to 1570* (1848-49).[39] He was long known to have tampered but proof positive came only in the late 1950s when an American scholar with the aid of Cyprian Blagden compared the suspect pages in Liber B with Herbert's transcript made 60 years before Collier came on the scene.[40]

Access in the Inter-war Years

By the end of the First World War the Court accustomed itself to the occasional presence of *bona fide* scholars, and researchers ceased to be treated as if they 'came as spies into the [Company's] affairs', but according to Ellic Howe who first visited the Hall in 1937:

> The position about forty-five years ago was that it wasn't all that easy to have access to the Company's muniments and nobody connected with the Company had any very clear idea of what was or was not available ... I encountered the clerk [R.T. Rivington], whose welcome was not particularly warm. He produced a Register, which I inspected on payment of a guinea.[41]

The charge was allowed to the Clerk by Court Order. Later Ellic Howe worked on the volumes of apprentice records which were brought to him one by one in the Stock

---

34 Published in 'Ancient editions of Shakespere's plays' 1773, 'Plays ascribed to Shakespere' and 'Ancient translations from classick authors' (1778). See Myers, *Pioneers*, pp.40-58.

35 Court Book O, 6 November 1787 and 5 February 1788.

36 Court Book P, 5 July 1800.

37 For their supervision of the registry see Chapter Four, pp.73-7.

38 Collier was introduced by the 30-year-old Joshua Butterworth, donor of the Caxton window when Master in 1894.

39 He deceived Edward Arber and even Sir Walter Greg who wrote; 'Collier does not say where he found these documents, and if anyone can tell me where they are I shall be very grateful,' letter in *The Library*, Series V, 1955, p.53.

40 See Franklin Dickey, 'The old man at work', *Shakespeare Quarterly* winter 1960, pp.39-47 and Myers, *Pioneers in Bibliography*, pp.50-2.

41 Ellic Howe to Robin Myers, 1980.

74. The Queen
examines a display
of the archives laid
out on the Court
Room table, July
1981.

Room until he made friends with the Beadle, Ernest Mettrop, and whenever they could evade the Clerk, Mettrop let him poke about and find what he wanted for himself.

It is hardly surprising that the Clerk and Ellic Howe did not see eye to eye. Mr Rivington, bred to the law, was then a dignified 56-year-old while Ellic Howe (1909-91) was an upstart in his mid-20s with an impish manner unlikely to go down well with the older, more formal man. But after this bad start, Ellic became a staunch and generous supporter of the archives until his enthusiasm led him away from bibliography and printing history into the realms of astrology, Nostradamus and Freemasonry.

Graham Pollard (1903-77),[42] on the other hand, then a bookseller and most brilliant of the younger scholars in the inter-war years, who first came to the Hall in 1936, was more diplomatic and was never, he told Hodgson, asked to pay 'a penny ... but I went to Rivington with a host of introductions and I have always taken care ... to give him as little trouble as possible ... and can generally tell his clerk exactly what I want and where it is.'[43]

Sidney Hodgson seems to have had a free hand and in those far off days, before security became a buzz word, no one gave a thought to his taking archival items away to show to his entourage of bibliographers who frequented his saleroom in nearby Chancery Lane; he even let them borrow them.

42 Not to be confused with A.W. Pollard (1859-1944) of the British Museum, first secretary of the Bibliographical Society.
43 Bodleian MS Pollard, 2 January 1939.

The Bibliographical Society and the Archive

No description of the Company's archive can leave out of account the role of the Bibliographical Society. With its foundation in 1892 research into the Company's records had come of age. It had an impact on the Court's attitude from the very first. Its credentials impeccable, closely connected as it was with the British Museum, it disarmed, even overawed the Court. The Company's Clerk, C.R. Rivington, had been a founding member, Sidney Hodgson had sat on the Society's council, and R.A. Austen-Leigh (Master 1954) had been its president (1934-36). Rivington took the advice of A.W. Pollard, the Society's first Honorary Secretary, on editing and publishing the early records, Austen-Leigh discussed further publication with the Society, and Sidney Hodgson relied heavily on Sir Walter Greg, Graham Pollard and Frank Francis in such matters. In the 1940s and 1950s Blagden, Sidney Hodgson and Ellic Howe were members of council and there have been three Stationer presidents of the Society.[44] Most of the important Stationers' Company research in the inter-war years was done by members of the Society and published by it.

The Stationers' Company and Bibliography

In 1959 or 1960, Sidney Hodgson, having promoted bibliographical interest in the Stationers' Company over the years and, conscious of the Company's charitable obligations, suggested that some of the surplus money from the sale of the Simpkin Marshall site be used 'to endow a professorship of bibliography'. He thought that the University of London 'would welcome a chair in bibliography with particular reference to the study of the Company's records'.[45] Unsurprisingly, inside the Company his suggestion fell on deaf ears but, in the bibliographical community, interest in the Company gathered momentum.

Arber's Transcript of the Early Registers

The 18th-century pre-occupation with chronology and dating gave way to a general interest in the early records for the study of Elizabethan literature. There was a need for a reliable edition to make them available to the scholarly community but many years passed before anything, with a change of Clerk in 1869, was done. After 40 years as Clerk, Charles Rivington was succeeded by his son, Charles Robert Rivington (Clerk 1869-1916), then just such a keen 23-year-old as his father had been when he became Clerk in 1829. The very next year C.R. Rivington persuaded the Court to permit F.J. Furnivall to transcribe the entry books to 1700, which they would edit jointly and which Furnivall's recently founded Early English Text Society would publish.[46] This was a great step foward for hitherto, in Arber's words, 'the mere sight of the Registers had always been considered a great favour (they being actually the private property of the

44   R.A. Austen-Leigh (1934-36), Peter Isaac (1994-96), and Robin Myers (1996-98).
45   Memorandum see note 1.
46   Founded in 1864.

Company)'. But by the summer of 1872 Furnivall had given up; at which point the eager young Clerk started retranscribing part of Register A until he too found that his work as Clerk and as partner in his father's law practice did not give him the time for 'a project of such magnitude'.

Finally, in 1873, Edward Arber (1836-1912) stepped into the breach and went doggedly on for 20 years.[47] His interest in the records was, like all the scholars of the day, for the study of Elizabethan literature. Against all odds, fully occupied with university work, hedged about with restrictions and limitations by an ambivalent Court which wanted the work done yet still had an ingrained suspicion of the motives of outsiders, Arber worked single-handed on his monumental edition of the registers (1554-1640) amplifying his transcript with a wealth of contemporary documents in the British Museum, Public Record Office and elsewhere. But he was denied even the sight of the Court Orders and had to make do with reprinting a paper of the Clerk's which drew on material in Court Book C and Liber A which, in Blagden's words, 'underlines ... the mistake of denying it to Arber'.[48] Without any funding from the Court he published 300 copies of his *Transcript of the Registers of the Stationers' Company, 1554-1640*, by subscription.[49] By the 1890s the Court's attitude had changed and they were all for his continuing to 1800, but after 20 years even he had had enough.

Although only 230 copies of Arber's transcript, with its elaborate editorial paraphernalia were published, it circulated far and wide through scholarly libraries, public and private, and proved a springboard for research into the early trade in printed books by providing a text which could be quarried by those unable to use the original records. A case in point was E. Hyder Rollins, a scholar of ballad and Renaissance literature, who extracted all the ballad entries from Arber, at a time when it was impossible for him to come and work on the original records at Stationers' Hall. His *Old English Ballads, 1553 to 1625, chiefly from manuscript* (1924), superseded the suspect work of John Payne Collier, whose scholarship was so flawed by forgery as to be unusable.

After Arber; Eyre and Rivington; Greg and Boswell; Jackson; Editing Liber A

Next, the Clerk engaged H.R. Plomer to transcribe the entry books from 1640 to 1708, which he and Colonel Briscoe Eyre edited. *A Transcript of the Registers ... 1640-1708* (1913-4) was printed for the Roxburghe Club and published on the eve of the First World War.[50]

In the 1920s, the Livery Committee, led by R.A. Austen-Leigh, obtained Court permission for the Bibliographical Society to publish more of the early Court Books. W.W. (later Sir Walter) Greg took on the 'very interesting but rather exacting task of editing, in collaboration with my American friend, Eleanor Boswell, the part of

---

47   He was founding professor of English at Birmingham University (1877-94).
48   Blagden, p.261.
49   See Appendix 4.
50   See Appendix 4; in 1980 W.P. Williams, of the University of Northern Illinois at Dekalb, published an *Index to a Transcript of the Registers ... 1640-1708* (1980).

Register B [1575-1602] ... that for some reason Arber had not been allowed to print. When it appeared,' Greg recounted, 'we were both entertained at luncheon by the Court ... I received a silver medal and my colleague a handbag.'[51] After the Second War, W.A. Jackson, Librarian of the Houghton Library, Harvard University and an Elizabethan scholar, edited the Court Books from 1602 to 1640.[52]

The Bibliographical Society next planned an edition of Liber A, the last of the major early records to remain in manuscript. Graham Pollard had it transcribed in 1960 but, as Professor McKenzie told an audience at Stationers' Hall in 1996, 'while I was descending the staircase [from the Bodleian's Duke Humfrey Library] in the company of Graham Pollard twenty years ago, Pollard casually said it didn't look as if he would get round after all to editing Liber A for the Bibliographical Society as he had hoped to do, and asked if I would take it over'.[53] McKenzie had already proved his worth through more than twenty years' work on the Stationers' records (see below).[54] He put an M.A. student to index Liber A under his supervision, and worked on it off and on whenever he could but, as he commented in poignantly prophetic jest, 'This paper might well have been called "On *Not* Editing Liber A". Edward Arber was not allowed to, Graham Pollard didn't, and I am sorry to report that, as yet, I haven't.' His sudden death in March 1999 deprived the academic community of a great scholar and teacher and the Stationers' Company of an editor for Liber A of the equal of Graham Pollard.

The Company Before Incorporation

Graham Pollard's role in Stationers' Company bibliography is far greater than his small output of published work suggests. Throughout the late 1930s until his last years, he advised the Court and the Bibliographical Society on publication of the records, helping and encouraging Jackson, Blagden, Ellic Howe and many younger scholars by passing on discoveries he had made among the records at Stationers' Hall and elsewhere. Until recent years he was the only scholar to realise the importance of the Company before incorporation for understanding events after 1557; his two classic papers in *The Library* have never been superseded.[55] Dr Peter Blayney, who never knew Pollard, is one of the few scholars to work on the early history and pre-history of the Company; he has been at work on 'The Stationers' Company and the printers of London, 1501-1616' for many years. He has made extensive use of the Company's records and has discovered hitherto unknown material in the Corporation Record Office and Public Record Office.

---

51 *W.W. Greg, Biographical Notes* (1877-1947), p.14.

52 See Appendix 4.

53 D.F. McKenzie, 'Stationers' Company Liber A: an Apologia' 1996, see Myers and Harris, *The Stationers and Book Trade*; Appendix 4.

54 But his extensive working papers are being put at the disposal of one of his postdoctoral students and there are plans for the work to be completed under the supervision of Dr Peter Blayney.

55 Graham Pollard, 'The Company of Stationers before 1557', *The Library*, Series 4, 1937, pp.1-39, and 'The Early Constitution of the Stationers' Company', *The Library*, Series 4, 1937, pp.235-60.

Traditional Areas of Research

The years from 1557 to the expiry of licensing in 1695 were the traditional areas of research. The major records up to 1640 were in print, and Greg, above all others, continued to influence bibliographical thinking for some years after his death in 1959. During the 40 years he spent on his monumental bibliography of the English printed drama to the Restoration, he published a number of important books and papers on the records, some of which are, in effect, finding aids.[56]

D.F. McKenzie (1931-99), Professor of English at Wellington, New Zealand, and latterly of Bibliography and Textual Criticism at Oxford was as influential in his own generation as Greg had been in his. He did a great deal of work on the Stationers' records, some of which he incorporated in his unpublished Sandars lectures in Cambridge in 1976 on 'the London Book Trade in the late 17th century', and his Oxford Lyell lectures of 1988. His Panizzi lectures on the sociology of texts challenged Greg's ideas of textual criticism.[57] They have had a wide impact on bibliographical thinking, even on interpretation of the Stationers' records.

Michael Treadwell (1942-99), Professor of English at Trent University, Peterborough, Ontario, first came to Stationers' Hall in 1974, to research the Restoration book trade. His sudden death in his 57th year, one month after that of Don McKenzie, was a second terrible blow to Stationers' Company research. He was a scholar of like calibre, though more traditional. For 25 years he worked steadily on the Stationers' records from the Restoration to the mid-18th century. His 40 published papers were but a fraction of his working notes, meticulously hand-written and now preserved in a locked file on his university computer.[58] Most of these were assembled for a dictionary of London printers and typefounders (1666 to 1723) which the Bibliographical Society hopes to be able to publish. Like Graham Pollard before him, Michael Treadwell was unfailingly generous in sharing with fellow scholars and students his vast knowledge of the London trade, much of which died with him.[59] He and Michael Turner, head of conservation at the Bodleian Library, were preparing a detailed study of the composition of the Court (1600-1800) extracted from the membership records and Court Books, which it is hoped will still be published.

In July 1989 Michael Treadwell took part in the festive and scholarly celebration of the tercentenary of the birth of Samuel Richardson, Master of the Company 1754-5, reading a splendid paper on 'Samuel Richardson, Citizen and Stationer' to a lively audience of academics and members of the Court and Livery.[60]

---

56 In particular, his Sandars and Lyell Lectures and posthumous *Companion to Arber*, for fuller list see Appendix 4.
57 *Bibliography and the Sociology of Texts*, British Library (1986).
58 See Appendix 4. His 'London Printers and Printing Houses in 1705' (1980), 'London Trade Publishers 1675-1750' (1982), 'A List of Master Printers; the Size of the London Book Trade, 1637-1729' (1987), 'Printers in the Court of the Stationers' Company in the Seventeenth and Eighteenth Centuries' (1992) were particularly authoritative.
59 See Robin Myers, 'Michael Treadwell (1942-99)', *The Stationer and Newspaper Maker*, 77, August 1999, p.9.
60 Organised jointly by the Company and Messrs Longman.

Microfilming the Records (1951-88)

Up until now, the initiative for publication had always come from outside the Company, but in 1984 Robin Myers the honorary archivist approached Messrs Chadwyck-Healey with a proposal for microfilming almost the entire archive, 1554-1920s, which gave world-wide access through sales to libraries. In 1951 University Microfilms had filmed a large part as it stood on the shelves, for the University of Southern Illinois, extra sets being allowed to a handful of libraries in Britain and overseas, but a complete, well-organised edition was overdue.

The major re-arrangement and cataloguing of the records in the new muniment room enabled a new microfilm, in 115 reels, to be made; it has sold to some 60 libraries, world-wide. There were three objectives; to protect the originals from overuse, to generate royalties for the Company and, perhaps most important and long-lasting of all, to stimulate interest among scholars who could not hope to come to Stationers' Hall, allowing them to do most of their research in their own libraries. In this way, many new areas have been opened up—in English literature, book trade history, economic history, music publishing and the history of science—which has put the Stationers' Company on the scholarly map as never before.[61] The microfilm is used in combination with various finding aids (see p.177) by genealogists and amateur family historians, and helps to stem the rising tide of enquiries received at Stationers' Hall. In 1990 Robin Myers published a companion guide to the archives, *The Stationers' Company Archive 1554-1984*, with a complete description of the records keyed to reel numbers, an historical account of their scholarly use and a glossary of terms.

By now, the Company's library was a useful resource and, as it became more widely known that scholars were welcome to use it, so the above-stairs activity generated by outside enquiries and visitors steadily increased year by year; the Livery, who could seldom be persuaded to venture upstairs, remained largely unaware of what went on. The three trustees, Allen Thompson as chairman, Christopher Rivington[62] and George Mandl, fully understood that it was the archives which represented the public face of the Company, and Allen Thompson set out to raise its profile inside the Company in the practical way of securing the finances. Nothing can be effective if it lacks the tools of its trade, and bibliographical reference works are costly. As money from royalties on the Chadwyck-Healey microfilm was now rolling into the Company's coffers, the time seemed ripe for negotiating improved archive funding as well as administrative change.[63]

Writing the Company's History: from John Nichols to Blagden (1804-1960)

The start of the 19th century had seen the beginnings of interest in the company's past. In 1812, John Nichols (1745-1826), Master 1804, published an account in the *Literary*

61 It has earned some £35,000 in royalties.
62 Charles's younger cousin.
63 The archives were loaned to the trust and with joint funding, the library and archive could function as a unit.

Anecdotes of the Eighteenth Century which was, in the words of the Clerk, Charles Rivington, 'the only approach to a history of the Company so far published'; although hardly what the Clerk calls a 'concise and amusing history of the Company'.[64] It is a gallimaufry of extracts from the records, rumours of the company's origins, descriptions of rooms and furnishings extended by a mass of anecdotal footnotes about members of the Company[65] which would otherwise be lost to posterity.

In 1842, three years after attempting to get the records safely stowed, another committee advised on 'the propriety of publishing such Particulars of [the Company's] Literary and other History as may be likely to prove interesting to the Reading Public and which may not be found injurious to the dignity of the Company'.[66] It was ordered to 'point out a Gentleman for Editor on whose experience, ability, integrity and honour the Court may place the most implicit reliance'. The Clerk, Charles Rivington, whose report of 29 April described the records category by category, showed a grasp of their extent and importance and a realisation of their essential unity. He reviewed the work of Steevens, Herbert, Malone, Nichols and others and advised that there was 'ample material for the compilation of a moderate sized volume which would possess much interest for the Members of the Company and ... illustrate the history of literature in this country.' But he warned of the dangers of 'printing what (when once given to the public) can never be recalled; and that if undertaken by a stranger it would require strict superintendence on the part of the Court.' The offer of his own services was gladly accepted when no 'gentleman in whom the court could place the most implicit trust' was found.[67] There is no further evidence, in Blagden's words, 'that the Company, after the initial burst of enthusiasm in 1842, showed any corporate interest in its history' until 103 years later.[68]

The Quatercentenary of the Granting of the Charter and Blagden's History of the Company (1403-1959)

After the Second World War, there grew a feeling, both inside the Company and among the scholarly community, that the time had at last come for a full narrative history. With the repair of the Hall after its wartime damage under way and the quatercentenary of the granting of the Company's Charter in 1557 not far off, the time seemed ripe. If well done, a published history would bring the Company prestige and fill a long-felt scholarly gap; that at least was the intention.

In March 1947, Ellic Howe wrote to Mr Hodgson:

> You have been so kind as to discuss with me the possibility of publishing a new and full
> scale 'History of the Stationers' Company' to celebrate the 400th anniversary of the granting

64 Court Book V, 3 May 1842.
65 John Nichols, *Literary Anecdotes of the Eighteenth Century*, vol. III, pp.345-68.
66 Court Book V, 3 May 1842.
67 Court Book V, 3 May 1842.
68 Blagden, p.261.

of our Charter ... in 1957. I raise the matter thus early, since the compilation of such a work, if a decent standard of scholarship is required, is necessarily a slow and arduous undertaking ...[69]

Alas, it turned out to be the old story—deliberations, started in 1947, were not much farther forward in 1956.

Cyprian Blagden (1906-62), who taught history at Uppingham (1928-32), had been a schools inspector (1933-39) before joining Longman's at the start of the war. He had recently published a paper on the origins of the English Stock, and was working on other aspects of the 17th- and 18th-century Company. As an historian and a Liveryman, he was the ideal man to produce a readable and authoritative account of the Company's history.

'As you know,' he wrote to Hodgson, ' I am all for the history, and ready to discuss it with you at any time.'[70] Sidney Hodgson for the Company, Frank Francis for the Bibliographical Society, and Ellic Howe were poised for action but the Court continued to shilly-shally, wanting a history but not wanting to spend the money.

In 1956, Mr Hodgson wrote dryly to a Texan correspondent:

As to the history of the Company, I am sorry to say nothing definite has been done about it. Some five or six years ago a Committee was formed to discuss the matter and a suitable person was found who we had reason to believe could have undertaken the work and, indeed, would still do so. However, when it came before the Court of the Company, they did not see their way to putting up the money to guarantee the cost of its production ... To compile a history worthy of the Company would occupy a very long time ... We shall certainly be having some celebrations during next summer ...[71]

In the event Jackson's admirable but hardly festive edition of the Court Books, 1602-40, took the place meant for Blagden's history.[72] Meanwhile, Mr Hodgson went on trying to get the Court to subsidise the work until, in 1958, Blagden lost patience and set to work with a Leverhulme Fellowship. The Court launched *The Stationers' Company; a history 1403-1959*, with a sherry party in 1960.[73] For many years a copy was given to every new Liveryman.

Blagden's meticulous scholarship established an interpretation of the Company's history which has stood the test of time. Drawing on discoveries in the archives of the Corporation of London and in the Public Record Office, he set in context what had previously been seen in isolation and shed further light on the London book trade of the 17th and 18th centuries. His individual papers on specific aspects of the Company's history, above all those on the English Stock in the 18th century, contributed to changing attitudes

69 Ellic Howe to Sidney Hodgson, 20 March 1947, Sidney Hodgson papers, Muniment Room.
70 Blagden to Hodgson, 4 August 1953.
71 Sidney Hodgson to Dean Ransom, University of Texas, 22 August 1956, Sidney Hodgson papers, Muniment Room.
72 Published by the Bibliographical Society, 1957.
73 Published by Allen and Unwin 1960; it has been reprinted by Stanford University Press, USA.

to the importance of the Company's 18th-century records. His premature death was a loss to the scholarly world. David Foxon, Reader in Bibliography and Textual Criticism at Oxford, worked for many years on the crucial register 1710-46, which follows the passing of the first Copyright Act, which he intended for publication. In his important 1975-6 Lyell Lectures on Alexander Pope he made use of some of his work on the register.[74]

Dictionaries of the Book Trade

In the early 20th century, H.R. Plomer and others built on the work of Joseph Ames and William Herbert in documenting the lives and output of the London printers. The London trade, and thus the Stationers' Company, was the hub, but the four volumes of the *Dictionaries of Booksellers and Printers, 1557-1775* include the rest of England, Scotland, Ireland and Englishmen printing abroad.[75] The Stationers' records were one of the major sources. Ambitious plans to revise Plomer have stalled, but in the past 50 years a great deal of work has been, and is being, done on sections of the trade—Ellic Howe on London bookbinders, 1648-1815; Ian Maxted on the London book trades, 1775-1800; Mary Pollard, former Keeper of Rare Books at Trinity College, Dublin, on the Dublin book trade to 1800—the fruit of 40 years' work.[76] Two huge computerised indexes to the trade to 1850 have been created by two Liverymen—Professor Peter Isaac's *British Book Trade Index* currently contains 71,000 English and Welsh members of the trade at work to 1851; Michael Turner in Oxford, latterly in collaboration with Dr Christine Ferdinand, Fellow Librarian of Magdalen College, Oxford, has indexed a similar number of Stationers and non-Stationers in the London trade, which incorporates McKenzie's *Stationers' Company Apprentices, 1605-1800*.

D. F. McKenzie first came to Stationers' Hall in 1957 in pursuit of documentation on the working conditions of Elizabethan printers, which he originally intended to use for a doctoral thesis. It led him, over 20 years, to forge a bibliographical tool which gives easy access to the Company's apprentices and masters from 1605 to 1800.[77] It is the most constantly used of all his works. In the cognate discipline of demography, Christine Ferdinand extracted statistical evidence for her demographic study, 'Towards a demography of the Stationers' Company 1601-1700'.[78]

Later Developments

Blagden, then Foxon and Treadwell, developed the scholarly potential of the 18th-century Company, and it is hoped that the present work will point the way to research in the long neglected area of the 19th century. As the 19th and 20th centuries grow more

---

74 Published as *Pope and the early eighteenth century book trade*, edited by James McLaverty, 1991.
75 Published by the Bibliographical Society, 1905-32.
76 Ellic Howe, *London Book Binders 1648-1815*, Bibliographical Society, 1950; Ian Maxted, *The London book trades 1775-1800: a Preliminary Checklist of Members*, 1977; Mary Pollard, *Dictionary of the Dublin Book Trade to 1800*, Bibliographical Society, 2000.
77 *Stationers' Company Apprentices* (1605-1800) 3 volumes (1961-78), is based on the interlocking registers of members of the Company, the court orders, pension lists and English Stock dividend books.
78 *Journal of the Printing Historical Society*, 1992. See Appendix 4.

distant from the present, they will be seen to be rich sources of research and the very weaknesses of the 19th-century Company—loss of influence in the trade, negligent copyright administration, inefficient management of the English Stock—makes research the more interesting.

A whole new research area beckons from outside the walls of Stationers' Hall or the microfilm of the records housed there. Simon Eliot has described the sequence of copyright registers from 1842, now at the Public Record Office in 1912.[79] After the passing of the Copyright Act of 1842, the single register was replaced by two, called 'Books Commercial' (intended for the entry of ephemeral and jobbing printing) and 'Books Literary'; with the Fine Art Copyright Act of 1862 further special registers were opened, such as a register of 'Paintings, Drawings and Photographs', which contains a mass of ephemeral, commercial and visual material. Whereas the older registers merely record publication details, with no copy of the work appended, the later sequences, which have another purpose altogether, are accompanied by albums of sample labels, drawings, photographs and theatre programmes. Towards the end of the 19th century, commercial and visual material predominated and it is a prime source for an entirely new field of sociological, typographical and graphic research.

The records from 1914 are already providing data for statistical, genealogical and demographic research and it remains to be seen what other uses they will be put to. Whatever the verdict on the Company's role in relation to its trades in the past two centuries, there can be no doubt that its archive plays an increasingly important part in the development of book trade scholarship.

PART 2: THE COMPANY'S LIBRARY (1934-99)

Background

It is not uncommonly supposed that the Company's library is richly stocked with books and, latterly, printed ephemera submitted for entry at Stationers' Hall, or at the very least, with copies of everything once published by the English Stock. Alas, this is not so, although books may have been quietly sold off from time to time. In the later 17th and early 18th centuries, there were various proposals for the foundation of a public library in London. William Oldys, herald and antiquary, writing in 1740, suggested that Stationers' Hall, then in the centre of a commercial and literary area, would be a suitable location.

> It were to be wished the Stationers' Company would erect a library to their Hall, it being commodiously enough situated for resort to all parts. So many of them having got estates by the learned, it would demonstrate some gratitude to the sciences, and repay their expenses sufficiently in honour and reputation.[80]

79 See Simon Eliot, '"Mr. Greenhill, whom you cannot get rid of": copyright, legal deposit and the Stationers' Company in the 19th century' in *Libraries and the Book Trade*, ed. Robin Myers, Michael Harris and Giles Mandelbrote (2000), pp.57-77.
80 [J.Yeowell] *A literary antiquary: a memoir of William Oldys*, 1862, cited by Don McKenzie in 'Stationers Company Liber A', *The Stationers' Company and the Book Trade* (1996), p.54.

One hundred and ninety years came and went before the Company itself gave the idea any consideration. Even though books were the Company's business, the first mention of a collection of books was in 1872, when the General Purposes Committee was ordered 'to provide a proper receptacle for the Books belonging to the Company',[81] and in 1889: 'The Master and Wardens to provide such bookcase or other receptacle for Books presented to the Company as they may think requisite'.[82] The late 19th- and early 20th-century Court Orders record a number of book presentations which have all since disappeared.

Charles Rivington in his article on the library's first ten years (1974-84) mentions a 'small but useful collection of books, mainly ... connected with the Company's history',[83] which had been donated to the Company in years past and made over to the new library...[84] They are a miscellaneous collection which include some very fine things such as the *New History of London* ... (1773), which the author presented to the Court with a letter, tipped into the front fly-leaf:

> Gentlemen, I take the liberty ... of your acceptance of the History of London herewith sent ... I hope you will not think it unworthy a place on your table, for occasional reference to, and for the amusement of the members of the court; which will be considered as an honour done to, Gentlemen, your obedient and humble servant, J. Noorthouck.

Noorthouck (*c*.1735-1816), who earned his living by writing for the trade, was a Liveryman and son of a Liveryman and bookseller, who was voted £80 for compiling the admirable abstract of the orders to 1778 which is still in use.

William Caslon's type specimen books, 1785, 1786 and 1798, 3 volumes, octavo, bound in red morocco, gold tooled and protected by chemises, deserve special mention. Their provenance is unrecorded but they may have been the gift of one of the Caslon family who were liverymen in the 18th century.

The Library of the Newspaper Makers

We hear no more about the Company's books until the Newspaper Makers joined the Company, bringing a library of books with them whose disposition the Court discussed on 6 November 1934 and ordered: 'As regards the Library which had been taken over from the Company of Newspaper Makers Sir Percy Greenaway and the members of the Newspaper Makers Company should be consulted as ... to the disposal' of about 75 per cent of it.[85]

Although none of the Newspaper Makers' books can be identified in the present library nor is its extent known, an Honorary Librarian, Mr Frederick Dorling Bone, was

---

81 Court Book a, 9 April 1872.
82 Court Book d, 1 March 1889.
83 Charles Rivington, 'The Stationers' Company's library; the first ten years', *The Stationer and Newspaper Maker*, 34, winter 1984, and 35, spring 1985.
84 In the 1960s, Sidney Hodgson, first honorary archivist, asked the Beadle, Stanley Osborne (1909-98), to make a catalogue of books belonging to the Company.
85 Court Book j, 6 November 1934.

75. John
Noorthouck's
letter presenting
his *History of
London* to the
Court, 6 April 1773.

75. John Noorthouck's letter presenting his *History of London* to the Court, 6 April 1773.

appointed 'during the pleasure of the court' on 7 September 1937. He was a journalist and among the first of the Newspaper Makers to be cloathed in 1934. The next year, in September 1938, he produced a design for a library to be built round the plane tree, an attractive edifice, seemingly inspired by the British Museum's famous round reading room.

Dorling Bone took his appointment seriously enough to send a letter to the Livery Committee, in June 1939, 'venturing to cite', among other suggestions, the promotion of 'a scheme whereby a bungalow is built around the tree in the garden to house the library, and have accommodation for a reading room ... a luncheon club in the garden pavilion

76. F.D. Bone's sketch for a proposed new library, 1938. (See Illustration 4, p.16.)

SECTION AT A-B

for the members of the Livery and their guests.' The War no doubt put paid to the scheme once and for all.[86]

The Trust

There was no more talk of a library until James Moran (1920-78) came on the scene in the late 1960s and proposed that the Stationers' Company ought to have its own reference library for the use of the Livery and of visiting scholars, who had previously had to use the St Bride Printing Library down the road. Mr Moran was editor of *Printing World*, founder of the Printing Historical Society and active in printing history circles; he was admitted to the Livery in 1960. He was very much a live wire, full of bright ideas for starting new things.

He galvanised the Court into setting up a library which was to be an autonomous charitable trust. On 14 March 1974 it was formally established, with Charles Rivington, Wilfrid Hodgson and James Moran as the trustees, and James Moran as Honorary Librarian.

The Attic Conversion

In 1972 the Court decided that, as a quiet place out of the public eye, the attics, where the parcels of quarterage books, during the Blitz, had been stored, should be converted, as economically as possible, into a library.

---

86 Dorling Bone served on the Livery Committee until 1956 but is not reported as saying another word about the library or anything else.

The Company provided a Victorian mahogany glass-fronted bookcase (probably the 'receptacle' of the 1889 Court Orders), chairs and a massive oak trestle table dating back to the original furnishing of the Hall. Charles Rivington donated the Victorian partners' desk at which a succession of legal Rivingtons had sat, and his office captain's bow chair.

Sir Derek Greenaway obtained a pair of solid free-standing, double-sided book presses and the room was ready for the books.

The Book Stock: Donations, Bequests and Purchases

From the 1920s, Sidney Hodgson, the premier book auctioneer of his day, assembled and gave to the Company a collection of books with Stationers' Company associations. In the 1970s and 1980s, Charles Rivington built on these donations with other well-chosen gifts. Both Sidney Hodgson and Charles Rivington added a number of antiquarian works on the history of the book including the 17 volumes of John Nichols, *Literary Anecdotes of the Eighteenth Century*, and *Illustrations of the Literary History of the Eighteenth Century*. Among other rarities inherited by the library were four volumes, 1835-80, of London and County sheet almanacks, many with engraved headpieces; interspersed in the volumes are some Raven's miniature sheet almanacks, most frequently found in presentation bindings, of which the archive contains a collection and a volume of proof pulls. The provenance of the bound volumes is unknown; they may have been the English Stock's file sets.[87] The library's section on paper and papermakers has one of the few complete runs of the *Paper Trades Review*.

The library's principal objects were defined by the trust deed as 'the advancement of education by the establishment, equipment, maintenance and administration of a library for the use of persons engaged in historical research in ... printing, publishing, bookselling, bookbinding and other allied trades'.[88] The trustees drew up a list of desiderata which was circulated among the Livery; books rolled in and were initially accepted whether or not they fell within the scope of the terms of the trust. There was not yet the thought that space would run short soon enough. By 1984, when Charles Rivington reviewed the library's first ten years, he calculated that there were 3,000 books (perhaps over-estimating), 60 boxes of pamphlets, offprints and typescripts.

Funding

Books and volunteer labour can go a long way towards producing a library, but it cannot run effectively without funding. There was next to none until Lord Leverhulme's gift of £5,000 in 1990, which constituted riches beyond the dreams of library and archive avarice and permitted the librarian to have a purchasing policy instead of relying on gifts of books.

87 A hand-written catalogue of the Company's collection of almanacks was compiled by Miss Hope Verschoyle, a NADFAS volunteer, in 1980.
88 Court Book O, 5 March 1974.

The Bibliographical Society's Library

The Company had had close links with the Society since its foundation in 1892. In 1981 the association between the two bodies was further cemented when the present honorary archivist, Robin Myers, was elected the Society's honorary librarian; Council enquired whether the Stationers' Company could house the Society's library alongside its own. Robin Myers and Charles Rivington were quick to see that this would be mutually advantageous; the Company was, in effect, being offered a windfall, a collection of some 8,000 books on bibliography and book history, with remarkably little serious duplication of the Company's bookstock, apart from the essential and long-out-of-print transcripts of the early registers and a few major bibliographical tools, such as the *STC*.[89] There was much in the Society's library which the Company could never have afforded to buy—the two series of its own *Proceedings* contain most of the important research papers on the Company's history;[90] there were also runs of several other important bibliographical serials. The Society's library also possesses a very fine collection of 18th- and 19th-century sale catalogues, some of them very rare, as well as valuable antiquarian works of relevance to the study of book history.

The trustees, led by Charles Rivington, convinced the Court of the wisdom of accepting the Society's proposal and bore down the initial opposition of the Clerk and Treasurer who wanted to charge rent. The trustees explained that this was out of the question, but the Court stipulated (and the Society readily agreed) that the library become, in effect, an honorary corporate member receiving all the Society's publications free of charge, and enjoying reciprocal borrowing and user rights.

The back of the attic was cleared and cleaned up and the Society's books and archive were moved in one weekend by a team of stalwart Bibliographical Society volunteers.[91]

Eleven years later, on 11 July 1992, the Society held its grand centenary dinner at Stationers' Hall, and afterwards swept up the library stairs in a cheerful, well dined, unstoppable body, gaily chattering bibliographical details, to inspect the Company's recently refurbished library and flood into the muniment room.

Librarians and Trustees

Less than two months before the official opening of the Company's library James Moran died suddenly, aged 57.[92] It was a great blow and a disappointment that he could not live to preside over and see the development of his brain-child. Kenneth Day (1912-81), recently elected Court Assistant (1979), took his place as the third trustee.

89 *A short-title catalogue of books printed in England, Scotland and Ireland and of English books printed abroad*, Bibliographical Society, 2nd edition by Katharine Panzer, 3 volumes (1976, 1986 and 1991).

90 The Society's proceedings were published as *Transactions*, 15 vols, 1893-1920, thereafter quarterly as *The Library*, 6 series, 1920-99. Series 7 began January 2000.

91 For a full description of the move see M.M. Foot, 'The Bibliographical Society' in *The book trade and its customers; historical essays for Robin Myers* (1997), p.300.

92 Obituary article, *The Stationer and Newspaper Maker*, 17, spring 1978.

Kenneth Day was educated at the Stationers' School (see p.141) and admitted to the Livery (1965), and edited *The Stationer and Newspaper Maker* (1977-81). For many years, he was typographic designer at Ernest Benn. He built up an excellent collection of type specimens, advertising ephemera and books on book design, which he bequeathed to the library when he died, barely three years after being appointed trustee.[93] This put the trust in something of a quandary because 'the Master hoped that the aim of the library, which was mainly to be concerned with the history of the Stationers' and other livery companies, would not be changed by the influx of Kenneth Day's books and it was agreed that there should not be an over-emphasis on typography.'[94] It was resolved by selling at auction the duplicates and books quite outside the library's range and using the proceeds for works more central to it—the printed ephemera and type specimens, though marginal to the library's specialities, were not too bulky to be boxed and catalogued. A plaque recording 'Kenneth Day (1912-81) Benefactor to the Library' was put up on the wall.

Charles Rivington, the second librarian (1978-84); Keith Fletcher, the third librarian (1984-)

Charles Rivington was appointed honorary librarian in James Moran's stead. His background was quite different; a man of open mind and wide culture, educated in classics and the law, and steeped in the traditions of the Company and the City. He came to the bibliographical scene with enthusiasm and, in the six years that he ran the library, it made strides. He left his mark on it in a number of ways; through exchange with other livery companies, he expanded the section on livery company histories and books on the City which the present librarian has developed further. He instigated a file of book trade obituaries, from *The Times* and elsewhere, now bound into volumes, and he started box files of ephemeral, pamphlet and typescript material relating to the Company and its trades of the guild. His hand-written index cards still proliferate in the unautomated library catalogue, in two sequences, one by classmark, one by author/title. He also made an abstract and index of the 18th-century Baskett family papers, which the archive acquired at auction in 1986. In 1984, Charles Rivington, then 82 years of age, decided to retire as librarian while continuing as chairman of the trust for another three years. In his second retirement he made good use of the library and archive for his research on Sir John Davies, John Barber and Pepys's booksellers.[95]

Keith Fletcher had advised on book purchasing policy in 1981, and Charles Rivington recommended him to the Court as his successor, though a youngish man and junior in the Livery. Keith Fletcher brought bookselling and bibliographical skills to the job and could sniff out rare items for the library which few members of the Company had the expertise to find. He and Robin Myers quickly formed a working partnership, as she had

93   Obituary article, *The Stationer and Newspaper Maker*, 27, spring 1982.
94   Court Book p, 1 February 1983.
95   'Sir Thomas Davies; the first bookseller Lord Mayor', *The Library*, September 1981, pp.187-201, read before the Bibliographical Society, 21 October 1980, *'Tyrant', The Story of John Barber Jacobite Lord Mayor of London, & Printer and Friend to Dr Swift* (1989), and *Pepys and the Booksellers* (1992).

77. Type specimen books of William Caslon, 3 vols. 1785-8, bound in scarlet morocco, gilt, green watered silk doublures, in chemises. They are among the treasures of the Company's archive and library. Actual size 9½in. by 6in.

previously done with Charles Rivington, and they discussed bibliographical and archival policy together from the start.

New Brooms: Changes and Additions (1984-98)

Keith Fletcher became librarian in 1984, by which time it was no longer a question of furnishing the room and he showed great expertise in making the best use of a modest amount of regular funding, which he spent on important reference works. The section on livery company and Corporation of London histories, inaugurated by Charles Rivington by exchange with other livery companies, was continually expanded as new histories were published and several costly, standard works on the corporation added to the shelves which stand beside the printed *Reports* of the Charity Commissioners, 1830, and the *Reports* of Commission of Enquiry into the livery companies of London, 1837 and 1884, which must once have lived in the Clerk's office.[96]

In 1992, the room itself was redesigned and reshelved and formally opened by Charles Rivington.

The Library as Research Centre

During the library's first 25 years there have been many additions to the bookstock. There are currently some 5,000 volumes including periodicals, slightly fewer than that of the Bibliographical Society. From the resources of the two collections scholars at work on the Company's records are provided with most of the books they need to check biographical and bibliographical references. They also have useful antiquarian material in the run of almanacks, the *Gentleman's Magazine*, 1790-1815, and books formerly published by the Company. The pattern of use is documented by a loan book and a visitors' book. It shows that the Livery hardly ever visits the library or borrows a book, despite considerable internal publicity. It is, however, increasingly used by visiting scholars searching the archives under the archivist's supervision and consulting her on archival matters, for which the resources of the two libraries are needed to deal with their enquiries. In effect, the attic room has become a small research centre where scholars exchange ideas and offer each other advice, and can work with the reference tools to hand.

---

96 George Unwin, The *Gilds and Companies of London*, 2nd edition (1925), and W.C. Hazlitt, *The Livery Companies of the City of London* (1892). Further desiderata include William Herbert's commentary on the commission reports, *The History of the Twelve Great Livery Companies of London*, 2 vols. (1834 and 1837).

CHAPTER TEN

Networks and Hierarchies

The Stationers' Company in the City of London

Michael Harris

In outline the history of the Stationers' Company conformed to that of the majority of the Livery Companies based in the City of London. Medieval or early-modern incorporation; active engagement in the monitoring and control of the main London trades running into and through the 17th century; some limitation in the exercise of this role during the 18th as the scale and character of London and its trading community changed; a general shift towards educational and charitable activity in the 19th; and, finally, a calm and usually low-key consolidation around the traditional political and social rituals of the City during the 20th century. Within this framework the ebb and flow of creation, reconstruction and dissolution continued to manifest themselves by fits and starts within the Company structure. As trades became obsolete, were divided by function or were stimulated by new technology or simply by changing fashion, the process was mirrored in changes in the number, form and character of the London companies. The pattern of experience from 1800 was shaped and changed by two very different external pressures: firstly, the clamour for reform which broke over the City and all its constituent institutions, stimulating what has come to be described as the Great Awakening of the 1870s. Secondly, the devastation caused through the first half of the 20th century by international conflict, in particular by the Second World War, and the sweeping social and economic changes that came in its wake. Though apparently locked into a self-contained world of commercial and social exclusivity, the London companies formed part of a wider system which contained its own interactive dynamics. This chapter considers how the Stationers' Company formed part of a community within the City of London and how within this sphere of influence it related to its fellow companies, to the Corporation of London and more generally to the outside world of politics and power.

The London companies engaged with the shared pattern of historical experience, but they were not a homogeneous group. In detail they were divided by broad distinctions in character, organisation and background. The Great Twelve companies, themselves graded by size, wealth and status, remained distinct from the rest. Outside the Great Twelve, the large and amorphous group of other companies fluctuated in number and membership across the period. In the late 1830s, a total of 89 companies were identified of which 13 were pronounced extinct in 1884.[1] In 1909 the first new creation for 200

78. The Court of Common Council in session in 1957.

---

1   I.G. Doolittle, *The City of London and its Livery Companies* (London: Gavin Press, 1982), p.89.

years, the Solicitors' Company, was not incorporated until 1944 and later in the 20th century the process of company creation speeded up. Between 1977 and 1982, nine new livery companies were created bringing the total, including the Great Twelve, to 93; by 1998 this number had risen to 100. This erratic sequence with activity accelerating in the recent past was clearly visible in the shifts in the size of the Livery. Based on the numbers provided by Ian Doolittle, a chronological listing of the total membership shows a generally upward trend, extracted from the Common Hall Register, 1998:

1832	12,000
1855	5,500
1918	c.8,000
1939	c.10,000
1945	9,500
1955	13,000
1982	20,000
1998	23,742

The Stationers' Company was located at a middling point among the companies outside the Great Twelve standing at number 47 in precedence. In terms of gross annual income it was cited as the 15th richest Company and in 1882 it boasted the fifth largest Livery. Among the companies the relationship with the individual trades which they had historically represented also varied a good deal. Some companies sloughed off their economic responsibilities and interests well before 1800. Others doggedly continued to engage with the practice, management and control of commercial activities into the mid-20th century. The Goldsmiths, the Brewers and the Vintners were among the most durable in this respect, becoming part of a government-sponsored supervision of the products in which their members had traditionally dealt.[2] The Stationers' Company fought a long rearguard action against the loss of its historically defined book-trade functions. As the last of the City Livery trading companies, through the management of the English Stock, and as the official guardian of copyright by registration, its membership continued to have an unusual coherence.[3] The restriction of access to those working in the different branches in the trade still marks out the membership of the Company from most of the other related institutions in the City.

In the quality of their organisation the individual companies were equally heterodox. Some were effective and successful; others rapidly developed a tendency to disintegration and self-destruction. Here again external circumstances could play a part. Some of the City companies in the course of the 19th century found themselves in possession of

---

2 In 1973 the Vintners' Company, under a new charter, set up the Wine Standards Board which took over some government responsibilities for enforcing the regulations on wine quality issued by the EEC. Anne Crawford, *A History of the Vintners' Company* (London: Constable, 1973), p.248.

3 That is not to say that the organisation always worked nor that all the individuals with financial responsibilities were entirely scrupulous in their dealings.

land which was rising in value, not only because of the upward trend in the price of City property—which benefited the Haberdashers—but also if their estates lay on the route of a projected railway. The Carpenters were particularly fortunate in this respect and received a series of railway-related windfalls from the 1830s to the 1860s.[4] Financial viability clearly contributed to internal stability and the Stationers' Company with its active commercial interests stood out as a resilient and business-like organisation. It was never likely that its Master would bolt to New Zealand to escape his creditors nor that the Company regalia would be pawned—misfortunes experienced by the Curriers during that company's erratic progress through the 19th century.[5] The Curriers were hit financially by changes in the market which undermined their constituent trades. The Stationers had no such problems. Print was proliferating and its members experienced not only the benefits of a generally buoyant market but also the associated status of a commodity with high cultural value.

Like the other London companies, the Stationers were active participants in the conventional rituals of City life. Important to the structure of internal organisation as well as to external relationships was the increasingly notorious timetable of recurrent dinners. These events, usually organised within a framework of long-established dates, were far more than an excuse for a popular form of self-indulgence. They became an effective forum for the expression of views and opinions, often implicit rather than explicit, which were conveyed to a wider public through coverage in the newspaper press. Dinners provided the opportunity for expressing various forms of group solidarity as well as political and ideological difference.[6]

In the heightened political atmosphere of the 1820s and 1830s it was difference that was more often displayed in this setting. When the Master of the Stationers' Company, John Key, a supporter of reforming principles, was elected Lord Mayor in 1830 he became involved in a series of events which caused some heartache within the City's trading community. Hearing rumours of possible crowd trouble on Lord Mayor's Day, Key warned the government, who immediately cancelled a scheduled visit by the King. As a result, the expected crowds failed to materialise, shops remained closed and Key was blamed for making a premature intervention which lost City tradesmen a valuable commercial opportunity. At the celebratory dinner at Stationers' Hall two days after his inauguration, the toast to the Lord Mayor (not present) was greeted by dead silence. Alderman Venables appealed for tolerance, to be met by 'hisses mingled with cries of "No, no".' This was fully reported in *The Times* and readers can have been in no doubt of the Company's view of its own Master.[7]

4   B.W.E. Alford and T.C. Barker, *A History of the Carpenters' Company* (London: George Allen and Unwin, 1968), pp.148, 151-3.
5   Edward Mayer, *The Curriers of the City of London* (London: Worshipful Company of Curriers, 1968), pp.151, 159.
6   The formation of a Dinners Committee within the Company structure suggests the continuing importance of these events. See for example the report to the Court by this Committee in Court Book c, 4 October 1881.
7   *The Times* 14,381, Thursday, 11 November 1830.

The expression of corporate opinion in relation to the wider political sphere recurred at the equivalent dinner in November 1839. On this occasion the health of 'Her Majesty's Ministers' was proposed. *The Times* reporter struggled to convey the spirit of the occasion. 'Those only who were present', he wrote 'can judge of the sensation produced on announcing the toast—Yells, hisses, groans, and other discordant noises continued for at least ten minutes, mingled with cries of "No, no, it shall not be drunk! Turn the Whig ministers out," &c.' A vigorous, shouted dispute ensued which only ended when the Chairman intervened—'I will give you something you like better—the dessert', and on this jocular note the conflict subsided.[8] By mid-century the forms of physical violence that sometimes broke out at Livery dinners had become a thing of the past. Dinners involving the Stationers' Company continued to carry a symbolic force, but increasingly this was used to embody alliances within the general organisation of the City rather than hostility or confrontation.

The expression of disagreements within the Stationers' Company could sometimes turn on participation in the primary rituals of City life, the processions associated with the inauguration of the Sheriffs as well as of the Lord Mayor. Between 1800 and 1980 22 Stationers served as Lord Mayor and the arrangements for Company participation were routinely recorded in the minutes of the Court. Some elements of the general debate about the lavish displays which characterised the event up to the middle of the 19th century divided the Stationers. The last procession by water was held in 1856 and subsequently the extravagance of the land-based ritual came under attack. William Ferneley Allen, Stationer and publisher to the East India Company, was elected Lord Mayor in 1867. He was said to be 'generally opposed to the grotesque and cumbrous pageantry of Lord Mayor's day as now conducted' and he certainly refused to use the ornate state coach at his inauguration. This action ran directly counter to the form of traditional liberalism adopted by his fellow Stationer Sydney Waterlow, himself elected Lord Mayor five years later. At a Court dinner held in December 1867, Waterlow expressed his regret at Allen's actions and hoped they would be reversed on the next occasion. His remarks, reported in the *Printers' Journal*, were modest enough but suggest a local manifestation of a line of ideological disagreement which ran across the City at large.[9]

Dinners, processions and the superficial trappings of authority provided a soft target for the individuals and groups who continuously promoted a programme of reform or who looked for the total disestablishment of the Corporation of London. To the reformers, the companies represented an integral part of the political structure, however much they might claim to exist as free-standing institutions within it. Whatever conflicts can be identified within and between the companies themselves, the series of variably critical enquiries which ran through the 19th century provided a crucial counterpoint to the history of the companies individually and collectively.

---

8   *The Times* 17,198, Wednesday, 13 November 1839.
9   *Printers' Journal* 72, Monday, 16 December 1867.

From the 1820s the Stationers' Company shared the experience of being required to respond to investigations organised by the Charity Commissioners, specially created Royal Commissions and parliamentary committees. The sequence has been traced in outline by Ian Doolittle, who seldom in the course of his book refers to the Stationers. This reflects the generally low profile adopted by the Company. To some extent, the Stationers were caught up in the generalised resistance to external probing as the groans noted above may suggest. The Court was certainly not anxious to provide more than a minimum response to whatever questionnaires and other calls for information it received. Even so, the Stationers appear to have been less exercised about their position than many of the other City companies, possibly because of their continued involvement in the organisation of the print trades. The enquiries do not figure very extensively in the records and occasionally the wish to remain aloof from some forms of opposition does surface. In the 1850s the Mercers' Company sent round a demand for money to be used as a fighting fund to resist the most recent of the bills introduced in Parliament to reform the Corporation. The response from the Stationers was a cool one. The Clerk was ordered to reply 'that the Court do not feel called upon to make the contribution requested' and a subsequent attempt to drum up the modest amount of cash was met by a stony silence.[10]

The Stationers seem to have responded to each of the enquiries in a calm and cautiously co-operative way, although they continued to fight a long and ultimately pointless battle to prevent public access to their records. One problem which they faced in trying to exclude outsiders was the difficulty of separating sensitive material from information which lay legitimately within the public domain. As a trading company, the Stationers particularly resented any attempt by external interests to examine the accounts of the English Stock. This was a reasonable commercial position defended by the Company throughout the 19th century. In 1880 Lord John Manners, Postmaster-General, who had recently chaired an enquiry into copyright, referred at a Stationers' Company dinner to the forthcoming Royal Commission on the London Livery Companies. During his flattering remarks on the Company's management of the registers, he stated that 'it would be most unfair to require them to submit their trading books to investigation'. Not surprisingly *The Times* recorded cries of 'Hear, hear' from the membership.[11]

However, the Stationers' efforts to prevent access extended across all other areas of their records. From the 1830s special care was taken for their preservation but simultaneously a high level of supervision was also introduced. Pressure for access was in some cases entirely reasonable. The high literary and cultural value of the material

10 Court Book X, 13 November 1839. A similar indication of detachment, this time in relation to action proposed by the Mayor and Common Council, appeared in a letter to *The Times* from John Dickinson, one of the Wardens. *The Times* 22,346, Tuesday, 15 April 1856.

11 *The Times* 29,795, Wednesday, 4 February 1880. The Stationers' Company had petitioned Manners in 1879 to support their continued registration of copyright.

assembled under the registration requirements of three centuries meant that the demands to record and publish were likely to grow. At the same time, the archive contained the more ambiguous material concerned with the internal organisation of the Company and with its relationship to the City. This was exactly the sort of information that the enquiries were seeking to dig out: and if scholars such as Edward Arber had the greatest difficulty in obtaining permission to view and then to publish the early registers, it has to be acknowledged that the Company saw itself as almost continuously under siege. By the mid-20th century the position had altered so radically that the Stationers' records could be described as one of the prime justifications for the existence of the Company itself.[12]

If in response to enquirers the Stationers were watchful and restrained, they took a similar rather prickly line with their fellow companies. Property was a mutual preoccupation and the London companies were inextricably bound up in the most complex networks of leasing and ownership. One area which stood out in this respect and suggests the character of many of the relationships, was centred on the estates in Ulster purchased during the plantation of Ireland in the early 17th century. Managed by the Irish Society, a committee of the Corporation, each estate was held by a tenant-in-chief drawn from the Great Twelve companies. Leases in the property were offered to two or three of the rest and the shared estate was then run to their proportional advantage.[13]

The Stationers' Company was involved in one such syndicate. The 'Pellipar' estate, named from the Irish word for skinner, was held in chief by the Skinners' Company which retained control over the bulk of the property. The Stationers held about one-sixth, while the White Bakers and the Girdlers each held about one-eighth.[14] Through most of the 19th century the Pellipar estate formed one of the elements in the shifting relationship between these companies and betweeen the companies and the Corporation. The ebb and flow of negotiation, which can be tracked through the Stationers' records, was again part of the general pattern in which the main institutions of the City of London were involved both independently and collectively.

Signs of a form of benevolent co-operation between the partners in the Pellipar estate cropped up in 1827 when the Master of the Stationers reported to the Court that he had attended a dinner at the Skinners' Hall with the Masters of the Bakers and Girdlers. So hospitable was the entertainment that the Court resolved to issue invitations to all concerned to the next Court dinner.[15] Even so, the Skinners were already looking to buy out their partners, a proposal rejected by the Stationers and the other 'associated companies'. The first signs of real tension appeared in the Stationers' records during the

---

12 Unwin, p.55.
13 For an account of the history and management of the Irish Society see Raymond Smith, *The Irish Society, 1613-1963* (London: for the Irish Society, 1966) and James Stevens Curl, *The Honourable The Irish Society and the Plantation of Ulster, 1608-2000* (Chichester: Phillimore, 2000).
14 An account of the arrangements between the Skinners, the Stationers and the associated companies appears in *The Stationer and Papermakers', Printers' and Bookbinders' Circular*, 10 January 1860.
15 Court Book T, 12 June 1827.

79. The manor of
Pellipar, London-
derry, belonging to
the Company, from
a map in the
Muniment Room.

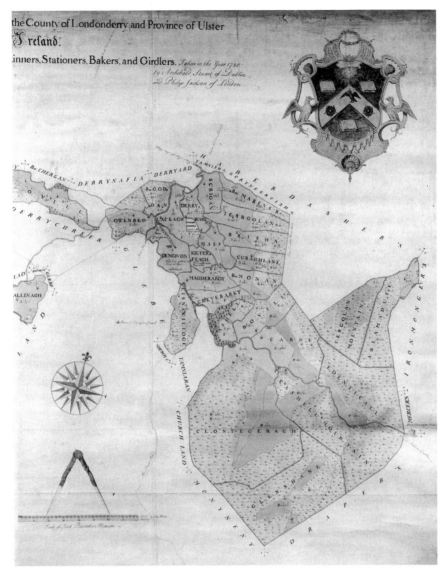

long-drawn-out and finally unsuccessful Chancery suit between the Skinners and the
Irish Society over the distribution of money and accounting procedures. The Skinners
were acting, at least in part, on behalf of the Great Twelve and its associates in Pellipar
were drawn in apparently without much, if any, consultation. As the case, launched in
1833, dragged on year after year some stirrings of discontent became evident. In 1839,
when the Skinners embarked on an appeal against an initial judgement to the House of
Lords, the Stationers' Court 'explicitly but respectfully' dissented from this line of
action, taken without consultation. In return the Skinners' Court expressed astonishment at this intervention which it described as unnecessary and inappropriate, and the
emphatic pulling of rank on the associates seems to have pre-empted any further disagreement before the long-delayed final judgement in 1845.[16] Whether or not things were

16   Court Book V, 1 October 1839.

patched up, the issue of control and the rights of the Stationers, Bakers and Girdlers continued to crop up and some degree of mutual distrust seems to have formed part of the background to the sale of the subordinate interests in Pellipar in the 1870s.

The negotiations which followed the expiry of the underleases in 1874 involved some close negotiation. The Skinners on one hand and a committee of the Stationers, Bakers and Girdlers on the other skirmished over the disposal of the shared interests. The Stationers called on their most high-profile officers, the ex-Lord Mayor Sir Sydney Waterlow and Sir J.H. Truscott, to support the process which seems in the end to have been undertaken by the associates independently. In June 1875 the Stationers asked the Skinners for £48,000 for their share in Pellipar, a claim which was linked to criticism of the Skinners' management and was only to remain valid for a month. The Skinners replied with a counter offer of £34,000 and after further haggling the deal was settled at £40,000, the Stationers to receive the money in instalments of £10,000. The return from the investment of this money began to appear in the English Stock accounts in 1879.[17]

There is something in this which suggests changing times. In the 1870s the London companies generally were experiencing some unusual pangs of activity and even growth as the 'Great Awakening ' spread across the City. Under the lash of the enquiries and almost constant attacks in the newspapers, the pressure to construct a positive image was becoming crucial. This was compounded by the fact that the companies were losing their political grip on traditional areas of control. Their trading monopoly had been weakened in 1835 when Freedom of the City was made available at a modest fee outside the company structure. It was given the *coup-de-grâce* in 1856 when, under an Act of Common Council, the Freedom itself ceased to be a requirement to trade in the City. Similarly, areas of political influence were increasingly undermined. In 1867 the Freemen were replaced by £10 ratepayers as voters in ward elections and the gradual erosion of franchise privileges continued. The Livery lost the last vestiges of the right to elect members of parliament for the City in 1918, although some commercial qualifications lingered until 1948.

Self-justification through the Company's educational and charitable functions became increasingly essential. However, in some respects the companies remained locked into the primary centre of political power and influence represented by the Corporation of London. The link was sustained by the interchange between the companies and the Court of Aldermen. The upper chamber of the Corporation had been losing ground over a long period to the more open and quasi-democratic Court of Common Council but it still retained considerable authority. Consisting of one representative for each of the 26 wards, elected for life and satisfying a massive property qualification, Aldermen were drawn from the companies and exercised both a specific and a general control over their actions. Any increase in the size of the Livery, change in the by-laws or in the terms

---

17 Discussion of terms run through the records of the Court from 1872. See, for example, details of negotiations in Court Book a, 2 June 1874; Court Book b, 3 August 1875. Also the accounts printed in Blagden, pp.270-1.

of apprenticeship required ratification by the Court of Aldermen. The two-way move-ment was visible in the general and semi-automatic transfer of individuals elected as Alderman onto the ruling bodies of their respective companies.[18] The Livery continued to exercise its traditional rights in the election of City officers through their general meeting in Common Hall. However, the primary routes for the exercise of civic duty, personal advancement and political influence were located at the upper levels of the Corporation, which in turn led into the wider sphere of national government.

The way this worked in practice in relation to the Stationers' Company can be seen most clearly in the experience of individual members. During the second half of the 19th century and the early years of the 20th it would be hard to find a better case history of movement within the complex but well-defined networks and hierarchies than in the experiences of Sydney Hedley Waterlow.[19] The Waterlows became one of the great nonconformist (Unitarian) dynasties whose presence dominated the commercial structure of the City during the 18th and 19th centuries. They easily satisfied the basic requirement of number. In the 1870s, 200 members of the Waterlow family were invited to a banquet at the Guildhall and 180 turned up.[20]

The basis of this traditional, capitalist success story was located in the law stationery business founded at the end of the 18th century by the patriarch James Waterlow at 24 Birchin Lane in the City. He apprenticed his sons through the Stationers' Company and Sydney Waterlow was apprenticed to the successful government printer Thomas Harrison (1836-43). Waterlow revelled in his traditional City background and wanted his biography to be called 'The Life of a London Apprentice'. After a short spell in Paris with Galignani, he was offered a partnership in his father's business and given respon-sibility for developing the printing side. This proved the starting point for an acceler-ating commercial success. In tandem with the legal business, Sydney Waterlow moved into one of the most profitable areas of non-book printing, work for the railways. Subsequent diversification into the printing of stamps and currency, combined with a general wholesale and export stationery business, gave the firm a high visibility and status in the City. Starting with 20 employees, Waterlow's was by 1898 working from 10 separate establishments in the City, one in Westminster and one in Dunstable and had 4,000 employees on the payroll.[21]

This was the launch pad for Sydney Waterlow's career in a wider sphere. By the late 1860s he was becoming less closely involved in running the business and had already

18 This form of access to the governing body of a parent company is identified in several of the company histories and any Alderman subsequently admitted to other companies seems to have been granted a similar privilege. This was the case of the Stationer Sir Sydney Waterlow who was given immediate access to the Court of the Clothworkers' Company.

19 The main source of information on the life and career of Sir Sydney Waterlow is George Smalley, *The Life of Sydney H. Waterlow Bart.* (London: Edward Arnold, 1909). See also Alfred B. Beaven, *The Aldermen of the City of London* (London: Corporation of London, 2 vols., 1908-13).

20 John Boon, *Under Six Reigns: Being some Account of 114 Years of Progress and Development of the House of Waterlow under Continuous Family Management* (Waterlow and Sons, 1925), pp.3-4.

21 Boon, *Under Six Reigns*, p.32.

begun to turn his attention to City politics, where his membership of the Stationers' Company was an important ingredient. Several other members of his family combined elements of civic and commercial life across the century. James Waterlow was elected to the Common Council for Cornhill in 1843 and chaired the City Lands Committee in the 1850s.[22] On one occasion he was involved on behalf of the City in a hearing directed at Waterlow Brothers for smoke pollution from their Finsbury factory.[23] However, none moved so effectively through the structures of the City as his son Sydney Waterlow.

He was elected in 1853 to the Common Council as a representative for the Broad Street ward. Here he displayed a particular kind of pragmatic energy in which public and private interest were neatly combined. By encouraging the introduction of the telegraph to the City to link police stations, using wires strung between church belfries, he was able to bring this effective means of communication to bear on the scattered elements of the Waterlow printing and stationery business. The next step in his political progression came in 1863 with his nomination and election as Alderman for Langbourn ward. He was immediately elected to the Court, along with the dour Alderman Allen, though, as was conventionally the case, without receiving any privileged access to shares in the English Stock.[24] His smooth progress through the interlocking stages of City and Company organisation was uninterrupted. Elected as Sheriff in 1866 and knighted at the end of his term, he became Renter Warden of the Stationers' Company, Under Warden and Warden in consecutive years before being elected Master in 1872.

Although attempts had been made in the 1820s to avoid a simultaneous conjunction of roles, Sir Sydney Waterlow was elected Lord Mayor in 1872 and combined this with the Mastership of the Company to the general satisfaction of members.[25] Though it was no longer a requirement for the Lord Mayor to be a member of one of the Great Twelve companies, he joined the Clothworkers and was immediately elected to their Court. This accumulation of office marked the apotheosis of Sydney Waterlow within the City. His subsequent career as M.P. (1874-85) and Governor of the Irish Society (1873-83), as well as membership of a variety of committees and commissions, gave him a presence that carried him onto the Royal Commission enquiring into the Livery Companies (1880-84). There is no evidence that the Stationers objected to this, though the Clothworkers found it an unacceptable fraternisation with the representatives of state interest.[26]

Waterlow continued to be active within the Stationers' Company and his name appears with regularity in the Court minutes. In July 1906 he attended the Court and was elected First Assistant.[27] He died a month later. His career reflected both the force that

22 *The House of Waterlows of Birchin Lane from 1811 to 1911* (nd), pp.3-4. Publicity material held by the St Bride Institute Library and used by Boon in *Under Six Reigns*.

23 *The Times* 21,961, Friday, 26 January 1855.

24 Court Book Z, 1 December 1863.

25 Court Book a, 5 July 1873.

26 Tom Girtin, *The Golden Ram: a Narrative History of the Clothworkers' Company, 1528-1958* (London: Clothworkers' Company, 1958), p.245.

27 Court Book e, 3 July 1906. He had resigned as Alderman in 1893.

80. Sydney Hedley
Waterlow as Lord
Mayor, 1872.

an individual Stationer could have in exploiting and extending the networks of influence within the City and beyond, but it also suggests something about the increasing importance of the London companies in the later 19th century. From being what had been described as a combination of shopkeepers, the companies, including the Stationers, were attracting and involving some of the commercial high-flyers in the City. Sir Sydney Waterlow 'apprentice, Lord Mayor, captain of industry and philanthropist', as the title of his biography described him, provided the essential elements of status and influence. If, as his biographer, the American journalist George Smalley, remarked in an ironic aside, few people could make a joke go such a long way, this reflected an inherent seriousness of purpose which was required in the defence of the companies and the Corporation.

The combination of characteristics embodied in Sir Sydney Waterlow's personality and career can be seen at play in his dynamic engagement with the movement for technical education which formed a crucial strand in the 'Great Awakening' of the 1870s. Against the background of recurrent charges of inertia and self-indulgence, energetic individuals within the company structure began to explore new lines of social and economic activity. In this context technical education became a primary arena for a redefinition of the companies' trade-based interests. The movement to give working people effective access to education geared to the needs of trade and particularly to the use of new technologies had been pioneered by George Birkbeck through the mechanics' institutes of the 1820s. By the mid-19th century the momentum for this form of educational provision had begun to shift to the industrialising nations of continental Europe. The impulse stirring in the City companies was therefore both practical and patriotic.

Sir Sydney Waterlow was the man for the moment. By the early 1870s he had achieved substantial commercial success, held a string of offices at the highest level of the City hierarchy and as Lord Mayor had established an international presence.[28] A man of liberal principles, he combined a deep veneration for City institutions with a practical concern for the conditions of working people and such key social issues as housing and education.[29] The first official moves in 'the encouragement of Art, Manufacture and Technical Education in connection with the City of London' were made by the Lord Mayor, Sills Gibbons, in 1872. Three Stationers, including the Master of the Company William Tyler, were present at the initial meeting but it was not until Waterlow had embarked on his term as Mayor that things began to speed up.[30]

It was characteristic perhaps that the Stationers were not the prime movers in the development of technical education in spite of Waterlow's position as Master of the Company. Immediately after his year of office he was elected onto the Court of the richer Clothworkers and it was through their organisation that much of the City-wide activity was coordinated. Even so, the Stationers contributed to the networks of activity through their participation in the provision of public lectures. At a meeting of the committee to promote technical education held in February 1873, Waterlow proposed that evening lectures should be held in the halls of the livery companies generally, 'and that a fund be formed for founding a College to develop technical education'.[31] The Stationers agreed to the use of their Hall but it was the representatives of the Great Twelve, the Mercers, Drapers, Clothworkers, Goldsmiths and Fishmongers, who

28 As Lord Mayor, Waterlow visited France and entertained both the Viceroy of Egypt and Sultan Abdul Aziz.
29 Waterlow's interest in housing was reflected in his speeches as reported in the newspapers. For an early example of his interventionist approach see J.A. Mayo, *Improved Dwellings for the Industrial Classes, Ground Plan and Elevation of Langbourn Buildings, Mark Street, Paul Street, Finsbury Square, Designed and Erected for Mr Alderman Waterlow by Mr Matthew Allen,* ... (London: 1863). He was chairman of the United Westminster Schools from 1873 to 1893.
30 Waterlow took the chair for the first time in February 1873, Guildhall MS 22,000. I am grateful to Penelope Hunting for this reference and for other information relating to technical education.
31 *Ibid.*

pledged an annual £2,000 (from 1876) to support what was to become the City and Guilds of London Institute.

The lectures at Stationers' Hall proved a very successful experiment. In the *Journal of the Society of Arts* it was reported that, 'In the matter of instruction in technical matters the Stationers' Company may (says the *City Press*) claim to being first in the field'.[32] The provision was advertised in the *Press* and Ellis A. Davidson of Cassells and author of technical manuals agreed to lecture on printing, its history and progress, engraving and lithography. The lectures were free and the Clerk was overwhelmed by 2,400 applications for tickets, 2,100 from City workmen. Such was the demand that one lecture had to be repeated and Stationers' Hall was regularly packed to capacity 'with as orderly audiences as ever came together, all seemingly bent on instruction'.[33]

Proposals for further series on the printing and book trades were made and the London Booksellers Assistants went so far as to suggest that, as well as follow-up lectures, a club for its members might be based at the Hall with a dedicated library.[34] However, with the ending of Waterlow's term as Lord Mayor, interest among the Stationers evaporated. In 1884 the Company received an appeal on behalf of the new College which had recently been opened by the Prince of Wales in a new building in South Kensington. It was read aloud at a Court meeting whereupon Sir Sydney Waterlow moved that the Company should give a donation of £52 10s. to the Institute. This proposal was adopted 'during the pleasure of the Court' and was paid annually (increasing to £100 in 1886 at Waterlow's suggestion). Such benevolence had its limits. In March 1888, at a Court meeting from which Waterlow was conspicuously absent, it was resolved not to make any further payments.[35] This was not entirely an arbitrary act of self-interest. Doubts had arisen over the organisation of the Institute following the withdrawal of support by the Drapers, while the strong tradition of apprenticeship in printing and the allied trades must have made external provision appear less important. The Stationers continued to be involved in the movement for technical education particularly through the creation of the St Bride Foundation Institute (1891) with its workshop-based printing school. This remained a favoured project and after the First World War pains were taken through the Stationers' Company and Printing Industry Technical Board to improve the quality of the provision. Meantime, through the 1890s, the Court remained deaf to appeals for financial support from such outside bodies as the L.C.C. and the City and Guilds Institute. Individual members of the Company, notably J.R. Riddell, the first Principal of the St Bride Institute, were active in the wider world. The Company tended to have its own internal priorities which superseded the initiatives of Sir Sydney Waterlow.

32 *Journal of the Society of Arts*, 18 April 1873.
33 *Ibid.*, 21 March 1873, 18 April 1873. References to the lectures and to their success appear in Court Book a, 4 March, 6 May, 10 June 1873.
34 Court Book a, 14 April 1874.
35 Court Book c, 1 April 1884, 6 April 1886, 26 March 1888.

81. Sir Clive Martin, Lord Mayor, 1999-2000, by David Cobley.

Nevertheless, the need for public endorsement of the company structure was acknowledged in other ways. Waterlow's financial and political success had brought their own benefits to the standing of the Stationers' Company and increasingly attempts were made across the livery companies to develop associations with the rich and powerful. The mechanism by which this object was pursued was the Honorary Freedom and out of it came what might be described as status by association. In the Stationers' Company this form of external public relations was tailored to an institution which was unusually close to the conduct of its original trade. While the Clothworkers and Merchant Taylors dallied with various princes and dukes, the Stationers offered the freedom to W.H.

Smith, the M.P. and first Lord of the Admiralty, whose family fortune had been established through the wholesale distribution of newspapers and the creation of the railway bookstall.[36] Honorary status within the Company remained linked to the cultural product. Authors had never been identified as a suitable category for membership. However, in the changing circumstances of the mid-1920s the Company acknowledged that authors 'fulfil an important function in the production and making of a book' and should therefore be eligible for the Freedom and Livery. This followed the admission to the Company in 1925, according to what *The Times* described as 'quaint observances', of Lord Balfour, Rudyard Kipling and Sir James Barrie.[37] Subsequently, very few individuals were admitted to the Company on the grounds of authorship alone, and the practice of literature in any of its branches remained outside the orbit of the Company until the advent of a troop of journalists in 1932.

As the Stationers moved into the 20th century the recurrent preoccupation was with the identification of a new role in relation to the trade, particularly after the ending of official registration in 1912, and in the search for new members. Externally, the Stationers' Company in the City was most directly influenced by war.

Before 1939 the effects of conflict were only tangentially experienced. Like many other companies at the turn of the century, the Stationers had contributed to the Lord Mayor's fund in support of the City volunteer regiment and their families. After the Boer War ended, the Stationers, along with the Saddlers, Clothworkers, Wax Chandlers and others, received the corporate award of a South African medal. This was a modest extension of an established form of group solidarity. Even the First World War registered only obliquely in the Stationers' records; apart from occasional references to the use of the Hall for drill and the death of a few individuals related to the Company, little direct comment was made on the cataclysmic events taking place overseas. Only on one occasion was the orderly business of the Court disrupted. The meeting held in October 1917 came to an abrupt end when members were forced to take cover in the basement after 'warning was given on the attempted approach of hostile aircraft'.[38]

It was the experience of the Second World War that transcended the limitations of company routine. The general mayhem created by the blitz led to a hiatus in the organisation of all the London companies. During the First World War only the Wax Chandlers' Hall had been destroyed. During the Second, many halls were knocked over in short periods. On the night of 29 December 1940, eight company halls were lost, while on 10 and 11 May 1941 a further six were burned out. As companies regrouped and moved into alternative accommodation this in turn was sometimes bombed in the next wave of attacks. By the end of hostilities, 18 of the 36 halls were destroyed, with 15

36 Charles Wilson, *First with the News: the History of W.H. Smith, 1792-1972* (London: Jonathan Cape, 1985). Smith probably struck a chord in his audience when, at a celebratory dinner, he regretted that the trade in publishing was not eminently prosperous 'and large fortunes were rarely realized by following it', *The Times* 29,904, Thursday, 10 June 1880.

37 *The Times* 44,005, Saturday, 4 July 1925. See also Court Book i, 26 May, 6 October 1925.

38 Court Book g, 2 October 1917.

82. Aerial view of
Ludgate Hill and
Fleet Street, in the
1930s.

variably damaged among which was Stationers'.[39] After serious fire damage on 15 October 1940, Stationers' Hall and the neighbouring Cutlers' Hall had an almost miraculous escape on 29 December as fire swept through the adjacent streets.[40] The Stationers were at least able to salvage something from the wreck, though the loss of adjacent property cast a shadow over the company finances for many years. None of the City companies which lost their halls and other property in the blitz was able to make a rapid return to normality after the war. Priorities for rebuilding and planning restraints delayed the reconstruction of Company premises into the late 1950s.

War, in particular the Second World War, accelerated the process of social and commercial change. The City remained afloat, however, while the companies continued to form a durable part of its infrastructure, even experiencing an unexpected renaissance in the late 20th century. Ian Doolittle suggested that the emergence of a sharp party political divide at the end of the 19th century provided the mechanism for survival. Proposals for reform on one side would almost automatically be met by a rejection on the other. Even the formation of the L.C.C. and the G.L.C. left the Corporation and its constituent parts virtually untouched.

Within the City of London, the Stationers' Company quietly continues about its business. Since 1800 it has provided 23 Lord Mayors, the last holder of the office being Clive Martin, a printer (Master 1997-8). Still linked to its trade of origin, it continues to play its part in civic ceremonies and the life of the City, providing a local habitation for a specific cultural and commercial history embodied in the records which are its greatest treasure. At the same time the Company continues to provide a focus for members of the various trades still centred on print. Its trade activities mark it out at the end of the 20th century as an organisation which has kept faith with its past.

---

39   Early on the morning of 15 October 1940 incendiary bombs fell on the roof of the lobby of the Court Room. The subsequent fire destroyed the roof of the Hall, Blagden, p.282.

40   A good account of the events of 29 December 1940 based on the report of the Clerk to the Cutlers appears in Tom Girtin, *The Mark of the Sword: a Narrative History of the Cutlers' Company, 1189-1975* (London: Hutchinson Benham, 1975), 398-401. Included in the general destruction was Simpkin's 'with its great stock of books', Blagden, p.282.

APPENDIXES

APPENDIX 1

Annals of the Company, City and the Trades of the Guild

YEAR	THE COMPANY	THE TRADE AND PUBLIC EVENTS	YEAR	THE COMPANY	THE TRADE AND PUBLIC EVENTS
1800	Henry Rivington elected Clerk: Work on the Hall completed Robert Mylne's alterations to Hall complete Hall refurbished	Combination Acts prohibit formation of trade unions	1835 (contd.) 1837		Municipal Corporations Act London Union of Compositors becomes National Federation of Compositors Commissioners' report on London municipal corporations
1801	Painted glass window donated by Alderman Cadell inserted in north wall of the Hall—bequest of Alderman Cadell		1839	J.J. Lawson gaoled for printing libellous article in *The Times*	London Printing Machine Managers Trade Society founded
1804		Henry & Sealy Fourdrinier establish self-acting paper-making machines at Frogmore & Two-Waters, Hertfordshire	1840		Messrs Clowes introduces mechanised printing for production of the *Penny Magazine*
1806		Frederick Koenig's steam machine press brought to England	1842	Court considers commissioning a history of the Company Clerk's report on importance of the records	Royal Literary Fund founded at Stationers' Hall (founded as the Literary Fund, 1788) Copyright Act passed
1810	Livery reaches 510, the largest ever recorded Stone repository for records built		1844	John Battiscomb's abstract of the Court Books 1779-1844 completed Company's fire engine scrapped	National Typographical Association founded
1811	Robert Mylne dies. His son, William Chadwick Mylne, appointed Surveyor		1849	George Greenhill dies. His son, Joseph Greenhill, elected Treasurer or Warehouse Keeper and Copyright Registrar	
1813		Statute of Apprentices (1563) repealed	1850	Barge sold to Exeter College, Oxford	
1814		Copyright Act passed *The Times* adopts Koenig's steam machine	1851		Sörenson's type machine displayed at the Great Exhibition
1818		Select Committee on Copyright set up	1852		Abolition of Stamp Duty: beginning of mass circulation newspapers *The Daily Telegraph* established The issue of Free Trade in Books versus price control debated by booksellers, publishers and authors
1822		William Church patents composing machine			
1824		Combination Acts repealed—trade unions increase			
1825-6	General overhaul of premises; creation of Card Room		1853		C. Watt & H. Burgess' patent for manufacture and use of wood pulp London Corporation Commission
1826		London General Trade Society of Compositors founded			
1828		Charles Knight attacks Company's almanack publishing	1855		Newspaper Stamp Duty repealed
1829	Henry Rivington dies Charles Rivington elected Clerk		1856		Requirement of Freedom of the City in order to trade in the City 'square mile' abolished
1830	Clerk reports on state of the records				
1833	Committee set up to consider erecting a record repository		1858	Stationers' Company's School founded	
1834		Stamp duty on almanacks abolished Municipal Corporation Enquiry Association of Pressmen founded London Union of Compositors founded	1860		Society of Day-Working Printers of London founded
1835		Bookbinders & Machine Rulers' Consolidated Union founded	1861	Stationers' Company's School opens at Bolt Court, Fleet Street	
			1862	Copyright registers reorganised	Fine Art Copyright Act passed

YEAR	THE COMPANY	THE TRADE AND PUBLIC EVENTS	YEAR	THE COMPANY	THE TRADE AND PUBLIC EVENTS
1862 (contd.)	Start of increased registration of photographs, drawings, visual devices, and commercial ephemera	Children's Employment Commission highlights working conditions in print trade	1888 (contd.)	J. Butterfield donates stained glass portrait of Shakespeare to complete set of worthies in the west windows	
1863	W.C. Mylne dies. His son, Robert William Mylne, appointed surveyor		1889		Act of Common Council allowing Company to vary lengths of apprenticeships and pay wages
1867		Printing, book binding and papermaking brought under control of Factory Acts Extension Act: working hours regulated for women and children			National Society of Operative Printers and Assistants founded
			1890	Death of Robert William Mylne	The Associated Booksellers changed their name to the Booksellers Association
1869	Charles Rivington retires Charles Robert Rivington elected Clerk	London Society of Lithographic Printers founded	1890s		Mergenthaler Linotype Machine introduced from United States
1871	Anonymous pamphlet 'Entered at Stationers' Hall' attacks Stationers' Company and operation of Registry		1891		London Booksellers' Society founded, meeting held at Stationers' Hall St Bride Institute founded
1872	Sir Sydney Waterlow elected Lord Mayor		1892	Rev. Henry Greenhill appointed first Company chaplain	Bookfolders Union founded Bibliographical Society founded
1873	Edward Arber given leave to transcribe early records		1893	Sir William Tyler elected Company Treasurer, Master and Lord Mayor	Royal Commission on the amalgamation of the City and London County Council
1874		Society of Women Employed in Book-binding founded	1894	Cadell's painted glass in north window replaced by stained glass of Caxton Arber, vol.5 (index) published	The St Bride Printing School founded in the St Bride Institute
1875	Company's share in the Irish estate sold to Skinners' Company for £40,000		1895		The London Booksellers change name to Associated Booksellers of Great Britain and Ireland
1875-94	Arber's Transcript of the Registers ... 1554-1640 5 vols., published		1896		Publishers Association founded Daily Mail established
1876		Royal Commission on Copyright	1898		Printing and Kindred Trades Federation of the United Kingdom founded
1877		The Hattersley composing machine is displayed at the Caxton exhibition Library Association is founded	1899		Metropolitan Boroughs Act
1879		Composing machine perfected by Charles Kastenbein of The Times	1900		British Federation of Master Printers founded
			1902	'New men' let into the Company by the fast track	
1880	W.H. Smith M.P. becomes first Hon. Freeman and Liveryman	Second Royal Commission on livery companies City & Guilds London Institute begins technical examinations in printing Cheap Trains Act	1903	500th anniversary of founding of guild of lymners and textwriters	
			1904	Exhibition of books illustrating the history of printing mounted in the Hall for the congress of the International League of Antiquarian Booksellers	
1883	Joseph Greenhill retires as Copyright registration officer: Clerk takes over running of Registry				
1884	Quarterage abolished	Society of Authors founded Livery Companies Commission	1906		Antiquarian Booksellers' Association founded 'Offset' printing introduced from the United States of America
1885	Stained glass portraits of Tyndale, St Cecilia, Cranmer and Caxton installed in the west windows	Society of Lithographic Artists, Designers, Engravers and Process Workers founded	1907	Cassell takes over remaining almanack publishing for the Company	
1886		National Society of Lithographic Artists, Designers, Writers, Copperplate and Wood Engravers (London) founded, collapses 1898	1909	Silver medal awarded with £5 prize for apprentices of City & Guilds Institute	
			1911	Stationers' Company Copyright registry no longer registers works published in Great Britain	Imperial Copyright Act makes copyright a contract between publisher and author
1887	East Wing remodelled to form Stock Room		1912	Copyright registers (1842-1911) deposited at Public Record Office	
1888	Completion of the rebuilt eastern wing of the hall buildings, including Stock Room		1913-14	Eyre & Rivington, Registers of the Stationers' Company 1640-1708, published	

YEAR	THE COMPANY	THE TRADE AND PUBLIC EVENTS	YEAR	THE COMPANY	THE TRADE AND PUBLIC EVENTS
1916	C.R. Rivington retires Reginald Thurston Rivington elected Clerk		1940	Ernest Mettrop appointed Beadle	
1919	C.R. Rivington completes abstract of Court Books to 1919		1941	Court Room damaged by incendiary bombs	
1920	Livery Committee founded The Company and the Printing Industry Technical Board take over craft examinations from the City & Guilds Institute		1944	Miscellaneous records discovered and described by Sidney Hodgson	National Book Council becomes National Book League
1921	Silver Medal set up First silver medal awarded to George Duke for introducing 200 liverymen	Society of Bookmen founded Society of Scribes and Illuminators founded	1946	Archives returned from wartime safe deposit	
			1947		Society of Archivists founded
1922	Craft Lectures (1922-39) held in the Hall	The St Bride Printing School moves to Stamford Street; renamed London School of Printing	1948	Repair work begins: ceiling of Hall reinforced with steel joists: Court Room refurbished and carving restored but pillars to Card Room not replaced	
1924	Voluntary registry of books and printed material set up at Stationers' Hall	Joint Industrial Council of the Printing and Allied Trades draws up scheme for technical schooling of apprentices	1949	Admission of women rejected Main archives moved to safe closet at back of Hall, opened as a muniment room by Hilary Jenkinson, Keeper of the Public Record Office Sidney Hodgson becomes Hon. Archivist	LCC merges London School of Printing with School of Photo-engraving
1925	Sir James Barrie, Lord Balfour and Rudyard Kipling receive Hon. Freedom		1950	Major Hall indexes legal documents	
1926	First Livery representatives on the Court	Society of Bookmen founded General Strike	1951	(August) exhibition of the Company's archives and its treasures is held in the Hall to celebrate the Festival of Britain Revised coat of arms approved by College of Arms	
1927	*Old Moore* sold to Cassell				
1928	First dinner with ladies held in Hall				
1929	Livery Committee decides against admitting women on the Livery				
1930	W.W. Greg and E. Boswell, *Records of the Court ... 1575-1602*, published by Bibliographical Society	Printing Industries Research Association (PIRA) founded	1953	University Microfilms make private microfilm of Company's principal records in 29 reels for the University of Southern Illinois	
1931		Newspaper Makers' Company founded	1957	Restoration of Hall completed Quatercentenary celebrations of granting of 1557 charter held, including (4 May) dinner in newly restored Hall *Records of the Court of the Stationers' Company (1602-40)* published; editor, W.A. Jackson, awarded Silver Medal R.T. Rivington retires Gordon St Patrick Wells elected Clerk Sir Denis Truscott elected Lord Mayor First annual livery lecture Peak post-war year for bindings of Stationers' Company apprentices	Wynkyn de Worde Society founded; luncheons held at Stationers' Hall
1932	W.W. Greg given Silver Medal for edition of Court Book 1575-1602 Sir Percy Greenaway elected Lord Mayor				
1933	Dent Memorial Lectures held annually in the Hall from 1933 to 1938 Amalgamation of Stationers' and Newspaper Makers' Companies; 162 new liverymen admitted	Commissioners appointed to examine municipal corporation and livery companies			
1934-6 1936	Prince of Wales Master				
1937	Company of Stationers and Newspaper Makers receives new Charter Graham Pollard's 'Company before 1557' and 'Early constitution' published in *The Library*		1958		Carr Committee on Apprenticeship: apprenticeship downgraded
1940	Dec 29/30: Stationers' Hall roof destroyed Quarterage books destroyed in blitz William Poulten retires	National Book Committee founded to protect books from Purchase Tax, deriving from the National Book Council (founded 1925)	1959	Ludgate Hill property sold for £663,000 Master and Wardens Committee formed	
			1960	Cyprian Blagden, *The Stationers' Company, a History 1403-1959*, published	

YEAR	THE COMPANY	THE TRADE AND PUBLIC EVENTS	YEAR	THE COMPANY	THE TRADE AND PUBLIC EVENTS
1961	English Stock extinguished by act of parliament D.F. McKenzie, *Stationers' Company Apprentices, 1605-1640*, published	Institute of Printing founded 'to further the science and art of printing'	1978 (contd.) 1980	D.F. McKenzie, *Stationers' Company Apprentices, 1701-1800*, published Archives installed in room near the library above the Court Room	 National Book League becomes Book Trust
1963		Typographical Association and London Typographical Society merge to become the National Graphical Association	1981	Bibliographical Society library installed in back attic	'The Year of the Receiver'—a year of many bankruptcies in the printing industry
1964		London College of Printing (LCP) moves to the Elephant and Castle Industrial Training Act effectively ends apprenticeship	1982		Sun Printers & Odhams merge to become the British Printing Corporation (BPC) taken over by Robert Maxwell
1965	Stanley Osborne elected Beadle	Wolvercote Mill installs the first computer to control papermaking	1983 1984	Stationers' Company's School closed by order of the local authority Supernumerary List for Livery set up	Eddie Shah, chairman of Messenger group of Newspapers, challenges closed shop by encouraging non-union staff
1966	Rules to allow 'merit' elections to Court out of seniority approved by Court			Charles Rivington retires Keith Fletcher appointed Hon. Librarian	
1967		Standard Book Numbering Agency founded Books identified by an unique code or International Standard Book Number or ISBN		Colonel Alexander Rubens retires Captain Peter Hames elected Clerk	
1969	Pippa Woodman becomes the first woman to be called into Court Exhibition of archive held in Hall for National Library Week	 National Library Week	1985	Dudley Ward retires as Beadle Committee of the Future proposed Size of Livery is limited to 450 Clerk instigates a schedule of annual repair and refurbishment during the summer closure	
1970	First issue of *The Stationer & Newspaper Maker*			Report of the Committee of the Future	
1972	Stanley Osborne retires as Beadle Dudley Ward elected Beadle			Archive from 1554 catalogued by Hon. Archivist and microfilmed as a commercial venture by Chadwyck-Healey, bringing the Company £35,000 in royalties	
1973	Trades of the Guild Committee founded	The British Library Act (1972) separates British Museum Library from the British Museum	1986	Entry by 'Family Redemption' added to entry by Patrimony	News International, printers of *The Times* and *The Sun*, strike after move to Wapping
1974	Rule requiring Clerk to have legal training is abolished Company founds Library Trust; attic designated for new library Stanley Osborne retires as Assistant Clerk	BFMP (founded 1900) changes name to the British Printing Industries Federation (BPIF)	1987 1988	 Stained glass commemorating 500 years of English paper-making inserted in an east window of the Hall	*Financial Times* buys site in Docklands for new print works Newspaper press abandons Fleet Street
	J. Moran appointed Hon. Librarian Gordon Wells retires Colonel Alexander Rubens elected Clerk D.F. McKenzie, *Stationers' Company Apprentices, 1641-1700*, published				'The end of Fleet Street' exhibition held at the Museum of London
1976		*Irish Times* first uses VDUs for editorial advertising and accounts	1989	Librarians and archivists eligible to join the Company	
1977	Rules and Ordinances amended to allow women to join Livery	First robotised reel handling system installed by Coventry Newspapers	1990	Robin Myers, *Stationers' Company Archive 1554-1984*, published Court Room ebonised Chippendale chairs, 1750, are sold	Robert Maxwell launches *The European*
1978	Library opened to the public James Moran dies Charles Rivington appointed Hon. Librarian Robin Myers appointed Hon. Archivist			Original 17th-century oak benches are sold Peter Rippon buys the benches and gives them back to the Company	

YEAR	THE COMPANY	THE TRADE AND PUBLIC EVENTS	YEAR	THE COMPANY	THE TRADE AND PUBLIC EVENTS
1990 (contd.)	Quarterage reintroduced Hall security tightened		1997	Captain Hames retires Brigadier Denzil Sharp appointed Clerk New Millennium Review Committee set up	The British Library moves from Bloomsbury to St Pancras
1991		Robert Maxwell dies; Maxwell empire collapses with world-wide repercussions	1998	Younger People Working Party set up	
1992	Library is refurbished, new ceiling, lighting and heating installed Bibliographical Society centenary dinner held at Stationers' Hall		1999	Clive Martin elected 29th Stationer Lord Mayor Livery Committee Working Party set up	
1993	The Livery limit is raised to 475		2000	Closure of Stationers' Hall Registry Forecourt re-paved, flood-lighting installed	
1994	Trades of the Guild Committee becomes Trade and Industry Forum		2001	Clive Martin appointed knight in New Year's Honours List	
1996	Conference on 'The Stationers' Company and the Book Trade' held in the Hall				

APPENDIX 2

Archival and Other Exhibitions held at Stationers' Hall 1912-95

June 1912	Major exhibition of rare books illustrating the history of English Printing held in the Hall by the International Antiquarian Booksellers' Association. [Court Book g, 7 May 1912.]
23 April 1923	Tercentenary Exhibition of Shakespeare's First Folio. [Court Book h, 5 June 1923, printed list of exhibits.]
August 1937	Exhibition of Books, Plate, Manuscripts etc. held in the Hall. [Court Book j, 1 June 1937.]
August 1951	Exhibition of Books, Manuscripts, Plate, held in the Stock Room to celebrate the Festival of Britain, with a printed catalogue by Sidney Hodgson preceded by a brief history of the Company. [Court Book l, 5 June 1951.]
13, 14 December 1954	Exhibition for the British Records Association. [Court Book m, 13 July 1953.]
19 March 1963	Exhibition of Books, Manuscripts and Artefacts for the AGM of the Bibliographical Society. [Court Book n, 8 January 1963.]
18 July 1963	Exhibition for those attending the International Printing Exhibition. Reception by the Master, John Mylne Rivington. [Court Book n, 30 July 1963.]
6 March 1969	Exhibition on the occasion of the inauguration of National Library Week: Invitation by the Master, Charles Arthur Rivington.
6 March 1979	Registers put on view for delegation of printers from the Chinese People's Republic visiting the Monotype Corporation.
25 November 1981	'The Sovereign & the Stationers' Company', Exhibition in the Court Room to celebrate the 75th anniversary of the Historical Association with visit by HM Queen Elizabeth and HRH Prince Philip. [Typed catalogue of the 27 items on display.]
23 September 1982	'The English Stock of the Stationers' Company', exhibition to accompany the archivist's talk to the Wynkyn de Worde Society. [Catalogue appended to printed edition of the talk.]
20 October 1982	'The Christian Roots of the the Worshipful Company of Stationers' put on for visit of the Senior Wives' Fellowship. [Sixteen items with typed catalogue.]
7 February-29 April 1984	Exhibition demonstrating the Company's role in the printing and publishing industries (1554-1984) held at the Science Museum. [Court Book q, 10 January and 6 March 1984.]
4 June 1984	'Feasts & Entertainments', an exhibition of 18th- to 20th-century bills, menus and invitations to celebrate the award of silver medal to Sir Derek Greenaway.
23 April 1985	'Caxtoniana' exhibition of Caxton items and minutes of the Caxton Celebration Committee (1877) on the occasion of *Caxton '85* trade fair.
June 1985	The Printing Ordinance (1679), warrant for payment to King's Printer (1742) and other Tottel family documents recently restored by conservation students at Camberwell College of Art and Design.

May 1986	Vellum bindings and Shakespeare entries in Liber B and Liber D.
May 1987	'Books of Excellence Entered at Stationers' Hall' to celebrate the *Excellence '87* exhibition opened by the Duchess of York and organised by the Master, Allen Thompson.
September 1987	'Bindings from the Company's Archive'.
March 1988	'The Crown and the Stationers' Company', exhibition on the occasion of the election of the Duchess of York to the Honorary Freedom with a short talk to the Duke and Duchess.
February 1988	'Windows' designs, engravings, minutes of the Caxton and the Prince of Wales windows.
July 1989	'Samuel Richardson, Citizen and Stationer' exhibition to mark the tercentenary of Samuel Richardson's birth.
October 1994	Exhibition of major records for the AGM of the Bibliographical Society.
October 1995	Exhibition of major records for the winter meeting of Lady Margaret Hall, Oxford in Court Room with a talk on the Company and its records by the Hon. Archivist.

APPENDIX 3A

Masters

NAME	LIVERY	MASTER	TRADE
STEPHENS, William (1739-1816)	1762	1800	Stationer
PARKER, Henry (1741?-1809)	1762	1801	Printseller
DILLY, Charles (1739-1807)	1763	1802	Bookseller
DOMVILLE, Sir William, Bt. (1741-1833)	1764	1803	Bookseller
NICHOLS, John (1745-1826)	1766	1804	Printer
RIVINGTON, Francis (1745-1828)	1766	1805	Bookseller
BLOXHAM, Sir Mathew, Kt. (1744?-1822)	1766	1806	
VALLANCE, Thomas (1747-1823)	1768	1807	Stationer
BYFIELD, Henry Woolsey (1750-1826)	1768	1808	Bookseller
HAWKSWORTH, Samuel (1749-1827?)	1770	1809	Stationer and Bookseller
CRICKITT, John (1749-1811)	1770	1810	Printer
BOYDELL, Josiah (1752-1817)	1773	1811	Engraver
SMITH, Thomas (1747-1829)	1768	1812	Stockbroker
BARKER, John (1751-1831)	1772	1813	Stationer
STREET, James Wallis (1750-1817)	1772	1814	Stationer
COLLYER, Joseph (1751-1827)	1772	1815	Engraver
MAGNAY, Christopher (1768-1826)	1807	1816	Stationer
PAYNE, Thomas (1752?-1831)	1774	1817	Bookseller
GARDINER, Joseph (1754-1829)	1775	1818	Stationer
RIVINGTON, Charles (1754-1831)	1775	1819	Bookseller
WALKER, William (1756-1830)	1777	1820	Tea Dealer
WITHERBY, William (1758-1840)	1779	1821	Law Stationer
DAVIDSON, Robert (1780?-1824)	1779	1822	Pocket Book Maker
WILKIE, George (1760-1826)	1780	1823	Bookseller
VENABLES, William (1793-1884)	1814	1824	Stationer
BENSLEY, Thomas (1761?-1835)	1781	1825	Printer
MARSH, Richard (1758?-1847)	1784	1826	Fancy Stationer
TURNER, Thomas (1766-1843)	1787	1827	Paperhanging manufacturer
HARRISON, James (1765-1847)	1787	1828	Printer
CROWDER, John (1756-1830)	1823	1829	Printer
KEY, Sir John, Bt. (1794-1858)	1815	1830	Stationer
PETTIWARD, Roger (1756-1833)	1776	1831	No Business
BAKER, Joseph (1767-1853)	1787	1832	Engraver
WOODFALL, George (1767-1844)	1788	1833	Printer
FOURDRINIER, Charles (1768-1844)	1788	1834	Stationer
WITTS, Edward London (1770?-1841)	1790	1835	Stationer
CHAPMAN, Thomas (1764-1849)	1790	1836	Printer and Bookseller
CHAPMAN, William Francis (1769-1849)	1790	1838	Stationer

NAME	LIVERY	MASTER	TRADE
ROWE, George (1770-1839)	1791	1839	Fancy Stationer
STEEL, Thomas (1770-1840)	1791	1840	Law Stationer
BARRON, William (1762-1851)	1790	1841	Stationer
BALDWIN, Charles (1774-1869)	1795	1842-3	Printer
BATE, Richard (1774-1856)	1796	1844	Stationer
CARPENTER, William (1770-1854)	1792	1845	Printer
WALTER, John (1776-1847)	1797	1846	Printer of *The Times*
MAGNAY, Sir William, Bt. (1797-1871)	1816	1847	Wholesale Stationer
COX, John Lewis (1777-1856)	1798	1848	Printer
GIBBONS, Benjamin (1775-1861)	1799	1849	Printer
NICHOLS, John Bowyer (1779-1863)	1800	1850	Printer
GARDINER, Thomas (1779-1866)	1800	1851	Printer
TAYLOR, Thomas (1779-1861)	1800	1852	Coal Merchant and Stationer
FARLOW, William (1781-1866)	1802	1853	Law Stationer
GYFFORD, Samuel (1780?-1856)	1802	1854	Stationer
MOON, Sir Francis Graham, Bt. (1796-1871)	1828	1855	Stationer
GRAHAM, Nathaniel (1782-1861)	1803	1856	Bookseller
DICKINSON, John (1781-1869)	1804	1857-8	Stationer
SADDINGTON, John (1785-1861)	1806	1859	Copper Plate Printer
FOSS, Henry (1790-1868)	1813	1860	Bookseller
ADLARD, James William (1795-1865)	1815	1861	Printer
SIMPSON, John (1794-1868)	1817	1863	Music Seller
DAIKERS, James (1777-1869)	1817	1864	Stationer
JONES, Thomas (1796-1876)	1818	1865	Paper Hanger
HODGSON, Edmund (1794-1875)	1819	1866-7	Stationer
ADLARD, Henry (1799-1893)	1821	1868	Engraver and Printer
GOOD, Henry (1800-74)	1821	1869	Stationer
BROWN, Henry George (1801-81)	1822	1870	Stationer
TYLER, William (1802-75)	1823	1871	Stationer
WATERLOW, Sir Sydney Hedley, Bt. (1822-1906)	1847	1872	Law Stationer and Printer
RIVINGTON, Francis (1805-1885)	1826	1873	Bookseller
WATSON, William (1806-86)	1827	1874	Stationer
GOOD, William (1806-84)	?	1875	Stationer, Rope and Twine Manufacturer
RIVINGTON, Charles (1806-76)	1827	1876	Solicitor
BROWN[1], Henry George		1876	
RIVINGTON, William (1807-1888)	1829	1877	Printer
CHATER, George (1808-92)	1829	1878	Stationer
TRUSCOTT, Sir Francis Wyatt, Bt. (1824-95)	1846	1879 & 1887	Printer and Stationer
FIGGINS, James (1811-84)	1832	1880	Type Founder
STARKEY, Richard William (1809-90)	1830	1881	Stationer

1 Charles Rivington died in August and H.G. Brown succeeded for the rest of the guild year (1876-7)

NAME	LIVERY	MASTER	TRADE
MILES, Joseph Johnson (1811-84)	1832	1882	Bookseller
MILES, John (1813-86)	1834	1883	Bookseller
LAYTON, Charles (1807-88)	1837	1884	Bookseller
WALKER, Edmund (1817-1904)	1886	1885	Fancy Stationer
HANSARD, Thomas Curson (1813-91)	1839	1886	Printer
HAWKSWORTH, William (1820-91)	1841	1888	Stationer and Bookseller
DIGGENS, James George Alexander (1820-1905)	1841	1889	Stationer
ADLARD, James Evan (1820-90)	1824	1890	Printer
GREENHILL, Joseph (1803-92)	1824	1890	Bookseller, Stationers' Hall Registry
SINGER, George (1821-1903)	1842	1891	Printer
RICHARDSON, Guildford Barker (1816-95)	1843	1892	Bookseller
TYLER, Sir George Robert, Bt. (1835-97)	1856	1893 & 1894	Stationer
BUTTERWORTH, Joshua Whitehead (1817-95)	1839	1894	Bookseller
SOTHERAN, Henry (1825-1905)	1846	1895	Bookseller and Stationer
STEPHENS, William Richard (1825-1913)	1896	1896	Stationer
CLAY, Charles John (1828-1905)	1849	1897	Printer
RIDER, William (1828-1905)	1849	1898	Printer
HUNT, Joseph (1829-1904)	1850	1899	Stationer
HARRISON, James William (1830-1912)	1851	1900	Printer
TRUSCOTT, Sir George Wyatt, Bt. (1857-1941)	1878	1901	Printer
ROE, Matthew Thomas (1831-1906)	1853	1902	Stationer
MILES, John (1835-1921)	1856	1902	Bookseller
STRONG, Sir Thomas Vezey, Kt. (1867-1920)	1888	1903	Wholesale Stationer
NORTH-COX, George (1836-1913)	1857	1904	Bookseller
ION, John (1837-1914)	1858	1905	Wholesale Stationer
STEVENS, Richard (1837-1930)	1858	1906	Law Stationer
HODGSON, Henry Hill (1838-1919)	1859	1907	Book Auctioneer
COX, Edward Webster (1839-1921)	1860	1908	Printer
CLOWES, William Charles Knight (1839-1917)	1860	1909	Printer
CHATER, George (1839-60)	1860	1910	Stationer
GREENAWAY, Daniel (1841-1917)	1862	1911	Stationer
EYRE, George Edward Briscoe (1841-1922)	1864	1912	Printer
HILL, Henry (1844-1927)	1865	1913	Quill Pen Maker
GOOD, Henry (1845-1926)	1866	1914	Stationer
WATERLOW, Herbert Jameson (1846-1921)	1867	1915	Printer and Stationer
COX, Edward Hanslope (1848-1938)	1869	1916	Law Stationer
MARSHALL, Lord Horace Brooks of Hampstead (1865-1936)	1866	1917	Newspaper Publisher
NICHOLS, John Bruce (1848-1929)	1869	1918	Printer
LAYTON, Edwin James (1850-1929)	1871	1919	Bookseller
UNWIN, Edward (1840-1933)	1871	1920	Printer and Stationer

NAME	LIVERY	MASTER	TRADE
RIVINGTON, Charles Robert (1846-1928)	1868	1921	Solicitor
FITCH, Herbert (1850-1933)	1871	1922	Fancy Stationer
VACHER, Edward Pinney (1850-1942)	1874	1923	Stationer
BENTLEY, Richard (1854-1936)	1873	1924	Bookseller
MILES, Frederick Harris (1854-1946)	1875	1925	Bookseller and Stationer
BLADES, Sir George Rowland (Lord Ebbisham) (1868-1953)	1917	1926	Printer
RIVINGTON, Arthur William (1854-1929)	1875	1927	Solicitor
HARRISON, Sir Cecil Reeves, Kt. (1856-1940)	1877	1928	Printer
WATERLOW, Sir William Alfred, Bt.	1914	1929	Printer and Stationer
HARRISON, Edgar Erat (1856-1933)	1877	1930	Printer
WILLIAMS, John Henry (1857-1937)	1878	1931 & 1932	Stationer
GREENAWAY, Sir Percy Walter, Bt. (1874-1972)	1895	1932	Printer
WALES, HRH The Prince of (later King Edward VIII, Duke of Windsor) (1894-1972)	Hon. Freedom 1933	1934 & 1935	
BLUMENFELD, Ralph David, *Deputy* (1864-1948)	1933	1934	Newspaper Editor
DAVY, John William, *Deputy* (1858-1942)	1879	1935	Printer
ADLARD, Robert Evan (1860-1941)	1881	1936	Printer
SANDLE, Sidney John (1898-1937)	1919		Wholesale Stationer
BADDELEY, Sir John William (1869-1951)	1927	1937	Printer and Stationer
MAUGER, Edward, Lord Iliffe (1877-1960)	1933	1937	Newspaper Proprietor
TRUSCOTT, Henry Dexter (1861-1950)	1882	1938	Printer
CLAY, Charles Felix (1861-1947)	1882	1938	Printer
AUSTEN-LEIGH, Edward Chenevix (1867-1949)	1888	1939	Printer
UNWIN, Edward (1870-1959)	1891	1939	Printer and Stationer
WATERLOW, Sir Edgar Lutwyche, Bt. (1870-1954)	1893	1940	Printer
LOW, Stanley (1873-1955)	1894	1940	Stationer
WILKINSON, Sir George Henry, Bt. (1885-1967)	1906	1941	Papermaker
ASTOR, John Jacob (Lord Astor of Hever) (1886-1971)	1933	1942	Newspaper Proprietor
Cox, Herbert Arthur (1877-1956)	1898	1943	Chartered Accountant, Printer
WATTS, Charles John (1866-1964)	1899	1944	Wholesale Stationer
BURT, Robert Kingston (1878-1945)	1899	1945	Papermaker's Agent
JORDAN, Herbert William (1874-1947)	1906	1946	Printer and Publisher
HARRISON, Victor Bobardt (1885-1959)	1906	1947	Printer

NAME	LIVERY	MASTER	TRADE
HARRISON, Sir Bernard Guy, Kt. (1885-1978)	1906	1948	Printer
HODGSON, Sidney (1876-1973)	1907	1949	Book Auctioneer
RIVINGTON, Reginald Thurston (1888-1971)	1909	1950	Solicitor
FOWLER, Arthur George (1889-1961)	1910	1951	Printer
TOLLIT, Charles Clifton (1892-1965)	1913	1952	Printer and Stationer
WILL, William (1892-1958)	1913	1953	General Manager and Proprietor of the *Graphic*
AUSTEN-LEIGH, Richard Arthur (1872-1961)	1901	1954	Printer
PENMAN, William (1893-1970)	1914	1955	Paper Agent
GRASEMANN, Cuthbert (d.1961)	1933	1956	Newspaper Agent
PENMAN, Victor Robert	1914	1957	Paper Agent
SIMON, George Percival (1893-1963)	1933	1958	Newspaper Publisher
TRUSCOTT, Sir Denis Henry, Kt. (1908-89)	1929	1959	Printer
OUSEY, James Edward (1882-1974)	1906	1960	Stationer
YOUNG, William Henry (1897-1967)	1918	1961	Printer
BETTS, John (d.1967)	1933	1962	Newspaperman
RIVINGTON, John Mylne (1897-1972)	1918	1963	Barrister
BAILEY, James Alexander (1899-1969)	1920	1964	Book Importer
JOHNSON, Henry Arthur (1899-1989)	1921	1965	Printers' Engineer
KELLIE, Donald Fores (1895-1974)	1923	1966	Bookbinder
THOMPSON, Henry Frank (1889-1972)	1923	1967	Manufacturing Stationer
RIVINGTON, Charles Arthur (1902-94)	1924	1968	Solicitor
HUBBARD, Alfred John (1902-76)	1926	1969	Printer
BURT, Eric (1906-74)	1927	1970	Printer
UNWIN, Philip Soundy (1905-81)	1929	1971	Publisher
RIDDELL, George Low (1907-98)	1929	1972	Printer
GREENAWAY, Alan Pearce (1913-94)	1931	1973	Printer
GREENAWAY, Sir Derek Burdick, Bt. (1910-94)	1931	1974	Printer
KENYON, Leonard Entwisle (1908-79)	1933	1975	Printer
MATSON, Jack (d.1980)	1958	1976	Accountant and Printer
BENN, Edward Glanvill (1905-2000)	1935	1977	Publisher
COULTON, Brian Trevena (b.1917)	1947	1978	Printer
HODGSON, Wilfrid Becket (b.1915)	1936	1979	Book Auctioneer
ROBINSON, Kenneth Buckingham (1911-99)	1942	1980	Printer
WYNDHAM-SMITH, David (b.1916)	1957	1981	Printer
COX, Peter (b.1923)	1945	1982	Book Distributor
RIVINGTON, Christopher Thurston (b.1920)	1942	1983	Publisher
VINEY, Laurence (b.1919)	1945	1984	Printer
TINDLE, Sir Ray, Kt. (b.1926)	1968	1985	Newspaper Proprietor
THOMPSON, Allen (1919-97)	1946	1986	Printer
TOLLITT, Mark (b.1925)	1948	1987	Stationer
LEIGHTON, Robert J. (b.1927)	1949	1988	Bookbinder

NAME	LIVERY	MASTER	TRADE
RYMAN, John Desmond (b.1929)	1948	1989	Stationer
CORRIGAN, Thomas (b.1932)	1973	1990	Papermaker
YOUNG, William (b.1919)	1952	1991	Printer
MANDL, George (1923-97)	1956	1992	Papermaker
RIPPON, Peter (b.1923)	1967	1993	Newspaper Proprietor
HASELDEN, Richard (b.1927)	1957	1994	Printer
BROOKER, Alan (b.1931)	1970	1995	Printer and Publisher
FULLICK, Roy (b.1925)	1973	1996	Printer
MARTIN, Sir Clive, Kt. (b.1935)	1960	1997	Printer
SULLIVAN, Vernon (b.1930)	1960	1998	Printer
HARRISON, Richard (b.1936)	1961	1999	Printer
CHAPPELL, Henry Frank (b.1940)	1963	2000	Printer

APPENDIX 3B

Silver Medallists

1922   GEORGE DUKE
First holder of the silver medal awarded 4 July 1922 in 'hearty appreciation of the very successful efforts you have made for many years past in gathering into the Company as freemen upwards of 200 members of the printing trade.' [Court Book h, 4 July 1922.]

1922   JOHN ROBERTSON RIDDELL
Presented 15 December 1922 at a lecture given by Mr Riddell in the Hall, 'in consideration of many services rendered during recent years and by which the Company has considerably benefited.' [Court Book h, 5 December 1922.]

1923   WILLIAM ARTHUR NEWSOME, BA
An assistant master at the Company's School. Presented 9 January 1923 as a recognition of his services to the Company's School on retiring after 33 years. [Court Book h, 17 November 1923.]

1931   SIR WALTER WILLIAM GREG, LITT.D, FBA
Presented at a court luncheon, 7 September 1931, 'as a recognition of his recent important work research work into the early history of the Company.' [Court Book i, 7 July 1931.]

1939   MAJOR JOHN HUCK, OBE
The former Head Master of the Company's School. Presented 10 January 1939. [Court Book k, 10 January 1939.]

1940   THE MAYOR, ALDERMEN AND BURGESSES OF THE BOROUGH OF WISBECH
Presented 'in recognition of the valued services rendered by the Borough of Wisbech in receiving the Staff and the Boys of the School in their homes and in providing the premises for carrying on the work of the School.' [Court Book k, 2 April 1940.]

1945   HENRY MAURICE WOTTON, MA
The Clerk to the Governors of the Company's School presented 'in consideration of the services rendered by him to the School.' [Court Book k, 10 April 1940.]

1958   PROFESSOR WILLIAM A. JACKSON
'... of Harvard University had completed his work of editing the Records of the Court of the Company from 1602-1640 for the Bibliographical Society of London and had presented a copy of the Book to the Company ... Mr. Hodgson ... strongly recommended that this valuable service to the Company be recognised by the award to Professor Jackson of the Company's Medal.' [Court Book m, 14 January 1958.]

1969   PAST MASTER SIDNEY HODGSON, FSA
The Master presented the Company's silver medal 'for highly valued and long service to the Company and for his great work in keeping and preserving the Company's historic records.' [Court Book o, 2 December 1969.]

1978   PAST MASTER CHARLES A. RIVINGTON, MA
Presented with the Company's Silver Medal, 2 May 1978 'in high appreciation of the long and outstanding services given to the Company.' [Court Book p, 4 April 1978; *The Stationer and Newspaper Maker*, 18 autumn 1978.]

1984   PAST MASTER SIR DEREK BURDICK GREENAWAY, BT, CBE, TD, JP, DL
'In view of the outstanding and distinguished service rendered to the Worshipful Company of

Stationers and Newspaper Makers over many years' awarded the Silver Medal of the Company 26 June 1984. [Court Book q, 6 March 1984; *The Stationer and Newspaper Maker*, 34 summer 1984.]

1985 PAST MASTER DR GEORGE LOW RIDDELL, OBE, B.SC, C.CHEM, FRSC
Awarded the Company's Silver Medal for 'outstanding services to the Company for more than 50 years', on Thursday, 9 May 1985. [Court Book q, 7 May 1985; *The Stationer and Newspaper Maker*, 37 summer 1985.]

1987 DAVID WYNDHAM-SMITH, MBE
In recognition of the 'outstanding contributions which he has made to enhance the status of the Company', awarded 1 December 1987. [Court Book q, 1 December 1987; *The Stationer and Newspaper Maker*, 45 spring 1988.]

APPENDIX 3C

Members of the Company who have served as Lord Mayor since 1800

1813-4	Sir William Domville, Bt. *
1821-2	Sir Christopher Magnay, Bt. *
1825-6	William Venables *
1829-30	John Crowder *
1830-1	Sir John Key, Bt. *
1843-4	Sir William Magnay, Bt. *
1854-5	Sir Francis Graham Moon, Bt. *
1867-8	William Ferneley Allen
1872-3	Sir Sydney Hedley Waterlow, Bt. *
1879-80	Sir Francis Wyatt Truscott, Bt. *
1893-4	Sir George Robert Tyler, Bt. *
1900-1	Sir Frank Green, Bt.
1908-9	Sir George Wyatt Truscott, Bt. *
1910-11	Sir Thomas Vezey Strong, Kt. *
1915-6	Sir Charles Wakefield, Bt.
1918-9	Sir Horace Marshall, Bt. *
1921-2	Sir John James Baddeley, Bt.
1926-7	Sir George Rowland Blades (Lord Ebbisham of Cobham) *
1929-30	Sir William Alfred Waterlow, Bt. *
1932-3	Sir Percy Walter Greenaway, Bt. *
1940-1	Sir George Henry Wilkinson, Bt. *
1957-8	Sir Denis Henry Truscott, Kt. *
1999-2000	Sir Clive Martin, Kt. *

* See 3A Masters of the Company

APPENDIX 3D

Honorary Freemen and Liverymen

1880	The Right Honourable W.H. Smith, MP
1893	Sir John Evans, KCB, DCL, FRS
1898	Sir E. Maunde Thompson, GCB, DCL, LLD
1899	J. Passmore Edwards, Esq
1901	General Sir James Willcocks, GCB, GCMG
1913	Henry Chettle, MA
1923	Sir Israel Gollancz, LITT D, FBA
1925	The Earl of Balfour, KG
1925	Rudyard Kipling, Esq
1925	Sir James Barrie, Bt., OM
1927	Earl Baldwin, KG
1929	The Right Revd Lord Davidson, PC
1931	Sir Frederic Kenyon, GBE, KCB
1933	HRH Edward, Prince of Wales
1934	Sir Henry B. Brackenbury, LPD, MD
1944	The Most Revd Lord Lang of Lambeth
1946	Lt-Gen Lord Freyberg, VC
1956	The Rt Hon The Earl of Stockton, OM, FRS
1957	Sir George Wilkinson, Bt., KCVO, LLD
1966	Sir Stanley Unwin, KCMG, LLD
1972	Sir Basil Blackwell, Kt
1983	HRH The Prince of Wales, KG, KT, PC, GCB
1984	Sir Edward Pickering, Kt
1988	HRH The Duchess of York
1996	Admiral of the Fleet, The Lord Lewin of Greenwich, KG, GCB, LVO, DSC

| 1998 | *Honorary Associate* |
| | Carl Landegger |

APPENDIX 3E

Warehouse Keepers and Treasurers[1]

	TREASURER	WAREHOUSE KEEPER AND TREASURER	REGISTRAR
George Greenhill (d.1849)		1798-1849	1798-1849
Joseph Greenhill (1803-1897)		1749-1783	
	1885-1889		1749-83
George Robert Tyler		1893-1894	
Henry Sotheran		1894-1896	
Thomas Harrison		1896-1897	
William Rider		1897-1899	
William H. Teulon		1899-1900	
William H. Miles		1900-1901	
Sir George Wyatt Truscott	1901-1941		
Herbert A. Cox	1941-1943		
Sir Percy Greenaway	1943-1953		
Sir George H. Wilkinson		1953-1961	
William Penman	1957-1959		
Sir Guy Harrison	1961-1964		
John M.Rivington	1964-1972		
Jack Matson	1972-1974		
H. Guy Virtue	1973-1979		
Geoffrey Hooper	1979-1983		
Peter King	1983-1991		
Robert Russell	1991-1998		
Dennis Osborne	1998-		

1   See p.112.

APPENDIX 3F

Chairmen of the Livery Committee

1920	R.A. Austen-Leigh	1954	C de Ryck	1980	R.F. Fullick
1927	G de L'E. Duckworth	1957	A.W. Last	1982	R.K. Haselden
1929	H.A. Cox	1960	G.L. Riddell	1982	A.J. Copley
1932	P.N. McFarlane	1962	H.W. Underhill	1984	A.T. Heyer
1934	R. Metghin	1964	A.G.L. Atkinson	1986	E.W. Haylock
1936	S. Hodgson	1966	N.C.B. Harrison	1988	A.H. Rodgers
1938	D.F. Kellie	1968	C.T. Rivington	1988	A.T. Heyer
1940	S.E. Sandle	1970	W.C. Young	1989	K.J. Hutton
1944	W.N. Bacon	1972	J.C. Moran	1991	R.B. Mountford
1947	J.A. Bailey	1974	K. Day	1993	L.G. Menhinick
1949	H.F. Thompson	1976	R.W. Read	1996	I.D.F. Fidler
1951	P. Unwin	1976	P.T. Rippon	1998	L.T. Lack
1953	F.A. Garrett	1978	J.E. Langford	2000	Sir Jeremy Elwes

APPENDIX 3G

Honorary Archivists and Librarians

Frederick Dorling Bone, Hon. Librarian, 1937, Journalist

James Moran, Chairman, Library Trust, 1972-74, Hon. Librarian 1974-8, Hon. Archivist 1972-8, Printing Journalist

Charles Rivington, Chairman, Library Trust and Hon. Librarian 1978-84, Solicitor

Keith Fletcher, Hon. Librarian 1984- , Antiquarian Bookseller

Sidney Hodgson, Hon. Archivist (officially appointed), 1951-1972, Book Auctioneer

Robin Myers, Hon. Archivist 1978- , Teacher and Bibliographer

APPENDIX 3H

The Company's Chaplains

1892-1907	The Revd Henry Greenhill
1907-1919	The Revd Joseph Miles
1919-1938	The Revd Henry Stewart Miles of All Saints, Whetstone
1938	The Revd William Coleman Percy (February to May)
1938-1966	The Revd George Henry Palmer, freeman and liveryman, Vicar of Benson, Oxfordshire
1966-1968	The Revd Dewi Morgan, Rector of St Bride's, Fleet Street
1968-1970	The Revd Canon Richard Tydeman, Rector of the Church of the Holy Sepulchre, Holborn
1970-1974	The Revd Peter Lillingston, Vicar of St Martin-within-Ludgate
1974-1976	The Revd Percy Coleman, Rector of St Andrew by the Wardrobe
1976-1979	The Revd Dewi Morgan, Rector of St Bride's, Fleet Street
1979-1984	The Revd Percy Coleman, Rector of St Andrew by the Wardrobe
1984-1987	The Revd John Williams, Chaplain of the Queen's Chapel in the Savoy
1987-1989	The Revd Chandos C.H.M. Morgan, Royal Navy, Rector of St Margaret, Lothbury
1989-2000	The Revd Canon John Oates, Rector of St Bride's, Fleet Street

APPENDIX 3J

Editors of The Stationer and Newspaper Maker

1970-1973	James Moran
1973-1977	Walter Cade
1977-1982	Kenneth Day
1982-1988	Alfred Peers
1988-1989	Robert Hedley Lewis
1989-1990	Alfred Peers
1990-1992	Robert Russell
1992-1994	Allen Thompson
1994-2000	Keith Hutton

APPENDIX 3K

Clerks

C: CLERK   L: LIVERY   M: MASTER

Henry Rivington (1765-1829), C.1800-1829, L.1786, Solicitor

Charles Rivington (1806-1876), C.1829-1869, L.1827, M.1876, Solicitor

Charles Robert Rivington (1846-1928), C.1869-1916, L.1868, M.1921, Solicitor

Reginald Thurston Rivington (1881-1971), C.1916-1965, L.1909, M.1950, Solicitor

Gordon St Patrick Wells, C.1957-1974, L.1974, Solicitor

Colonel Alexander Rubens (1919-1995), C.1974-1984, L.1976, Regular Army (retired)

Captain Peter Hames (b.1929), C.1984-1997, L.1995, Royal Navy (retired)

Brigadier Denzil Sharp, C.1997-, Regular Army (retired)

APPENDIX 3L

Beadles

F: FREE   L: LIVERY

Thomas Millis (d.1807), 1788-1807

William Lester (d.1833), 1807-1832

Thomas Hopkins (d.1838), 1832-1838

William Diggens (1796-1878), 1838-1869, L.1824, Law Stationer

Benjamin Manley (1869-97)

William Poulten (d.1943), 1897-1940, L.1897, Secretary (part time) Publishers Association, Stock-Keeper 1942

Ernest Mettrop, 1940-1959

John Nevill, 1959-63

Douglas Rowland, 1963-1965

Stanley Osborne (1909-98), 1965-1972, F.1964, Solicitors' Clerk, Assistant Clerk 1972-74

Dudley Ward (b.1920?), 1972-84, F.1985, Businessman

Simon Lawrence 'Tiny' Begley, 1986-88, Regular Soldier

Owen Whittaker, 1988-97, Bank Clerk

Bert Abel, 1997- , Accountant

APPENDIX 4

Principal Records in the Muniment Room

(For a complete catalogue of the records see Myers, *Stationers' Company Archive*, 1990, pp.5-332)

COPYRIGHT AND LEGAL DEPOSIT RECORDS

Entry Books and Copyright Registers (1556-1842), 34 vols.
Libraries Receiving Books of books sent to the legal deposit libraries 1860 to 1910, 8 vols.
Printed Indexes to Copyright Registers (now at the Public Record Office) 1842 to 1907, 4 vols.

MEMBERSHIP RECORDS

Apprentice Memorandum Books 1724 to 1962, 16 vols.
Apprentices Bound, Turned Over, Free and Cloathed from 1555 to 1900, 6 vols., chronological indexes
    of bindings
Master and Apprentice Calendars 1654 to 1807 approx., 6 vols. of indexes by master
Registers of Freemen 1605 to 1974
Declarations of Freemen 1831 to the present, 6 vols.
The Beadle's Book 1786-1973
Register of the Livery and English Stock annuitants preceded by additional material
Call of the Livery 1606 to 1853, 4 extant vols., those from 1812 to 1837 are lost
List of Common Hall Voters 1887 to 1922, 2 vols.
Printed Folio Lists of the Livery 1721 to 1965
Printed Octavo Livery Lists, annual from 1866 (incomplete set)

CATALOGUES, ABSTRACTS AND INDEXES

John Noorthouck, Abstract of the Orders of Court ... to 1779, 1780
John Battiscombe, Abstract of the Orders of Court ... 1779 to 1843, 1844
C.R. Rivington, Abstract of the Orders of Court ... 1844 to 1919
An Account of Writings in a Case of Drawers in the Court Room of the Hall ... 1772
Major A.C.S. Hall, Register of Documents at Stationers' Hall, 1950

COURT MINUTES

Waste Books or draft minutes of the Court 1661 to 1957 (incomplete run), 29 vols.
Typescript draft minutes from 1957 (unbound)
Court Books from 1602, 42 vols. in 2 alphabetical sequences (C to Z, a to r)
Liber A, a volume of 17th-century precepts, also contains Court minutes (1604-40)

LIVERY COMMITTEE

Minutes from 1920 to 1964, 3 vols.

FINANCIAL RECORDS

Books of Fines of money paid into Court 1605 to 1805, 4 vols.
Wardens' Accounts 1663 to 1907, 9 vols.
Renter Wardens' Accounts 1851 to 1966, 14 vols. (those before 1851 lost in the Blitz)

ENGLISH STOCK

Books in the Treasurers' Warehouse 1663 to 1723
Accounts of Books Delivered to the Warehouse 1723 to 1774, 3 vols.
Journal of English Stock Disbursements 1650 to 1698
Ledgers of English Stock Disbursements 1766 to 1871, 5 vols.
Dividend Books 1644 to 1961, 31 vols.
Gradus ad Parnassum Sold Ledger 1827 to 1963
Almanack Accounts 1789 to 1882 in various formats, some loose annual lists
Stock Board Minutes Books 1869 to 1972, 5 vols.

CHARITY RECORDS AND PENSION LISTS

Book of Bequests labelled 'Liber C2; extracts of wills where legacies are left to the Company' 1593-1679, with additions 1884 and 1908
Loan Book labelled 'Bonds for Moneye lent', loans to young Stationers under the bequests of John Norton and Evan Tyler
The Poor Book labelled 'Liber Computi pro Pauperibus' 1608 to 1676. The earliest list of Company and English Stock pensioners
Pension Lists 1677 to 1929, 4 vols.

PROPERTY RECORDS

William Leybourn, 'Survey of all the Land and Tenements belonging to the Worshipful Company of Stationers', 1674
'Rentals of Estates Distinguishing which Belong to the Corporation and which to the English Stock', 1773
Plan of the Manor of Pellipar, quarto album of 58 maps of the Company's Irish estate, 1792
Map of Manor of Pellipar, 1792

CHARTERS AND PATENTS, RULES AND ORDINANCES (SELECTION)

Inspeximus exemplification 10 August 1667 recital of Charter of Incorporation 4 May 1557
Exemplification of 1684
Inspeximus 10 August 1667 of Patent of English Stock of 29 October 1603
Bylaws of the Company 2 February 1678
Roll of Association 1793, declaration of loyalty signed by members of the Company

MISCELLANEOUS DOCUMENTS

Sequence I: some 15,000 miscellaneous documents contained in some 40 boxes, sorted and listed by Robin Myers, 1984
Sequence II: 664 mainly legal documents calendared by Major A.C.S. Hall (and Series II)

COLLECTIONS OF FAMILY PAPERS

Papers of the Baskett family 1740s to 1840s, acquired 1986, abstracted and calendared by C.A. Rivington
Papers of the Bentley and Nichols familes 1785 to 1877, deposited 1985
George Hawkins, English Stock Treasurer, papers 1737 to 1778
Richard Johnson Papers 1756 to 1857
John Kellie & Sons, Bookbinders 1767 to 1962, ledgers and papers, donated 1985
Rivington Family Papers—miscellaneous legal and other papers, 1787 to 1932
Tonson Family Papers 1741 to 1767, conveyance, lease and copy of will of Richard Tonson
Tottel Family Papers 1448 to 1719, acquired 1981

APPENDIX 5

Books and Major Articles on the Stationers' Company

EDITIONS OF THE RECORDS

Arber, Edward, *A Transcript of the Registers of the Company of Stationers of London, 1554-1640 A.D.*, 5 vols., 1875-94

Eyre, G.E., Plomer, H.R. and Rivington, C.R., *A Transcript of the Registers of the Worshipful Company of Stationers from 1640 to 1708*, 3 vols., Roxburghe Club, 1913-14

Ferguson, W. Craig, 'The Stationers' Company Poor Book', *The Library*, 1976

Ferguson, W. Craig, *The Loan Book of the Stationers' Company, with a List of Transactions 1592-1692*, Bibliographical Society Occasional Publications, no. 4, 1989

Greg, W.W. and Boswell, E., eds., *Records of the Court of the Stationers' Company, 1576-1602 from Register B*, Bibliographical Society, 1930

Greg, W.W. ed., *A Companion to Arber, being a Calendar of Documents in Edward Arber's Transcripts ... with text and calendar of supplementary documents*, 1967

Jackson, W.A., *Records of the Court of the Stationers' Company, 1602-1640*, Bibliographical Society, 1957

Rollins, E. Hyder, *An Analytical Index to the Ballad-Entries (1557-1709) in the Registers of the Company of Stationers of London*, 1924

BIOGRAPHICAL DICTIONARIES OF THE COMPANY AND OF THE BOOK TRADE

A Dictionary of the Printers and Booksellers who were at Work in England, Scotland and Ireland 1557-1775, 4 vols., Bibliographical Society, 1907-32, reprinted in 1 volume, 1977

Howe, Ellic, *A List of London Bookbinders 1648-1815*, Bibliographical Society, 1950

Maxted, Ian, *The London Book Trades, 1775-1800, a Preliminary Checklist*, 1977

McKenzie, D.F., *Stationers' Company Apprentices 1605-1800*, 3 vols., 1961-78

Turner, Michael, *The London Book Trade; a biographical database 1557-1830*, ongoing

CATALOGUES AND INDEXES OF THE COMPANY'S RECORDS

Hodgson, Sidney, 'Papers and Documents Recently Found at Stationers' Hall', *The Library*, 1944

Myers, Robin, *The Stationers' Company Archive; an Account of the Records, 1554-1984*, 1990

Plomer, H.R., 'A Catalogue of Records at Stationers' Hall', *The Library*, 1926

Shell, Alison and Emblow, Alison, *An Index to Court Books E and F (1679-1717)*, Bibliographical Society, forthcoming

Williams, W.P., *An Index to a Transcript of the Registers of the Stationers' Company 1640-1708*, De Kalb, Illinois, 1980

HISTORIES OF THE COMPANY

Blagden, Cyprian, *The Stationers' Company, a History 1403-1959*, 1960

Nichols, John, 'The Stationers' Company', *Literary Anecdotes of the Eighteenth Century*, vol.3, 1812

Unwin, Philip, *The Stationers' Company, 1918-1977, a Livery Company in the Modern World*, 1978

BOOKS AND ARTICLES (1935-97)

Blagden, Cyprian, 'Charter Trouble', *The Book Collector*, winter 1957

Blagden, Cyprian, 'The Accounts of the Wardens of the Stationers' Company (1557-96)', *Studies in Bibliography*, Charlottesville, 1957

Blagden, Cyprian, 'Early Cambridge Printers and the Stationers' Company', *Transactions of the Cambridge Bibliographical Society*, 1957

Blagden, Cyprian, 'The English Stock of the Stationers' Company in the Time of the Stuarts', *The Library*, 1957

Blagden, Cyprian, 'Book Trade Control in 1566', *The Library*, 1958

Blagden, Cyprian, 'The Stationers' Company in the Civil War Period', *The Library*, 1958

Blagden, Cyprian, 'The Distribution of Almanacks in the second half of the seventeenth century', *Studies in Bibliography*, Charlottesville, 1958

Blagden, Cyprian, 'The Stationers' Company in the eighteenth century', *Guildhall Miscellany*, 1959

Blagden, Cyprian, 'Thomas Carnan and the Almanack Monopoly', *Studies in Bibliography*, Charlottesville, 1960

Blagden, Cyprian, 'The "Company" of Stationers', *Transactions of the Cambridge Bibliographical Society*, 1960

Blayney, Peter, *The Bookshops in Paul's Cross Churchyard*, Bibliographical Society Occasional Monograph no.5, 1990 (not directly based on the Company's records, but of relevance to their use)

Blayney, Peter, 'William Cecil and the Stationers', *The Stationers' Company and the Book Trade 1550-1990*, eds. R. Myers and M. Harris, 1997

Ferdinand, C.Y., 'Towards a Demography of the Stationers' Company 1601-1700', *Journal of the Printing Historical Society*, no.21, 1992, ed. Robin Myers

Foot, Mirjam, 'Some Bookbinders' Price Lists of the Seventeenth and Eighteenth Centuries', *Economics of the British Booktrade 1605-1939*, eds. R. Myers and H. Harris, 1985

Greening, Anna, 'The Tottel family documents at Stationers' Hall', *The Book Trade and its Customers 1450-1900*, eds. A. Hunt, G. Mandelbrote and A. Shell, 1997

Greg, W.W., 'The Decrees and Ordinances of the Stationers' Company', *The Library*, 1928

Greg, W.W., 'Entrance, Licence and Publication', *The Library*, 1944

Greg, W.W., *Some Aspects and Problems of London Publishing between 1550 and 1650*, 1956

Hetet, John, 'The Wardens' Accounts of the Stationers' Company, 1663-79', *Economics of the British Booktrade 1605-1939*, eds. R. Myers and M. Harris, 1985

Lambert, Sheila, 'Printers and the Government, 1604-1640', *Aspects of Printing*, eds. R. Myers and M. Harris, 1987

Lambert, Sheila, 'State Control of Printing in Theory and Practice; the role of the Stationers' Company before 1640', *Censorship and the Control of Print in England and France 1600-1910*, eds. R. Myers and M. Harris, 1992

Lambert, Sheila, 'Journeymen and Master Printers in the early Seventeenth Century', *Journal of the Printing Historical Society*, no.21 1992, ed. Robin Myers

McKenzie, D.F., 'Stationers' Company Liber A; an Apologia', *The Stationers' Company and the Book Trade 1550-1990*, eds. R. Myers and M. Harris, 1997

Myers, Robin, 'The Financial Records of the Stationers' Company 1605-1811', *Economics of the British Booktrade 1605-1939*, eds. R. Myers and M. Harris, 1985

Myers, Robin, 'Stationers' Company bibliography 1892-1992', *The Book Encompassed*, ed. Peter Davison, 1992

Myers, Robin and Harris, Michael, eds., *The Stationers' Company and the Book Trade, 1550-1990*, 1997

Pollard, Graham, 'The Early Constitution of the Stationers' Company', *The Library*, 1937

Pollard, Graham, 'The Company of Stationers before 1557', *The Library*, 1937

Treadwell, Michael, 'London Printers and Printing Houses in 1705', *Publishing History*, 1980

Treadwell, Michael, 'A New List of Master Printers c.1686', *The Library*, March 1982

Treadwell, Michael, 'List of Master Printers; the Size of the London Book Trade, 1637-1729', *Aspects of Printing*, eds. R. Myers and M. Harris, 1987

Treadwell, Michael, 'Samuel Richardson, Citizen and Stationer,' unpublished lecture, 1989

Treadwell, Michael, 'Printers in the Court of the Stationers' Company in the Seventeenth and Eighteenth Centuries', *Journal of the Printing Historical Society*, no.21, 1992, ed. Robin Myers

Tsushima, Jean, 'Members of the Stationers' Company who served in the Artillery Company before the Civil War ...' *The Stationers' Company and the Book Trade 1550-1990*, eds. R. Myers and M. Harris, 1997

Turner, Michael, 'A "List of the Stockholders in the Worshipful Company of Stationers", 1785', *The Book Trade and its Customers 1450-1900*, eds. A. Hunt, G. Mandelbrote and A. Shell, 1997

APPENDIX 6

Glossary of Terms

Upper case denotes cross-reference to a term defined elsewhere

ANNUITANT An English Stock shareholder who held shares at the time that the Stock was wound up in 1961, and those who, being Liverymen at the time, acquired shares after that.

ASSIGNMENT/ASSIGNED 1. Transfer of a copyright, usually by purchase. 2. Transfer (until 1961) of a share in the English Stock on the death of a PARTNER or shareholder.

BEADLE The most ancient of the Company's officers who was the link between the various elements of the Company, the curator of its property and general factotum. In the 19th century his functions included responsibility for keeping a list of freemen and liverymen, taking account of the deaths of members, distributing pensions to the Company's poor. He was, and still is, in attendance, robed and bearing the mace, at Company and City functions and seeing that the court and livery are wearing gowns and badges. The Company's plate was, and still is, in his charge. He summoned members to meetings, feasts and funerals.

BINDING The establishment of a contract between a master and apprentice who was by custom bound on his fourteenth birthday and freed by SERVITUDE seven years later. Those who bound their own sons or daughters generally freed them by PATRIMONY. A PREMIUM was generally paid in earlier times.

CAKES AND ALE On Ash Wednesday, the Livery enjoy a modest repast by one of the terms of the bequest of John Norton, before processing, the Court and Officers being robed and gowned, and preceded by the beadle, to St Faith's church in the crypt of St Paul's for an Ash Wednesday service. Before the Second World War the 'cakes' were buns made to a special recipe, now lost. Hot soup, bread and cheese, wine or beer, and coffee has now replaced the traditional cakes and ale.

CALL 1. A summons or invitation to attend a meeting of the Livery or Court. 2. Formerly a list of those admitted to the Livery at any one time; the early Livery registers are labelled *call of the livery*.

CLERK The company's chief officer, who, like all the Company's officers, is re-appointed annually, now at the April court, now a mere formality. Until 1957 the clerkship was a part-time appointment. Until 1800, the Clerk was a bookseller who was required to have some legal training and from 1800 to 1974 he was a lawyer. The last three Clerks have been retired members of the services.

CLOATHING/CLOATHED Almost always spelt thus; admission to the Livery, which confers full membership and all the rights and privileges of the Company including eligibility for office, the right to vote at Company and City elections and attendance at Common Hall.

COMMON HALL 1. The annual assemblies of the Livery of the City Companies at Guildhall (but not the freemen who have no voting rights), to elect the Lord Mayor and Sheriffs. 2. The Common Hall of the Stationers' Livery is an innovation of recent years. The Assistants, robed, attend while the Master reviews the events of his year of office; and the Treasurer gives his financial report. The Master, Wardens and Court then retire while the meeting elects the members of the livery committee. Common Hall was held in April until 1986, when it was changed to the July Court day before the change of Master ceremony which the Livery is permitted to attend.

COMMONALTY A collective term for the whole Company, excepting the Master and Wardens. It is now only used in official documents.

CORPORATION/INCORPORATION The term properly applies to the corporation of the City of

London, but the corporation was also used to denote the Company of Stationers to differentiate its affairs from those of the English Stock The Company was incorporated, or given the status of a chartered company, by royal charter in 1557.

COURT BOOK OR ORDERS OF COURT The official records of Court meetings, written up from a typescript of the clerk's minutes, formerly from the *waste book*, in which the Clerk took down minutes during the course of a Court.

ENTRY BOOK OR COPYRIGHT REGISTER (1556-1924) The earliest books and pamphlets 'entered' at Stationers' Hall, partly to control seditious publishing and piracy, were inscribed in a volume called *Register A*, followed by so-called *Liber B* to *Liber G* (1576-1717); thereafter the registers are titled by date. They later became official copyright registers. So-called *Liber A* is not part of the series but a volume of early Mayoral precepts which also includes the Court Orders from 1604 to 1640.

FINE 1. Dues or fees for binding, freedom, cloathing being called to Court etc. 2. An increased due paid, in the past, by those declining to serve when called upon to do so. 3. Formerly a punitive payment for transgressing the Company's rules such as binding more than the permitted number of apprentices, printing 'another man's copy' or bad behaviour such as abusing or assaulting the Company's officers or fellow members.

FREEDOM/FREE Admission to/admitted to the Company, and to the City. Until 1856 a man or woman was debarred from trading in the city unless free of the City. The Freedom is now a mere formality, by tradition open to all who live or work in the city and a requirement for those seeking admission to the cloathing of a livery company.

Freedom is the collective term for the company's third estate, came to be used as more or less synonymous with the term Yeomanry (although it was not the same in origin) and has dropped out of use. (See YEOMANRY.) There are five ways of attaining the FREEDOM: 1. Servitude: Serving as apprentices was once the

commonest method of entry; after 1966 it virtually ceased. 2(a). Patrimony: Freedom by inheritance. The son (and now the daughter) of a man free of the Company at the time of his son's or daughter's birth can join the Company without having to satisfy the requirement of working in the book or allied trades (see also binding). 2(b). Matri-heritage: inheritance through a woman free of the Company at the time of her son's or daughter's birth. 2(c). Family Redemption: In 1986 inherited Freedom was extended to the sons and daughters under the age of 30 of Liverymen of more than ten years' standing. 3. Redemption: freedom by purchase, open to those already working in the book and allied trades. In 1986 the Court ruled that would-be redemptioners will normally only be accepted for the Freedom if they are prepared to proceed to the Livery as a vacancy occurs. 4. By virtue of being an Old Stationer or old boy of the Stationers' Company School. 5. Translation: transfer from another livery company, a method of entry into the Company that was moderately common when full trading rights were only accorded to those who belonged to the Company of that trade. Nowadays a man or woman may belong to more than one company so that translation has become very rare.

GILD/GUILD YEAR The Stationers' Company's year runs from the beginning of July, the Master and Wardens being appointed on the first Saturday after St Peter's Day, 29 June and taking office on the first Tuesday in July. The City's Gild Year runs from 9 November (before 1751 it ran from 30 October).

LIVERY REPRESENTATIVE Since 1926 two senior liverymen, nominated by the Livery attend Court for two years and vote on behalf of the Livery.

MASTER 1. The highest office in the Company. Past Master: one who has served the office of Master. 2. An employer who, in the past, having served an apprenticeship, employed journeymen and bound apprentices.

MASTER AND WARDENS COMMITTEE An inner cabinet, formed in 1959, consisting of the Master, Wardens, Treasurer, two Past Masters, with the Clerk in attendance; it initiates policy to be ratified by the whole Court. Since 1986 it has admitted Freemen but admission to the Cloathing continues to take place before the whole Court.

ORDINANCES/RULES AND ORDINANCES/BY LAWS
Originally, the rules for membership and conduct. The Company's first extant by laws were drawn up and printed February 1678. They were updated in 1877 and, in order to take account of the admission of women to the Livery in 1977, they were revised in 1981. There have been three new Rules and Ordinances since then, the latest being 1998.

PARTNER A shareholder in the English Stock, who, after 1961, became an ANNUITANT.

POOR BOX A box put out on Court days for the collection of charitable donations from those being freed or cloathed who are directed to place a donation in it as they leave the Court Room. Nowadays a minimum of £10 is acceptable.

PREMIUM A training fee paid by a parent or guardian for apprenticeship. During the 19th century the custom of paying a premium gradually died out.

QUARTERAGE A quarterly, later an annual, sub-scription levied on all members of the Company and recorded in the Quarterage or Renter War-dens' Book which provided a complete record of the names and addresses of both freemen and liverymen. Quarterage was abolished in 1884 until revived in 1990. In the early period the Renters accompanied by the Beadle collected Quarterage from the 'place of abode' of members, who could also make payment at quarterly Quarterage courts to which all freemen were summoned.

REGISTRAR/REGISTRY From 1842 to 1883, the Registrar or Registering Officer was in charge of keeping the copyright register, issuing certificates and receiving books for legal deposit. He was also the salaried English Stock Warehouse-Keeper and as such was an officer of the Company. A voluntary Registry was set up in 1924 and closed 2000. The Company's general office was until very recently still called Registry.

RENTER WARDEN There were originally two Renters or Collectors, now there are four, livery-men of twelve years' seniority, chosen annually on

Lady Day. Their traditional duties were to collect Quarterage, keep the accounts and maintain an up-to-date list of the names and addresses of freemen and liverymen. They also provided a VENISON or ELECTION FEAST for the election of the Master and Wardens and now make a presentation to the Company. Although their duties are now mainly social, they attend on Court days and meetings of the Livery.

ROTTEN ROW Those liverymen, at one time as many as a third of the entire Livery, who took no part in Company affairs and chose neither to fine nor serve as Renter Warden, came to be known as being in 'rotten row'.

SERVE/SERVICE/SERVITUDE 1. Hold office in the Company. 2. Serve an apprenticeship

STATIONER 1. A member of the Stationers' Company. 2. A dealer in stationery and office materials. 3. Old Stationer—an old boy of the Stationers' Company School. 4. An archaic term for bookseller or text-writer (professional book copyist of the manuscript period).

SUMMONS (archaic) An invitation or notice, in the past usually printed, and sent out by the Clerk or Beadle to attend a company or city function or feast.

SUPERNUMERARY LIST/COURT EMERITUS LIST
In 1984 a supernumerary list to which inactive Liverymen and those who decline to pay Quarterage transfer, reverting to the status of Freemen. ROTTEN Row formed its basis.
    In 1966, a Court Supernumerary List of Assistants above the age of 75, or those who cannot attend Court regularly was instigated, in order to make room for younger men on the Court. In 1997 it was re-named the Court Emeritus List. Emeritus Assistants may continue to attend, robed, at certain company functions, such as Common Hall and Cakes and Ale.

TREASURER Since 1899 the Treasurer has been a senior member of the Court and, since 1907, he has been in charge of the Company's finances. From 1684 to 1899, known as the Warehouse Keeper, he was also the salaried manager of the English Stock, responsible for entering books in the register books and, from 1842, for issuing copyright certificates as well as organising, with the Beadle, the books to be sent to, or collected on behalf of, the legal deposit libraries.

VENISON FEAST/ELECTION DINNER A dinner to celebrate the annual election of the Master and Wardens on the first Saturday after St Peter's Day, 29 June, when the Company dined off venison at the expense of the Renter Wardens. It has been replaced by two livery feasts, the Charter Dinner in May to celebrate the granting of the first charter, and the Civic Dinner in November to welcome the new Lord Mayor.

WARDEN Prior to incorporation in 1557, the Wardens were the Gild's controlling officers. Until 1695, it was the Upper Warden's responsibility to pass works for entry in the register while the Under Warden had charge of the Company's annual accounts until this was taken over by the TREASURER in 1899.

WHIFFLERS Hired by the Beadle, who furnished them with staves, chains and ribbons, they aided the progress of the Company's barge down the Thames on Lord Mayor's Day. They were, in effect, floating outriders and manned small tugs used to the keep the passage of the Company's barge clear of other craft and to tow it round the bends in the river.

YEOMANRY An obsolete term for the general body of freemen. It survived until 1961 in the term Yeomanry Share for the lowest denomination of share in the English Stock.

Index

J.D. Lee

Check under the specific name or term required.

Figures in **bold** show the captions to illustrations, tables etc. Asterisked * material is in the *Glossary*.

Abbreviations used are as follows (B) = Beadle; (C) = Clerk; (CLC) = Chairman, Livery Committee; (H) = Honorary Freemen and Liverymen; (LM) = Lord Mayor; (M) = Master; (SM) = Silver Medallist

Abel, Bert (B), 244

Abergavenny House, 79, 97, 152, 153

Adam Brothers, 151, 171

Adlard family, 39, 40

Adlard, Henry (M), 40, **95**, 233

Adlard, James (M), 77

Adlard, James Evan (M), 234

Adlard, James William (M), 233

Adlard, Robert Evan (M), 235

advertising, and newspapers, 52; *see also* publicists

Akerman, John, 56

Alexandra Palace, 124

Alfred, king, painting by Benjamin West, 158, 173

Allen, William Ferneley (LM), 208, 214, 239

Almanack Day, xx, 82-3, **83**, 85

almanacks, 79, 82-5, **87**; background 86-90; profits, 90-1, graph **91**; sales, 92, graph **94**, 96; in the library, **175**, 199

Althorp, John Charles Spencer, Lord, 90

Amen Corner, 116, 154, 165

Ames, Joseph, 182, 194

annuitant, 80, 102, 105, 118, *249

Antiquarian Booksellers' Association, 4n

antiquarian bookselling, 45, 47-8

Apprentice Register, transcript, 184, **184**

apprentices: binding, **21**; entry by servitude, 23-9, *250; living out, 22; D.F.McKenzie on, 194; numbers, 22, 24, **28**; occupations of fathers, table, **25**; offer of two, **23**; tradition, 21-7

Arber, Edward, 187-8, 189, 210

archive, 175-95, **180**; access and use, 182-6; care and conservation, 180-1; description, 175-7; list of exhibitions, 230-1; finding aids, 177; Keepers of the Records, 181; microfilming, 191; principal records in the Muniment Room, 245-6; secrecy in 19th century, 209-10; storage, 177-9

archivists, qualified for Freedom, 46

Archivists of the Company, 181; list, 242

Arding, James, Bolt Court school, 136-7

arms, *see* heraldry; Stationers' Company: arms

Arram, Bessie, 57

Arts and Library Committee, 114

Ash Wednesday service, **107**, 119, 121, 123, 141

Askey, Arthur, 13

assignment/assigned, *249

Associated Bookbinders of London and Westminster, 2

Associated Booksellers of Great Britain and Ireland, 4, 6

Astor, John Jacob, Lord Astor of Hever (M), 56, 127, 235

Astor, William Waldorf, Viscount Astor, 57

astrology, and almanacks, 86, **87**, 89, **93**, **94**

Athenaeum, 88

Atkinson, A.G.L.(CLC), 242

Austen-Leigh family 13, 25n, 39

Austen-Leigh, Cholmeley, 24, 41, 147

Austen-Leigh, Edward Chenevix (M), 40-1, 235

Austen Leigh, Richard Arthur (CLC, M), 15, 41-2, **42**, 114, 126, 177, 187, 188, 236, 242

authors, 3, 219; relations with publishers, 4-6

Ave Maria Lane 152; property in, 95, 98-9, 116, 117, 154, 161, 168, 173; and World War II, 165; *see also* Ludgate Hill

Bacon, W.N. (CLC), 242

Baddeley, Sir John William (M, LM), 235, 239

Bailey, James Alexander (CLC, M), 236, 242

Bailey & Son, 161

Baker, stationer, 8

Baker, Joseph (CA, M), 36, 232

Bakers, *see* White Bakers' Company

Baldwin, stationer, 8

Baldwin, Charles (M), 233

Baldwin, Mrs Elizabeth, charity, 131

Baldwin, Joseph (C), 185

Baldwin, Stanley, Earl Baldwin (M), 31, 240

Balfour, Arthur James, Earl of Balfour (H), 13, 31, 219, 240

Ballantine, Spottiswoode, 41

balls, 125-6, **125**

banners, armorial, 170

Barber, John, 201

barge, company, 113, 116, 122-3, 163, 169; housing, 125; in Lord Mayor's procession 1843, **122**, 123; sale 1850, 1, 124-5

barge master and mate, 113, 124

Barker, John (M), 232

Barrie, Sir James, bt (H), 13, 31, 215, 240